INTERNATIONAL DEVELOPMENT IN FOCUS

Social Protection Program Spending and Household Welfare in Ghana

DHUSHYANTH RAJU, STEPHEN D. YOUNGER,
AND CHRISTABEL E. DADZIE

WORLD BANK GROUP

Contents

Figures

Tables

Acknowledgments

The authors express their gratitude to several individuals, including Shanta Devarajan, Jeffrey Hammer, and Ritva Reinekka, for useful discussions on the scope, structure, and substance of the study, including on data and methods, and to Samik Adhikari, Oti Enoch Agyekum, Cynthia Nimo Ampredu, Christopher Burningham, Enrico Calvanese, Katherine Chen, Jed Friedman, Mawuko Fumey, Franklin Kuma Kwasi Gawu, Ugo Gentilini, Antonio Giuffrida, Sakshi Hallan, Vincent Van Halsema, Kwabena Gyan Kwakye, Lucy Liu, Patrick Mullen, Alex Nartey, Mpumelelo Nxumalo, Paul Rodas, Anita Schwarz, Iffath Sharif, Karishma Talitha Silva, Stephen Tettevie, Jennifer Yablonski, and Jonathan Nasonaa Zakaria for valuable discussions, feedback, and assistance at various stages during the production of this study.

We also thank several government officials for an excellent partnership, including (listing organizations and officials' last names in alphabetical order) Franklin Ashiadey, Ghana Jobs and Skills Project Coordinating Unit; Peter Peprah, Ghana Statistical Service; Alhassan Iddrisu and Yvonne Quansah, Ministry of Finance; Alhaji Ibrahim, Richard Nartey, Myles Ongoh, Chris Siaw-Darko, and Johnson Wegba, Ministry of Gender, Children, and Social Protection; Patrick Appiah, Adwoa Boakyewaa Asotia-Boakye, Henry Bosompem, Albert Dadze Dennis, Desmond Duametu, George Kwadwo Osei-Ababio, and Stephen Tekpertey, Ministry of Local Government, Decentralization, and Rural Development; Charlotte Norman, National Disaster Management Organization; Vivian Addo-Cobbiah, National Health Insurance Authority; and Evelyn Adjei and Jones Kennedy Luri, Social Security and National Insurance Trust.

We apologize to any individuals or organizations inadvertently omitted from the above list and express our gratitude to all who contributed to the study.

The study was funded by the World Bank.

Summary

Ghana administers multiple social protection programs. One of them, pensions provided by the Social Security and National Insurance Trust, has a long history, but the rest of the programs—the Ghana School Feeding Programme, Labor-Intensive Public Works program, Livelihood Empowerment Against Poverty program, and National Health Insurance Scheme—have been introduced and expanded only over the past two decades.

This study assesses the performance of the government of Ghana's main social assistance and social insurance programs. It discusses the main design and implementation parameters of the programs and summarizes existing evaluative and operational research.

The study also examines patterns and trends in program benefit spending, based on government administrative data, and the coverage rates of the programs, their incidence, and their effectiveness in reducing poverty and inequality, based on recent national household sample survey data.

Furthermore, the study examines the relationship between household participation in social assistance programs and exposure to adverse covariate shocks—specifically, possible weather-related shocks, based on high-resolution climate risk maps for the country.

Ghana spends little on public social protection programs, equivalent to about 1.4 percent of gross domestic product (GDP). This spending is predominantly through social insurance programs. Spending on social assistance programs is equivalent to about 0.2 percent of GDP, far below international averages. Until recently, social insurance pensions were limited to retirees who worked in the formal sector. National health insurance is meant to be universal. Except for these two programs, social assistance programs in Ghana are well targeted to the poor population, and the programs tend to cover households that are exposed to high drought risk (poor areas and high-drought-risk areas are correlated).

Yet, the effects of the social assistance programs on poverty and inequality are at best modest because their outlays are small. Population coverage rates are limited for most of the programs, and average benefit amounts are low by international standards, relative to the average consumption levels of beneficiary households and to the country's extreme and overall poverty lines per adult equivalent.

While expanding the coverage of the programs and more generous benefit amounts would have a salutary effect, the current macroeconomic and fiscal situation makes such changes difficult. Social Security and National Insurance Trust pension benefits are much more generous but basically are received by a population (formal sector workers) that is generally well off. While we find much that is positive about social protection programs in Ghana, an important and frequent criticism is that the National Health Insurance Scheme is slow to pay health care providers for the services they provide to the scheme's members. This issue discourages providers from treating members or leads them to charge fees even when health care services are supposed to be free, thus undermining the purpose of national health insurance.

About the Authors

Christabel E. Dadzie is a Senior Social Protection Specialist at the World Bank. She currently is the task team leader (TTL) of the Strengthen Ethiopia's Adaptive Safety Net Project (the Rural Productive Safety Net Program) and is outgoing TTL of the Ghana Productive Safety Net Project and the Gambia Social Safety Net Project. She previously has supported the Ghana Jobs and Skills Project, as well as the Liberia and Sierra Leone social protection and jobs portfolios. Before joining the World Bank, she worked on U.S. Agency for International Development projects, leading performance evaluations for their Economic Growth Office, and she has worked within the United Nations system as a gender and economic development specialist. She has a master's degree in international affairs from Columbia University in New York, NY, in the United States.

Dhushyanth Raju is Lead Economist, Social Protection and Jobs (SPJ) Global Practice, at the World Bank. In his current position, he works on lending, advisory, and analytical services related to the labor market and social welfare policies and programs in Europe and Central Asia. He previously has held technical positions in the Africa regional SPJ department, the South Asia regional chief economist and education departments, and the global social protection and labor and gender departments of the World Bank. In the South Asia regional chief economist office, he was responsible for research and advice on human development, labor markets, social welfare, and program evaluations. His research is mainly in public economics, labor, risk, poverty, gender, and human development. He has a PhD in economics from Cornell University in Ithaca, NY, in the United States.

Stephen D. Younger is a Research Associate at the Commitment to Equity Institute. He previously has worked at Williams College, Cornell University, Vrije Universiteit, Facultad Latinoamericana de Ciencias Sociales–Quito, and Ithaca College. His research focuses on public policy and poverty in developing countries, including the incidence of taxes and expenditures, nonincome dimensions of well-being, and multidimensional poverty and inequality measurement. He has a PhD in economics from Stanford University in Stanford, CA, in the United States.

Abbreviations

BWA	Beneficiary Welfare Association
CFSVA	Comprehensive Food Security and Vulnerability Analysis
CLASS	Complementary Livelihood and Asset Support Scheme
CLIC	Community LEAP Implementation Committee
DAs	District Assemblies
DIC	District Implementation Committees
DLIC	District LEAP Implementation Committee
FCDO	Foreign, Commonwealth & Development Office (United Kingdom)
GDP	gross domestic product
GhIPSS	Ghana Interbank Payment and Settlement Systems
GLSS	Ghana Living Standards Survey
GSFP	Ghana School Feeding Programme
GSS	Ghana Statistical Service
IMF	International Monetary Fund
LEAP	Livelihood Empowerment Against Poverty
LIPW	Labor-Intensive Public Works
LMIC	lower-middle-income country
MELR	Ministry of Employment and Labour Relations (Ghana)
MLGDRD	Ministry of Local Government, Decentralization, and Rural Development (Ghana)
MOGCSP	Ministry of Gender, Children, and Social Protection (Ghana)
NHIA	National Health Insurance Authority
NHIS	National Health Insurance Scheme
NSPP	National Social Protection Policy
PMT	proxy means test
PPP	purchasing power parity
RDCU	Rural Development Coordination Unit
SIC	School Implementation Committee
SSA	Sub-Saharan Africa
SSNIT	Social Security and National Insurance Trust
UNICEF	United Nations Children's Fund
USAID	United States Agency for International Development
WFP	World Food Programme

1 Introduction

Ghana has relatively low levels of poverty as compared to the averages for Sub-Saharan Africa and lower-middle-income countries. After steady and substantial declines from 1991/92 to 2012/13, poverty reduction stagnated between 2012/13 and 2016/17, the most recent year for which there is an actual poverty measurement—based on the Ghana Living Standards Survey (GLSS) 2016–17 (GSS 2019)—despite significant economic growth during the period. Inequality rose over the decade from 2005/06 to 2016/17. For 2016/17, the poverty rate stood at 12.7 percent based on the international poverty line of $1.90 in 2011 purchasing power parity dollars, 23.4 percent based on the country's overall poverty line, and 8.2 percent based on the country's extreme poverty line. The Gini index of consumption per capita was 43.0 percent.

Enabled by expanded fiscal space due to debt reduction and the discovery and exploitation of significant oil and gas resources, the government of Ghana has introduced or expanded multiple social protection programs over the past two decades. This study examines benefit spending performance in the following main social protection programs of the government:

a. The Livelihood Empowerment Against Poverty (LEAP) program offers an unconditional cash transfer to households with persons in certain vulnerable groups (orphans, elderly individuals, pregnant women, mothers of infants, and persons with disabilities) and low proxy means test (PMT) scores in geographic areas with high poverty rates.

b. The Labor-Intensive Public Works (LIPW) program, a public employment scheme, takes place in the agricultural off-season in rural areas and uses a combination of geographic targeting to poor areas, self-selection, and community selection of the poorest candidates.

c. The Ghana School Feeding Programme (GSFP) provides cooked lunches to preprimary and primary students in public schools in geographic areas with high poverty rates.

d. The National Health Insurance Scheme (NHIS), a highly subsidized health insurance program, covers 95 percent of conditions commonly found in Ghana, with no premium payments for those younger than age 18 and those age 70 or older, as well as "indigent" individuals, Social Security and National Insurance Trust (SSNIT) contributors and pensioners, pregnant women, and women with infants younger than 3 months. Indigent individuals, pregnant women, and women with infants also are not required to pay the registration or renewal fees.

e. SSNIT offers retirement, disability, and survivor pensions to its contributors, most of whom are or were in the formal sector.

The social assistance programs use a variety of targeting mechanisms to reach the poor population, including categories of vulnerable people (orphans, elderly individuals, pregnant women, mothers of infants, and persons with disabilities), a PMT, and geographic areas with high poverty rates. SSNIT, on the other hand, almost exclusively benefits formal sector workers, very few of whom are poor individuals. NHIS is meant to be universal.

LIPW program benefits are fully financed by donors. LEAP program benefits are jointly financed by the government (general revenues) and donors. The donor financing is explicitly specified for these programs and channeled through the government. GSFP, NHIS, and SSNIT pension benefits do not receive donor financing. GSFP benefits are financed through general government revenues. NHIS is funded primarily through an earmark of 2.5 percent of value added tax revenues (the National Health Insurance Levy), with additional funding from SSNIT, which pays the premia and fees for its contributors and pensioners. A small amount of NHIS funding comes from other members' premia and fees. SSNIT pension benefits are funded with contributions from members (salaried employees) and their employers.

In this study, we describe the main design and implementation parameters of each of the five programs and selectively review the available descriptive, diagnostic, and evaluative research on the programs. The study's main contributions are describing the patterns and trends of spending on each program and assessing its performance in terms of coverage, incidence, and effectiveness at reducing poverty and inequality, including through the use of microsimulation of selected reforms. The study also examines the relationship between social assistance program coverage and adverse covariate shocks—specifically, weather-related shocks. The analysis of incidence and effectiveness is based on standard methods (Bourguignon and Pereira da Silva 2003; Lustig 2018; Yemtsov et al. 2018), including standard microsimulation methods (Figari, Paulus, and Sutherland 2015).[1]

The descriptions of program design and implementation parameters, as well as the analysis of program spending patterns and trends, are based primarily on information shared with the authors by the administrators of the various programs. The analysis of incidence and effectiveness relies on the GLSS 2016–17, which is the latest available national household sample survey with relevant data for our performance review. The GLSS 2016–17 includes questions about participation in, and benefits from, the LEAP program, GSFP, NHIS, and SSNIT pensions (but not the LIPW program). Measures of poverty and inequality are based on household consumption data in the survey. The government administers and uses the GLSS for its official estimates of poverty and inequality.

While we examine the important relationship between social protection programs, poverty, and inequality,[2] we recognize that the primary aims of these programs may be different. For example, NHIS is mainly meant to improve access to health care, and GSFP is meant to improve school enrollment, attendance, and academic achievement. We summarize existing evidence on the relationship between social protection program participation and other outcomes.

This study follows a series of high-quality studies on the performance of social protection programs in Ghana, based on analyses of household sample survey and government administrative data on programs and through reviews of existing research. See, for example, International Labour Organization (ILO 2015), Wodon (2012), World Bank (2016, 2017), and Younger, Osei-Assibey, and Oppong (2017). Some of these studies have covered a larger set of interventions than does our review, including, for example, various subsidies and active labor market interventions. Furthermore, some of the studies have conducted benefit incidence analyses and microsimulations of hypothetical program reforms, using previous rounds of the GLSS (from 2005/06 and 2012/13)—just as our study does. Many of our findings and recommendations match those of these past studies.

Prior to the outbreak of the coronavirus pandemic, in 2019, total social protection program benefits amounted to GH¢4.5 billion. SSNIT pensions accounted for 65 percent of this spending, NHIS for 22 percent, GSFP for 10 percent, and the LEAP program for 3 percent. The LIPW program was inactive in 2019. Total benefit spending in all five social protection programs across recent years was equivalent to 6.7 percent of overall government spending and to 1.4 percent of gross domestic product (GDP).[3] Total spending on social assistance program benefits across recent years was equivalent to 0.9 percent of overall government spending and to 0.2 percent of GDP. This level of social assistance program benefit spending is substantially lower than the average for Sub-Saharan Africa and for developing countries more generally, at 1.5 percent for both groups of countries. The pandemic did not result in a marked increase in spending on these programs, as the government opted to mainly respond with other instruments (discussed later).

None of the social protection programs we review, except for NHIS, is meant to cover all Ghanaians. Coverage of the national population by NHIS has ranged between 30 percent and 40 percent over the past decade, based on government administrative data on end-of-year active membership numbers. Available evidence suggests that the costs of registration or renewal fees and premia are the main reason that people do not register, even though they are very low.

The other programs are restricted to poor areas (the LEAP program, the LIPW program, and GSFP) and to people with certain characteristics—infants, (school) children, elderly individuals, persons with disabilities, pregnant women, and mothers of infants (the LEAP program, GSFP, and SSNIT). The LEAP and LIPW programs also target the poorest households in poor areas. As a result, national coverage rates are low. Coverage rates jump when we restrict our analysis to population groups targeted by the programs but remain far from universal.

Based on survey data, the LEAP program covers only 1.5 percent of Ghanaians and 6.7 percent of the extreme-poor population nationally. The coverage rate increases to 22.7 percent of the overall population in LEAP program areas and to 27.8 percent of the extreme-poor population in these areas. However, receipt of LEAP program benefits reported by GLSS 2016–17 respondents, the basis for our analysis of coverage, is underreported by 67 percent. When we predict a set of additional LEAP program households to address underreporting in the survey data and add it to the set of actual LEAP program households (a collective set that we refer to as "LEAP+" households), coverage rates increase to 4.1 percent of all Ghanaians and 17.9 percent of the extreme-poor population. In LEAP+ program areas, the coverage rate increases to 28.8 percent of all residents and to 34.8 percent of the extreme-poor population.

GSFP coverage of the national population rose from 6 percent in 2016 to 8 percent in 2019, based on administrative data. The program covers 10 percent of the extreme-poor population, based on survey data. But among public preprimary and primary school students in targeted areas, the coverage rate is 61 percent overall and 64 percent for the extreme-poor population.

Over the past decade, SSNIT pensions' coverage of the national population has ranged between 0.4 percent and 0.7 percent, based on administrative data. The program covers 5.2 percent of those age 60 or older, based on survey data. SSNIT pensions do not reach the poor population. The main limitation here is that, until recently, SSNIT was available only to formal sector workers, which is a small share of the overall labor force.

Aside from SSNIT pensions, the levels of total benefits received by households from the various programs are low. As a percentage of total household consumption among program households, the LEAP program averages 12.8 percent, GSFP averages 5.2 percent, and NHIS averages 3.6 percent. For SSNIT pensions, the average is 60.3 percent. The average percentage increases for all programs when the sample is restricted to poor households, but it continues to remain low for all programs except for SSNIT pensions. The results are qualitatively similar when we examine total benefits as a percentage of the extreme and overall poverty lines (set at the household level) averaged across program households.

LEAP program and GSFP benefits are highly concentrated among the poor population, with concentration coefficients of –0.53 and –0.22, respectively. These compare favorably with similar social assistance programs in a large sample of low- and middle-income countries. The concentration coefficient for NHIS benefits is 0.19, which is not a pro-poor benefit but still is more concentrated among the poor population than household consumption in general. (The Gini coefficient of consumption per adult equivalent is 0.42.) Of course, if NHIS were truly universal as intended, it would have a concentration coefficient of 0. The concentration coefficient for SSNIT pensions is 0.74, which is highly regressive. This is not surprising, as SSNIT pensions are relatively generous and, until recently, available only to those with at least 15 years of employment in the formal sector.

Despite the strong targeting performance of the LEAP program and GSFP, these programs have only small effects on poverty (based on the country's extreme and overall poverty lines) and inequality (the Gini index), at about one-tenth of a percentage point or smaller. The effects are somewhat greater for LEAP+, GSFP in GSFP areas, and NHIS, at about one-fourth of a percentage point or smaller. The effects are greatest for the LEAP program in LEAP areas, at about four-fifths of a percentage point. Finally, SSNIT pensions have almost no effect on poverty and inequality.

We measure effectiveness at reducing poverty (based on the country's extreme and overall poverty lines) and inequality (Gini index) by comparing the actual changes induced by each program to a perfectly targeted transfer with the same outlay ("impact effectiveness") or a perfectly targeted transfer that achieves the same impact but with a smaller outlay ("spending effectiveness"). The LEAP program is 69 percent as effective at reducing the Gini index as a perfectly targeted program would be. It is 65 percent as effective as a perfect program at reducing the poverty gap but only 33 percent to 35 percent as effective at reducing poverty severity (both measures based on the overall poverty line). The effectiveness results for LEAP+ are similar.

GSFP is somewhat less effective than the LEAP program at reducing inequality and poverty: It is 57 percent as effective as a perfect program at reducing inequality, 48 percent as effective at reducing the poverty gap (based on the overall poverty line), and only 24 percent to 28 percent as effective at reducing poverty severity (based on the overall poverty line).

The LEAP program in LEAP program areas and GSFP in GSFP areas are much less effective at reducing inequality in these areas than they are nationally.

NHIS is 28 percent as effective as a perfectly targeted transfer at reducing the Gini index, 22 percent as effective at reducing the poverty gap (based on the overall poverty line), and 11 percent to 16 percent as effective at reducing poverty severity (based on the overall poverty line).

SSNIT pensions actually increase inequality and are completely ineffective at reducing poverty.

Because of the prominence of the LEAP program in the government's anti-poverty strategy, we simulate different reforms to the program's coverage and benefit levels, based on the LEAP+ sample. We find that using the government's PMT to target the extreme-poor population would improve the program's already impressive concentration coefficient from –0.49 to about –0.73, even if the LEAP program abandons its current multilevel, multimethod targeting strategy. Further, we estimate that scaling up the LEAP program to cover all areas nationally while restricting benefits to the PMT–extreme-poor population only would reduce the program's outlay by 65 percent. Notwithstanding, the program's effect on poverty remains small across various simulations of coverage expansions (based on PMT targeting) because of its very low benefit level. Simulations of benefit increases also show limited poverty effects because the existing benefit level is low.

In terms of survey data quality, the correspondence between the GLSS 2016–17 estimates and government administrative information on beneficiary numbers and benefit spending is not always good. Total beneficiaries and benefits are both underreported by 67 percent for the LEAP program in the survey data, by 33 percent and 30 percent for GSFP, by 12 percent and 22 percent for NHIS, and by 43 percent and 64 percent for SSNIT pensions, all respectively. It is especially important to keep this in mind when considering our estimates of coverage and the effects of each program on poverty and inequality, which will be biased downward. If the underreporting is distributed randomly across the income distribution, then it will not bias estimates of incidence or effectiveness. But if the underreporting is more heavily concentrated among richer (poorer) households, concentration coefficients and effectiveness estimates will be biased downward (upward) as well.

The GLSS 2016–17 does not include questions on shocks that respondents have experienced and thus does not allow for an examination of the correlation between shocks and social assistance program participation. We draw on Nxumalo and Raju (2022), who linked data on drought and flood risks with data on household program participation at the district level. District program participation rates in the LEAP and LIPW programs correlate with drought risk, while the results for flood risk are less clear. The association between program participation and drought risk is an indirect result, partly mediated through poverty. That is, social assistance programs target poor areas, and poor areas tend to be drought prone. The link between household participation in the LEAP and LIPW programs and drought risk stems from preshock program coverage of drought-prone areas, achieved indirectly through the intentional coverage of poor areas. However, in the case of the LIPW program, an element of ex post response might be at work. The location, type, and scale (including workforce size) of the public works subproject may be influenced by local drought-risk considerations.

Unlike social assistance programs in other low- and lower-middle-income countries, those in Ghana have been the subject of much academic research, including studies with careful designs that allow identification of causal effects. We selectively review this research in this study. In contrast, our own results are descriptive only, but the descriptions are nationally representative, which the causal studies are not. As such, they provide a useful complement to the existing literature on these programs' effects.

One positive aspect of the implementation of social protection in Ghana is that, unlike many other lower-middle-income countries, researchers and practitioners review the programs with some care and, at least for the LEAP program and NHIS, have made important adjustments to the programs in response to this information.

For the LEAP program, careful evaluations (Handa et al. 2014, 2017) have found significant problems with the distribution of payments, which were irregular and sometimes difficult to obtain. The LEAP program changed payment mechanisms to a more modern electronic distribution system, which greatly improved the regularity of payments. Handa et al. (2017) found large increases in consumption, fertilizer use, and agricultural assets (including livestock) among households that gained access to the LEAP program, but the researchers were unable to distinguish these gains from a control group that had similar gains.

Another evaluation of the LEAP 1000 intervention, which targeted LEAP program transfers and free NHIS membership to pregnant women and young infants and their mothers, found a modest and mixed impact on a variety of measures of well-being, but this was expected, as the study compared households that were just below and just above the PMT cutoff value for participation (LEAP 1000 Evaluation Study Team 2018). The rate of NHIS membership increased substantially.

Osei-Akoto et al. (2016), in evaluating the LIPW program based on a field experiment, found that the program increased individual employment and earnings outcomes, measured variously. These researchers also conducted focus group discussions to complement the quantitative data. Respondents mostly expressed satisfaction with the program, with the main complaints being long delays in receiving their payments and conflicts between the demands of LIPW program work and work on their own farms (which should not occur, because LIPW subprojects are meant to take place only in the off-season).

For GSFP, studies based on a field experiment of a significant expansion of the program found that the program increased height for age, a standard nutritional measure, for girls and for poorer students, as well as raised scores on standardized tests, with larger increases for poor students (Aurino et al. 2023; Gelli et al. 2019). Operational reviews have revealed that the government is often slow to pay the caterers who prepare the school meals and that the amount paid has been eroded by inflation to such an extent that the caterers can no longer make a profit if they provide the stipulated nutritionally adequate meal.

For NHIS, there is a much larger amount of literature. Blanchet and Acheampong (2013), Degroote, Ridde, and De Allegri (2020), and Okoroh et al. (2018) have provided useful literature reviews. There is a clear consensus on the following across studies based on a variety of methods:

a. NHIS membership increased utilization of health care services;
b. NHIS members had lower out-of-pocket health care expenditures than did nonmembers;
c. NHIS members had lower "catastrophic" health care expenditures, variously defined; and
d. NHIS members usually did not have better health outcomes than nonmembers.

There also have been many operational reviews and adjustments to NHIS operations, including a change from fee-for-service reimbursements to standardized diagnosis-related groupings and an experiment with capitation payments for outpatient services. An important theme in the operational reviews is that health care providers struggle with delays in claims reimbursement or outright rejection of their claims. This issue has caused some providers to refuse to see NHIS patients, others to charge "copays" that should not be charged to members, and still others to send their patients to pharmacies to buy medicine that should be provided under NHIS (for reviews, see Blanchet and Acheampong 2013; Christmals and Aidem 2020).

In terms of the response to the coronavirus pandemic, as noted earlier, the government did not resort to a large response through its main social protection programs. It did not make any major adjustments in coverage or benefits under GSFP, the LIPW program, NHIS, or SSNIT pensions. GSFP operations were disrupted when schools closed, and LIPW program operations were interrupted for a brief period around the 3-week lockdown of the Accra and Kumasi metropolitan areas in April 2020. Following the lockdown, the LEAP program intended to offer a special additional 2 months of benefits (that is, 14 months of benefits in 2020 instead of the stipulated 12 months of benefits every year). However, due to subsequent delays in budgetary releases to the program, it could only provide 10 months of benefits to program households by the end of 2020. Thus, instead of a bump up in total benefits in 2020, it transformed into a dip in the year.

Notwithstanding, from late 2020 to early 2021, the government, with financing from the World Food Programme (WFP), provided small cash transfers (in two installments) to daily wage earners in Accra and smallholder farmers in the Western and Ashanti regions (about 74,000 individuals in total). Financed by the World Bank, in late 2020, the government also started providing small, one-time cash transfers to people from Accra and Kumasi and those from other parts of the country who identified as poor, vulnerable, or pandemic-affected individuals based on data gathered under the Ghana National Household Registry. The intervention aimed to reach 124,000 individuals.

The main responses to the pandemic by the government included cooked meals and dry rations to poor and vulnerable individuals in Accra and Kumasi during the lockdown in April 2020 (2.7 million cooked meals; dry rations to 470,000 families). The government also provided free water to 10 million customers (9 months for regular customers; 12 months for low-consuming customers) from the Ghana Water Company Limited and free or subsidized electricity to 4.7 million customers (9 months for regular customers; 12 months for low-consuming customers) from the Electricity Company of Ghana and the Northern Electricity Department of the Volta River Authority. Both interventions were initiated in April 2020. Through the Coronavirus Alleviation Programme Business Support Scheme, launched in May 2020, the government also provided soft loans to over 300,000 micro-, small-, and medium-sized enterprises. In terms of scale and the volume of spending, these responses dwarfed the various cash transfer–based responses. All these interventions were concentrated in urban areas, particularly in Accra and Kumasi. See Hallan and Raju (2023) for a detailed description of the social protection responses to the pandemic in Ghana.

In setting social protection policy, the government benefits from an unusually large evaluative and operational research literature, which it appears to use to good effect. The targeting of the LEAP program and GSFP, in particular, is both technocratic and highly effective at reaching the poor population. The impact of these programs on poverty and inequality, however, is limited due to their restricted outlays and the stinginess of their benefits, which have been eroded by inflation in real terms and never have been generous. An obvious recommendation, then, is to increase outlays for these programs. Unfortunately, that runs head on into a difficult macroeconomic and budgetary environment that, because of high debt burdens, seems unlikely to improve in the medium term. General government debt is estimated at 89 percent of GDP for 2022.[4] Deficits have been persistent for over a decade, with double-digit deficits since the onset of the pandemic. Thus, the government is left with a frustrating trade-off: It has proven tools to reduce poverty and inequality effectively but must balance those with the exigencies of fiscal deficit reduction. The recent government announcements of large increases in the benefit amounts of the LEAP program and GSFP do not in any way imply that this trade-off is less severe.

The LEAP program, GSFP, and presumably the LIPW program have made good use of geographic targeting. Both the LEAP program and GSFP have better targeting nationally than they do within the geographic areas where they are active. That is, both programs have chosen the areas in which to operate well given their intention to reach the poor population. As these programs continue to expand their national coverage, as both have done over the past decade, they will lose their effective geographic targeting, which may worsen their targeting overall. On the other hand, the government uses a PMT to target the LEAP program to households within selected communities, and our simulations show that its sole use can be as effective or more so than the prior multilevel, multimethod targeting strategy used by the program, which includes targeting individuals with specific sociodemographic characteristics as well as those living in poor areas. Therefore, there is every reason to believe that the LEAP program will continue to have high pro-poor targeting.

GSFP, however, cannot target individual children; it is a school-level intervention. Expansion to nationwide coverage, then, will certainly dilute its targeting effectiveness. This suggests a policy adjustment: The government could concentrate its social assistance program spending meant to alter the distribution of income directly in the LEAP program and perhaps the LIPW program, where the PMT can be used to target the poor population effectively. GSFP, on the other hand, would cease to be a transfer program. Instead, it could be assigned to schools where it is most likely to improve children's health and education outcomes, based on the evaluation results in the academic literature. Of course, these schools would have many poor children, but the redistributional effects would be a side benefit, not the main purpose, which would be nutrition status, school enrollment and attendance, and academic achievement.

NHIS presents the most daunting problems we found in this study. Unlike the other social protection programs, NHIS is meant to be universal (that is, to provide health insurance for all). Yet over the past 15 years, enrollment has been 30 percent to 40 percent of the population, but even with this reduced population coverage, NHIS has difficulty covering its expenses. By far the most common criticism we found of any social protection program in Ghana is that NHIS pays health care providers late or not at all for the services they provide to NHIS members. If NHIS is to be truly universal, it will need substantially more resources, more than twice its current outlay. Once again, this collides with the macroeconomic and fiscal situation. It seems unlikely that the government can allocate the additional resources needed to make NHIS universal.

What other options are there? Raising fees and premia might seem to be the obvious answer. They are very low, covering less than 5 percent of NHIS expenditures. Yet, it is also true that operational evaluations and survey data suggest that fees and premia, however small, are the main impediment to people registering or reregistering for NHIS. Lacking this, NHIS must accept that it will not cover everyone, reduce the scope of the coverage it offers, or obtain an implausibly large allocation from the central budget, perhaps by increasing the national health insurance levy.

SSNIT is also far from universal. In the past few years, it has tried to draw in more informal sector workers, but the response has been minimal. Also, there is a lesson from the NHIS experience: The government probably cannot and will not fund a universal pension, so any expansion of membership will require actuarially fair premia payments from new members, something that will probably keep them from joining.

An important observation from many operational reviews and the press is that the government has a pervasive and chronic problem: It often accumulates substantial arrears to its service providers. Over the previous decade, the government failed to pay more than GH¢3 billion it owed to SSNIT for its employees' premia. As noted, NHIS is so slow to reimburse health care providers that many now refuse to accept NHIS patients or charge them illegal copays. GSFP caterers and LIPW program participants have sometimes experienced long delays in payments as well.

The convenience of these arrears for a cash-strapped government is understandable: They constitute an interest-free loan and also hide the true size of the deficit, for a while. However, arrears have real costs in terms of program effectiveness. The arrears to SSNIT reduce its investment earnings, jeopardizing its already doubtful ability to pay future pensions. The arrears to health care providers cause them to deny NHIS members the free health care that NHIS is supposed to guarantee. Unpaid GSFP caterers must cut corners in the school meals they provide to children.

The rest of this book is organized as follows. To help contextualize the findings, chapter 2 presents background information on Ghana. Chapter 3 describes key design and implementation parameters of the social protection programs. Chapter 4 discusses results from the analysis of the performance of the programs. Chapter 5 concludes with thoughts on the future of social protection policy in Ghana.

This book also includes five appendices that discuss the construction of key variables for the program performance analysis (appendix A), analytical concepts for the analysis (appendix B), supplemental results (appendix C), the study's strategy for estimating counterfactual household consumption for households with SSNIT pensions in the absence of those pensions (appendix D), and the strategy for predicting additional LEAP program households to correct for underreporting of LEAP program households in the GLSS 2016–17 data (appendix E).

NOTES

1. For SSNIT pensions, the only program that offers substantial future benefits, an actuarial analysis would be appropriate. The International Labour Organization has conducted such analyses for SSNIT, but to our knowledge, they are not published or publicly available.
2. Given the sharp rise in world food prices, considering the association between program participation and food security status is also of interest, but the GLSS 2016–17 questions on food security are nonstandard and sufficiently limited that we cannot examine this association.
3. The noted percentage of overall government spending should be interpreted with caution given important nongovernment sources of financing of NHIS and SSNIT pensions, discussed later in the study.
4. Based on data from the World Bank, Macro Poverty Outlook for Sub-Sahara Africa, Ghana datasheet, April 2023, https://www.worldbank.org/en/publication/macro-poverty -outlook/mpo_ssa.

REFERENCES

Aurino, Elisabetta, Aulo Gelli, Clement Adamba, Isaac Osei-Akoto, and Harold Alderman. 2023. "Food for Thought? Experimental Evidence on the Learning Impacts of a Large-Scale School Feeding Program." *Journal of Human Resources* 58 (1): 74–111.

Blanchet, Nathan, and Osei B. Acheampong. 2013. *Building on Community-Based Health Insurance to Expand National Coverage: The Case of Ghana.* Bethesda, MD: Abt Associates.

Bourguignon, François, and Luiz A. Pereira da Silva, eds. 2003. *The Impact of Economic Policies on Poverty and Income Distribution: Evaluation Techniques and Tools.* Washington, DC: World Bank.

Christmals, Christmal Dela, and Kizito Aidem. 2020. "Implementation of the National Health Insurance Scheme (NHIS) in Ghana: Lessons for South Africa and Low- and Middle-Income Countries." *Risk Management and Healthcare Policy* 13: 1879–904.

Degroote, Stéphanie, Valery Ridde, and Manuel De Allegri. 2020. "Health Insurance in Sub-Saharan Africa: A Scoping Review of the Methods Used to Evaluate Its Impact." *Applied Health Economics and Health Policy* 18 (6): 825–40.

Figari, Francesco, Alari Paulus, and Holly Sutherland. 2015. "Microsimulation and Policy Analysis." In *Handbook of Income Distribution*, edited by A. B. Atkinson and F. Bourguignon, 2141–221. Vol. 2B. Amsterdam: Elsevier/North-Holland.

Gelli, Aulo, Elisabetta Aurino, Gloria Folson, Daniel Arhinful, Clement Adamba, Issac Osei-Akoto, Edoardo Masset, Kristie Watkins, Meena Fernandes, Lesley Drake, and Harold Alderman. 2019. "A School Meals Program Implemented at Scale in Ghana Increases Height-for-Age during Midchildhood in Girls and in Children from Poor Households: A Cluster Randomized Trial." *Journal of Nutrition* 149 (8): 1434–42.

GSS (Ghana Statistical Service). 2019. *Ghana Living Standards Survey (GLSS) 7: Main Report.* Accra: GSS.

Hallan, Sakshi, and Dhushyanth Raju. 2023. "Social Protection Response to the Coronavirus Pandemic in Ghana." Manuscript.

Handa, Sudhanshu, Michael Park, Robert Osei Darko, Isaac Osei-Akoto, Benjamin Davis, and Silvio Daidone. 2014. *Livelihood Empowerment Against Poverty Program: Impact Evaluation.* Chapel Hill: Carolina Population Center, University of North Carolina at Chapel Hill.

Handa, Sudhanshu, Gustavo Angeles, Gean Spektor, Robert Darko Osei, and Richard de Groot. 2017. *Livelihood Empowerment Against Poverty Programme: Endline Impact Evaluation Report.* Chapel Hill: Carolina Population Center, University of North Carolina at Chapel Hill.

ILO (International Labour Organization). 2015. *Rationalizing Social Protection Expenditures in Ghana.* Geneva: ILO.

LEAP 1000 Evaluation Study Team. 2018. *Ghana LEAP 1000 Programme: Endline Evaluation Report.* Chapel Hill: University of North Carolina Population Center. https://transfer.cpc.unc.edu/wp-content/uploads/2021/04/LEAP1000_Report_Final-2019-for-dissemination.pdf.

Lustig, Nora, ed. 2018. *Commitment to Equity Handbook: Estimating the Impact of Fiscal Policy on Inequality and Poverty.* New Orleans: CEQ Institute at Tulane University; Washington, DC: Brookings Institution Press.

Nxumalo, Mpumelelo, and Dhushyanth Raju. 2022. *Shocks and Social Safety Net Program Participation in Ghana: Descriptive Evidence from Linking Climate Risk Maps to Program Beneficiary Rolls.* Washington, DC: World Bank.

Okoroh, Juliet, Samuel Essoun, Anthony Seddoh, Hobart Harris, Joel S. Weissman, Lydia Dsane-Selby, and Robert Riviello. 2018. "Evaluating the Impact of the National Health Insurance Scheme of Ghana on Out of Pocket Expenditures: A Systematic Review." *BMC Health Services Research* 18 (1): 426.

Osei-Akoto, Isaac, Simon Bawakyillenuo, George Owusu, Felix Essilfie, and Innocent Agbelie. 2016. *Short Term Impact Evaluation Report: Labour Intensive Public Works (LIPW) of Ghana Social Opportunities Project (GSOP).* Accra: Institute of Statistical, Social, and Economic Research.

Wodon, Quentin. 2012. *Improving the Targeting of Social Programs in Ghana.* Washington, DC: World Bank.

World Bank. 2016. Ghana: *Social Protection Assessment and Public Expenditure Review.* Washington, DC: World Bank.

World Bank. 2017. *Ghana Public Expenditure Review: Fiscal Consolidation to Accelerate Growth and Support Inclusive Development.* Washington, DC: World Bank.

Yemtsov, Ruslan, Brooks Evans, Maddalena Honorati, Michael Lokshin, and Zurab Sajaia. 2018. *Measuring the Effectiveness of Social Protection: Concepts and Applications.* Streamlined Analysis with ADePT Software series. Washington, DC: World Bank.

Younger, Stephen D., Eric Osei-Assibey, and Felix Oppong. 2017. "Fiscal Incidence in Ghana." *Review of Development Economics* 21 (4): e47.

2 Background

INTRODUCTION

This chapter presents background information on Ghana to help contextualize the findings of our analysis on the performance of the government's main social protection programs, based on the Ghana Living Standards Survey 2016–17 (GSS 2019) data and program administrative data. This discussion covers population; national income and economic growth; consumption and income, poverty, and food insecurity; inequality; shocks; economic growth and poverty trends during the coronavirus pandemic; government revenues and expenditures; and social protection.

POPULATION

In 2021, Ghana had a total population of 30.83 million people, with 97.6 percent residing in households and 2.4 percent in institutional arrangements.[1] The average size of a household was 3.6 persons, a decline of about 1 person on average since 2010. Declines in average household size have been particularly large in the Northern, Savannah, North East, and Upper West regions, all in the north. Average household size was smaller in urban areas (3.3 persons) than in rural areas (4.0 persons) (GSS 2021a). In 2016/17, the average household size was 3.8 persons, with the average size decreasing with consumption quintile, from 6.2 persons in the poorest quintile to 2.4 persons in the richest (GSS 2019).

Four of the country's 16 regions accounted for more than half of the national population: Greater Accra (17.7 percent), Ashanti (17.6 percent), Eastern (9.5 percent), and Central (9.3 percent), all in the south (figure 2.1). Most of the national population was urban, at 56.7 percent, an increase from 50.9 percent in 2010. The urban share of the population ranged from a low of 25.4 percent in the Upper East region to a high of 91.7 percent in the Greater Accra region. Most regions in the south were majority urban, while the regions in the north were majority rural (GSS 2021a).

In terms of age structure, in 2021, 35.3 percent of the national population were ages 0–14; 60.4 percent were 15–64 (standard working age), and 4.3 percent

FIGURE 2.1

Population distribution in Ghana, by region and by area in each region, 2021

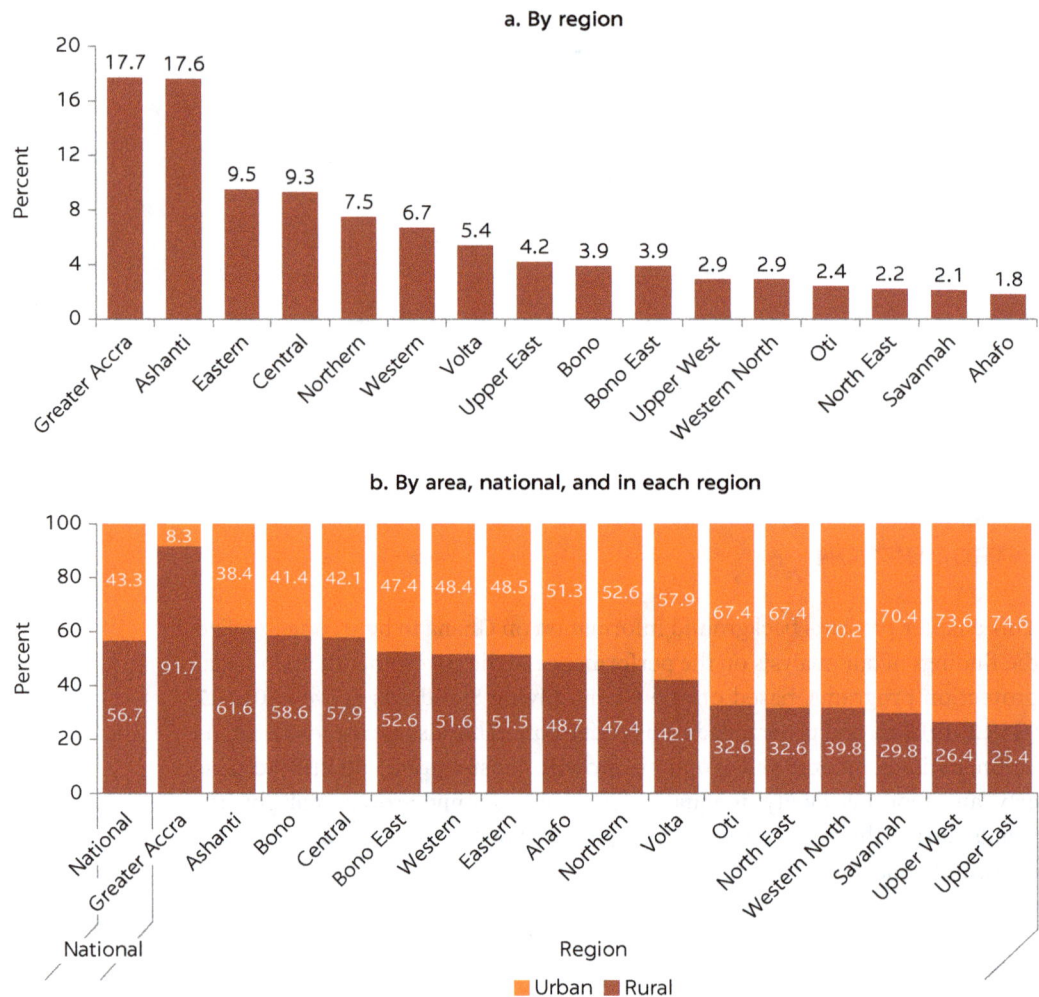

a. By region

b. By area, national, and in each region

Source: Statistics obtained from Ghana Statistical Service (2021a).

were 65 or older. The age structure varied markedly across regions. At the top end, 66.5 percent of the population in the Greater Accra region were ages 15–64, while at the bottom end, 51.4 percent were in this age group in the North East region (GSS 2021b). These patterns indicate strong rural-to-urban migration and north-to-south migration, importantly for work opportunities.

ECONOMIC GROWTH

The World Bank has classified Ghana as a lower-middle-income country. In 2021, the country's gross domestic product (GDP) per capita totaled $5,435 (in constant 2017 purchasing power parity [PPP] international dollars). Growth in GDP per capita averaged 4.3 percent annually between 2010 and 2019, buoyed by the discovery and exploitation of offshore oil and gas reserves (figure 2.2). Ghana began the 2010s with GDP per capita similar to the average for Sub-Saharan Africa but grew much faster than the region as a whole. The rapid growth nevertheless has been erratic, with large swings driven by the country's dependence

FIGURE 2.2

Ghana's national income trends, 2010–21

a. GDP per capita

b. GDP per capita growth

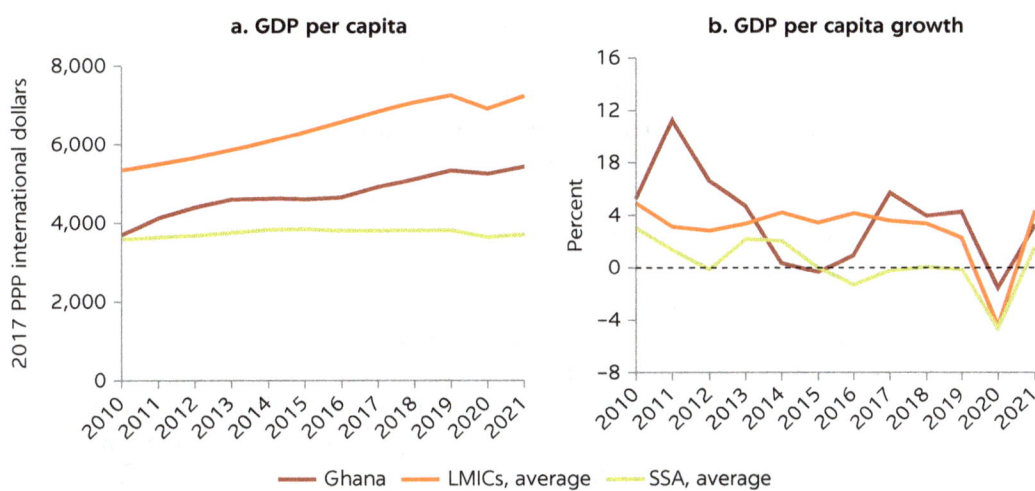

— Ghana   — LMICs, average   — SSA, average

Source: Statistics obtained from the World Bank, World Development Indicators database.
Note: The figure shows trends in annual GDP per capita in 2017 PPP international dollars and annual GDP per capita growth for Ghana. It also shows averages for these measures for Sub-Saharan Africa and lower-middle-income countries. GDP = gross domestic product; LMICs = lower-middle-income countries; PPP = purchasing power parity; SSA = Sub-Saharan Africa.

on mining, oil, and gas for national income; a serious drought that affected power supply; and perhaps a political business cycle.[2] Between 2010 and 2019, GDP growth rates ranged from a low of –0.3 percent (in 2015) to a high of 11.3 percent (in 2011). GDP per capita growth fell to –1.5 percent in 2020, due to the coronavirus pandemic, and rebounded to 3.3 percent in 2021.

Decomposition of Ghana's economic growth between 1970 and 2016 shows the main contributions of change—total factor productivity, capital accumulation, and labor accumulation (including labor quality as reflected by education)—during different subperiods. The analysis suggests that the change in labor accumulation has contributed meaningfully to the country's economic growth in all subperiods. The contribution to growth from the change in total factor productivity became positive and sizable roughly between 1990 and 2010. Meanwhile, the contribution from the change in capital accumulation became positive and sizable roughly between 2005 and 2015 (Nxumalo and Raju 2020).

CONSUMPTION AND INCOME

In 2016/17, Ghana's annual household consumption averaged GH¢12,900. Greater Accra ranked as the wealthiest region, with an annual household consumption level of GH¢21,300, while Upper West was the poorest, with an annual level of GH¢6,100—more than a threefold difference. In general, the regions in the north had the lowest consumption levels. The household consumption level was much higher in urban areas (at GH¢15,600) than in rural areas (GH¢9,400) (GSS 2019).

In terms of categories of goods and services consumed, food constituted 42.9 percent of total consumption for households nationally; housing, 15.8 percent; and other nonfood consumption, 41.3 percent. The food share in total consumption was higher in rural areas than in urban areas (50.6 percent versus 39.2 percent); the share also declined with consumption quintiles (from 49.2 percent in the poorest quintile to 38.2 percent in the richest) (GSS 2019).

Annual gross household income in Ghana averaged GH¢33,900 in 2016/17, with the income level for urban areas about 2.5 times higher than for rural areas. In terms of quintiles, the income level was about seven times higher for the richest than for the poorest income quintile. On average, across the country, earnings from nonfarm self-employment income constituted three-fourths of household income, followed by wage-employment earnings at 14.1 percent and agricultural earnings at 5.0 percent, rental income at 3.6 percent, and remittances at 1.4 percent. Transfers were a negligible source of household income. Compared with richer households, agricultural earnings were a much more important source of income for poorer households, while nonfarm self-employment earnings were a much less important source. There was no clear pattern with respect to the contribution of wage-employment earnings to household income across income quintiles (GSS 2019).

POVERTY AND FOOD INSECURITY

Poverty levels in Ghana declined steadily beginning in the 1990s through 2012/13, when they stopped falling despite significant economic growth between 2012/13 and 2016/17 (figure 2.3). The country's poverty rate was 12.7 percent in 2016/17, measured using the international poverty line of $1.90 per day per person in 2011 PPP international dollars. This level of poverty is lower than the average for Sub-Saharan Africa and for lower-middle-income countries in general (World Bank 2018). Measured using the country's poverty lines, the overall poverty rate in Ghana was 23.4 percent in 2016/17, whereas its extreme poverty rate was 8.2 percent. The country's overall and extreme poverty gaps were 8.4 percent and 2.8 percent, respectively (GSS 2018).

FIGURE 2.3

Ghana's poverty rate trends, based on international poverty line ($1.90 per day), 1990–2020

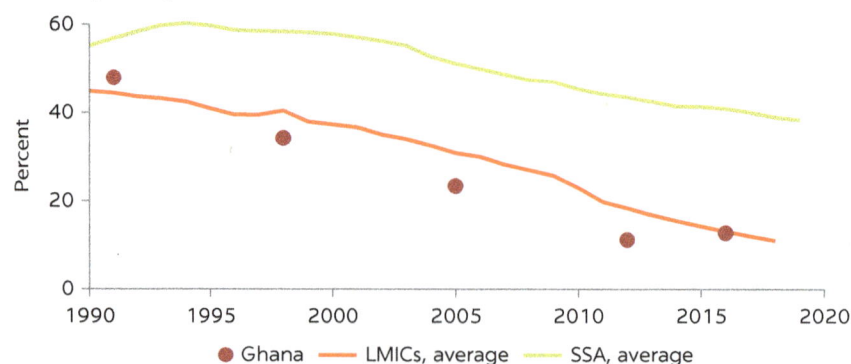

Source: Statistics obtained from the World Bank, World Development Indicators database.
Note: Figure shows the trend for the poverty rate based on the $1.90-per-day poverty line in 2011 PPP international dollars for Ghana. It also shows the average poverty rates based on the same poverty line for Sub-Saharan Africa and lower-middle-income countries. Each of the series end at a different year: Ghana, at 2016; LMIC average, at 2018; and SSA average, at 2019. LMICs = lower-middle-income countries; SSA = Sub-Saharan Africa.

FIGURE 2.4

Extreme and overall poverty rates in Ghana, national, by area, and by region, 2016/17

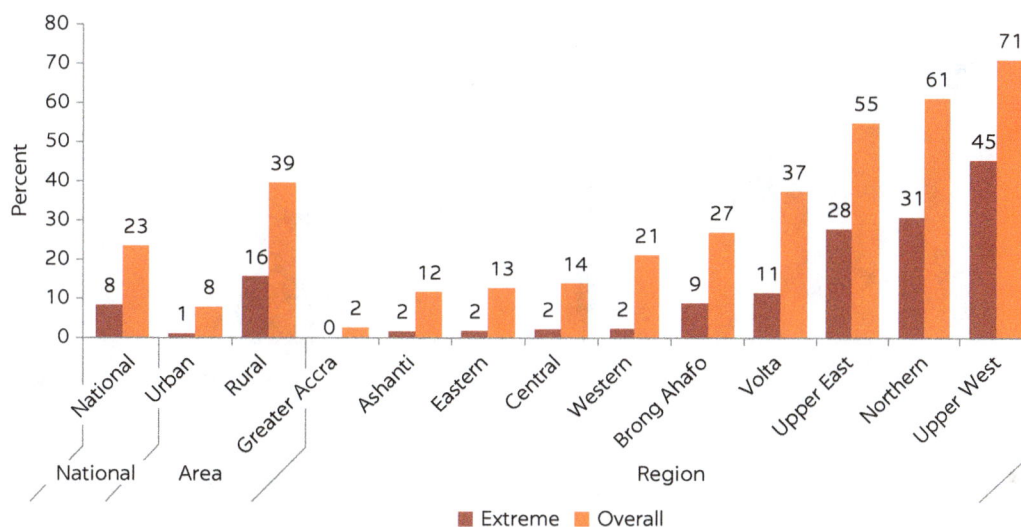

Source: Statistics obtained from GSS 2018.
Note: The classification of regions is per Ghana's 2010 population and housing census (GSS 2012).

Poverty rates appeared to differ markedly across areas within Ghana (figure 2.4). They were substantially higher in rural than in urban areas. In 2016/17, the overall poverty rate in rural areas was 39.5 percent, five times higher than the rate (7.8 percent) for urban areas. The extreme poverty rate was 15.6 percent in rural areas compared with 1 percent in urban areas. Overall and extreme poverty rates in 2016/17 were also markedly higher in the Volta, Upper East, Northern, and Upper West regions than in other parts of the country. These high-poverty regions are situated in northern and eastern Ghana.

Poverty levels also varied within high-poverty regions. Maps for 2010 show that poverty levels across administrative districts in the country appeared to be higher in the western parts of the high-poverty regions (figure 2.5). Spatial patterns where infrastructure, services, and markets are lacking show a strong overlap with the spatial pattern where poverty levels are high, suggesting that these factors may be constraining households from achieving sufficiently high incomes to escape poverty (World Bank 2018). High-poverty regions also face adverse ecological conditions, which are considered to play an important role in constraining growth, development, and poverty reduction (World Bank 2018).

The extent of households with an extreme-poor, a moderate-poor, or a near-poor classification in 2016/17 shows some differences across selected population subgroups (figure 2.6), with consumption (per adult equivalent) below the extreme poverty line for the extreme-poor population, between the extreme and overall poverty lines for the moderate-poor population, and above the overall poverty line but below 1.5 times the overall poverty line for the near-poor population.

No difference in poverty rates existed between men and women, accounted for by the fact that consumption per adult equivalent was measured at the household level and that households, on average, had roughly equal numbers of male and female members. Households headed by women were less likely to be

FIGURE 2.5

Distribution of poverty in Ghana based on various indicators, by district, 2010

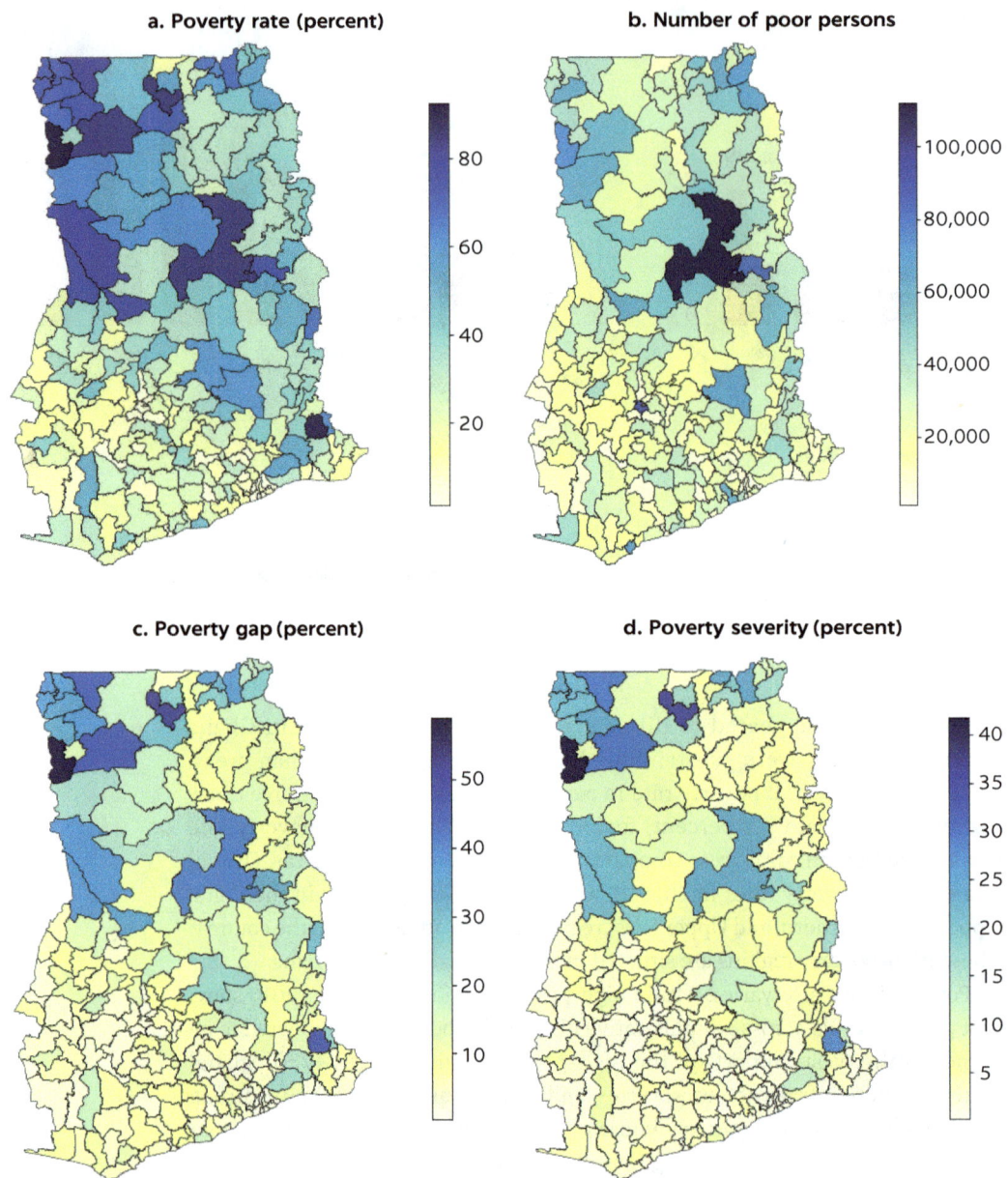

a. Poverty rate (percent)

b. Number of poor persons

c. Poverty gap (percent)

d. Poverty severity (percent)

Source: Statistics obtained from the Ghana Statistical Service, 2015.
Note: The poverty gap is a measure of how far the poor population is from the poverty line. Severity of poverty is the square of the poverty gap, which gives greater attention to the needs of the poorest individuals. It considers the distribution of poverty among the poor population, giving greater weight to the poorest of the poor. The classification of districts is per Ghana's 2010 population and housing census (GSS 2012).

moderate poor and much less likely to be extreme poor than were those headed by men. This pattern is often seen in countries where significant numbers of men migrate (internally or internationally) for work that pays relatively well and then send remittances back to their household.

Children younger than 15 years resided in households that were somewhat more likely to be poor than did people of working age. The same was true for people age 60 or older.

FIGURE 2.6

Poverty rates in Ghana, by selected subgroups, 2016/17

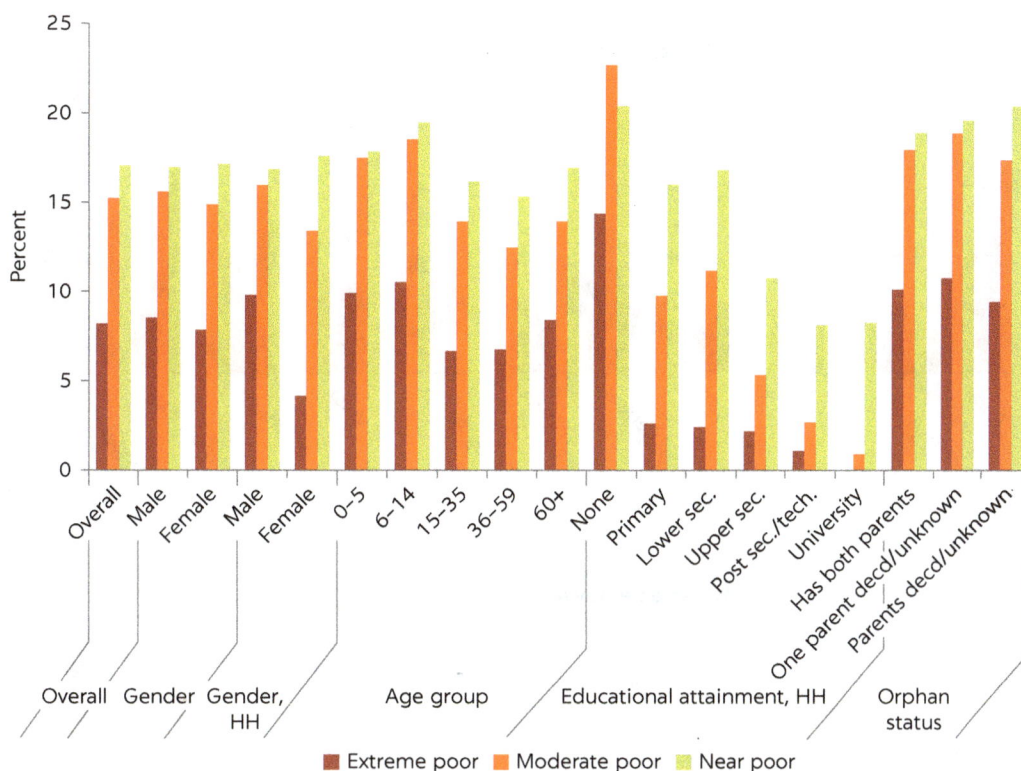

Source: World Bank compilation based on Ghana Living Standards Survey 2016–17 data.
Note: HH = household head, as defined by the household. Orphan status is restricted to children under age 18.
Decd = deceased. Lower sec. = lower secondary school. Upper sec. = upper secondary school. Post sec./tech. =
postsecondary or technical school.

Across all these age groups, the differences in the extreme poverty rate were greater than those for the moderate or near poverty rate. Extreme poverty was highly concentrated among households without formal education. Poverty rates also show a strong gradient across education attainment levels. The relationship between near poverty and education also had a negative correlation but was less strong than that for moderate poverty and, especially, for extreme poverty. Perhaps surprisingly, for children younger than 18 years, losing one or both parents had little relationship to their poverty status, a testament to the willingness of better-off Ghanaian families to take in orphans.

Even though extreme and overall poverty rates remained roughly constant across the country as a whole between 2012/13 and 2016/17, the rates in urban areas continued to decline apace, while those in rural areas increased (figure 2.7). These patterns are especially notable in the regions with large urban populations (Greater Accra and Ashanti) and some that are predominantly rural (Volta, Northern, and Upper East). This pattern may be explained by the fact that 2017 was an El Niño year, which tends to produce droughts in the northern areas of Ghana.

The small change in the overall poverty rate between 2012/13 and 2016/17 (−0.8 percentage points) can be decomposed into a "growth contribution" (that which is attributable to the increase in average consumption during the period)

FIGURE 2.7

Overall and extreme poverty rate trends in Ghana, national, by area, and by region, 2005/06, 2012/13, and 2016/17

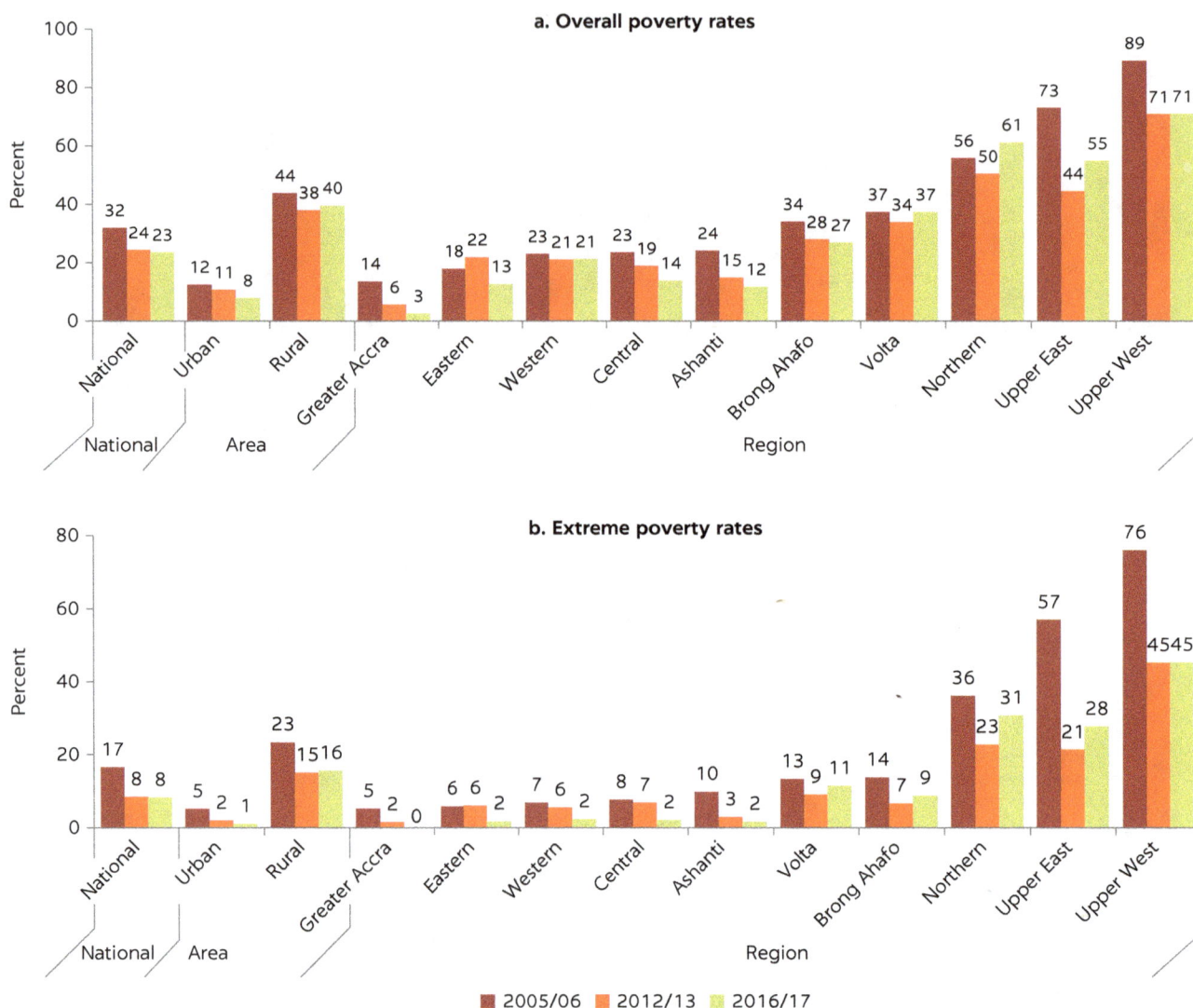

a. Overall poverty rates

b. Extreme poverty rates

■ 2005/06 ■ 2012/13 ■ 2016/17

Source: Statistics obtained from GSS 2018.
Note: The trends are shown for the country as a whole, by urban versus rural areas, and by region. The classification of regions is per Ghana's 2010 population and housing census (GSS 2012).

and a "redistribution contribution" (that which is attributable to a change in the share of consumption going to the poor or nonpoor populations) (figure 2.8). Nationally, economic growth contributed to a 2.3 percentage-point decline in the overall poverty rate, but this was offset by increasing inequality, which led to a 1.4 percentage-point increase in the overall poverty rate. Thus, overall consumption grew at a healthy pace over these four years, but the growth was uneven, favoring the nonpoor population.

Interestingly, though, this same pattern is not seen in most regions in the country. In urban areas, for example, both growth in consumption and a reduction in inequality contributed to a lower overall poverty rate. The same is true in many regions, the exceptions being Western, Volta, and Upper West, where the growth effect was negative but offset by decreasing inequality. Overall, these

FIGURE 2.8

Growth and redistribution decomposition of the change in poverty rate in Ghana, national, by area, and by region, 2012/13–2016/17

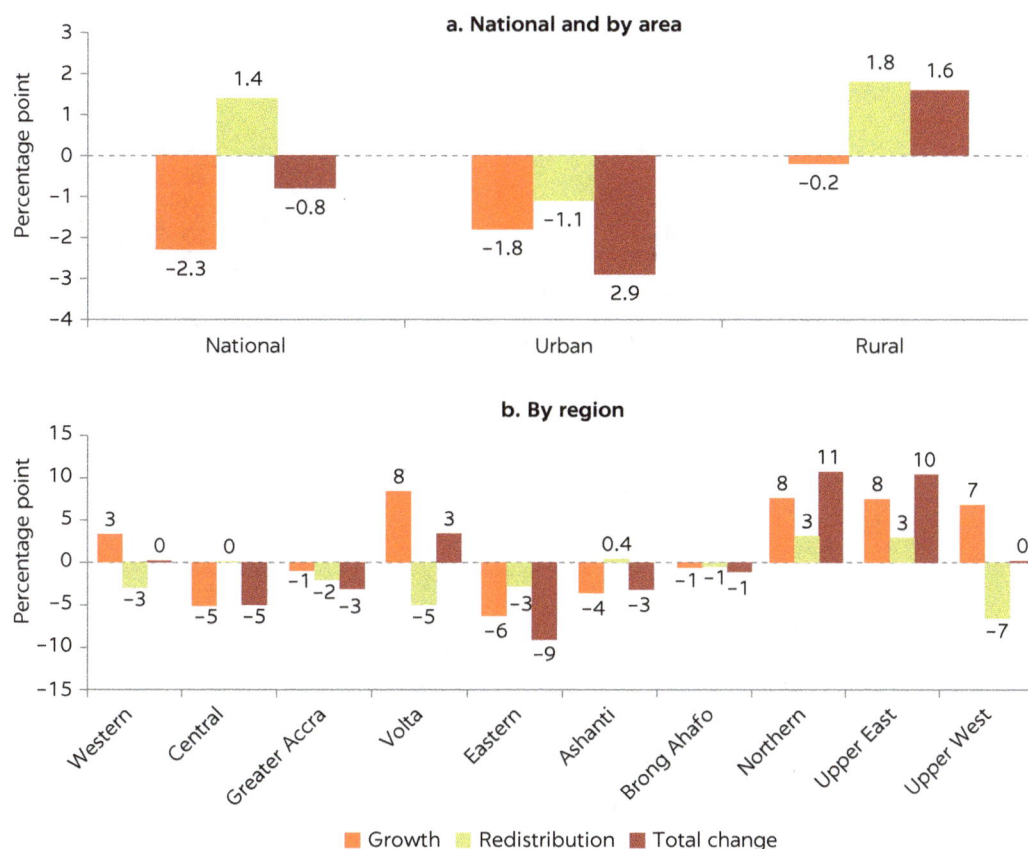

Source: Statistics obtained from GSS 2018.

Note: Figure shows the decomposition of the observed percentage-point change in the poverty rate between 2012/13 and 2016/17 into the percentage-point change in the mean value of consumption, assuming that inequality in welfare remained unchanged (the "growth" effect), and the percentage-point change in inequality of welfare, assuming that mean consumption remained unchanged (the "redistribution" effect). These decompositions were performed at the national, urban, rural, and regional levels. Classification of regions is per Ghana's 2010 population and housing census (GSS 2012).

patterns suggest a migration pattern in which people from poorer regions have migrated to richer ones, especially to cities. This migration has the effect of increasing consumption in the cities and decreasing it (relatively) in the poorer rural areas, but also increasing inequality in urban areas as the new migrants are poor relative to longtime urban residents.

In November–December 2020, a large-scale national household sample survey was fielded for a Comprehensive Food Security and Vulnerability Analysis (CFSVA), which captured data on household food insecurity. The survey report indicates that of the 11.6 percent of households across the country that were classified as food insecure, 6.5 percent were moderately food insecure and 5.2 percent were severely food insecure (GSS et al. 2021). The prevalence of food insecurity was higher in rural than in urban areas (18.2 percent versus 5.5 percent, a threefold difference) and much higher in the northern regions than in the southern regions (figure 2.9). Regional food insecurity prevalence rates ranged from a low of 3.5 percent in Greater Accra to a high of

FIGURE 2.9

Food insecurity rates in Ghana, national, by area, and by region, 2020

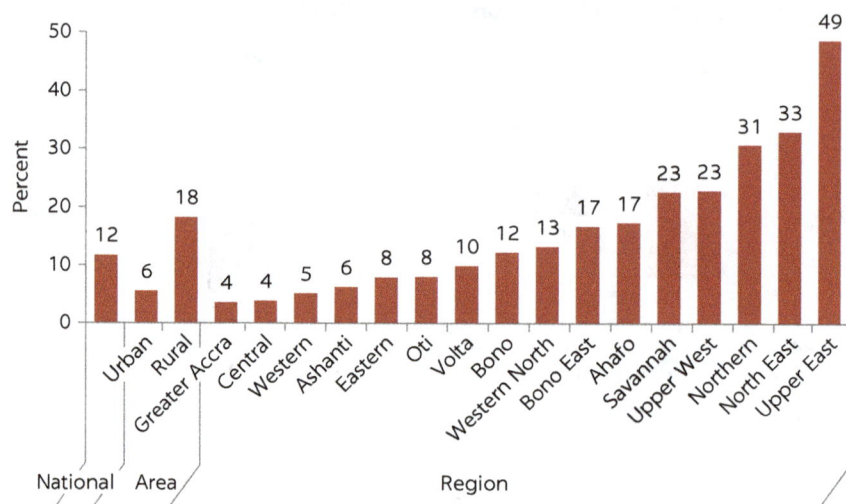

Source: Statistics obtained from GSS et al. 2021.

48.7 percent in Upper East (a 14-fold difference). The household correlates of the likelihood of food insecurity correspond qualitatively to the household correlates of the likelihood of poverty (GSS et al. 2021; World Bank 2018, 2020).

INEQUALITY

Ghana's level of inequality in household consumption per capita, measured by the Gini index, was 43.0 percent in 2016/17 (figure 2.10). It was higher in rural areas (41.8 percent) than in urban areas (37.9 percent). In terms of regions, it was lowest in Greater Accra (35.1 percent) and highest in the Upper East (48.1 percent). Indeed, inequality levels appeared to be lower in the richer, southern regions than in the poorer, northern regions. These patterns run counter to what is usually observed in other countries.

Between 2005/06 and 2016/17, the level of inequality increased in Ghana (by about 1 percentage point), driven by the increase in inequality in rural areas (figure 2.11).

SHOCKS

While Ghana has conducted several nationally representative household sample surveys in recent years, these surveys have lacked well-constructed modules to capture data on shocks experienced by individuals and households. However, the national household sample survey fielded for the 2020 CFSVA did administer a shocks module (GSS et al. 2021). The types of shocks surveyed appear to be a combination of presumably more chronic, adverse circumstances (for example, high food prices or lack of money to buy food or to cover basic needs) and sharp, acute developments (such as loss of employment by a household member), with the latter corresponding more closely to what is typically considered a shock.

FIGURE 2.10

Inequality in household consumption in Ghana, national, by area, and by region, 2016/17

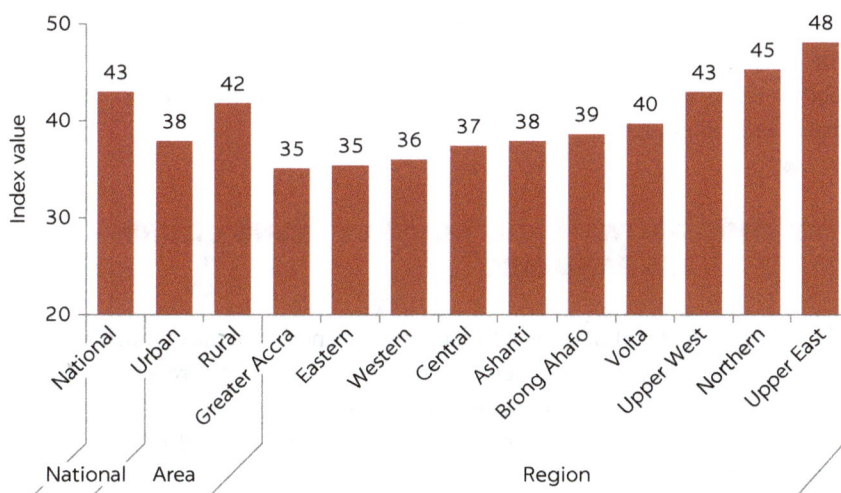

Source: Statistics obtained from GSS 2018.
Note: Figure shows inequality in consumption, measured by the Gini index, for the country as a whole, by urban versus rural areas and by region in 2016/17. Classification of regions is per Ghana's 2010 population and housing census (GSS 2012).

FIGURE 2.11

Inequality trends in consumption in Ghana, national, by area, and by region, 2005/06 to 2016/17

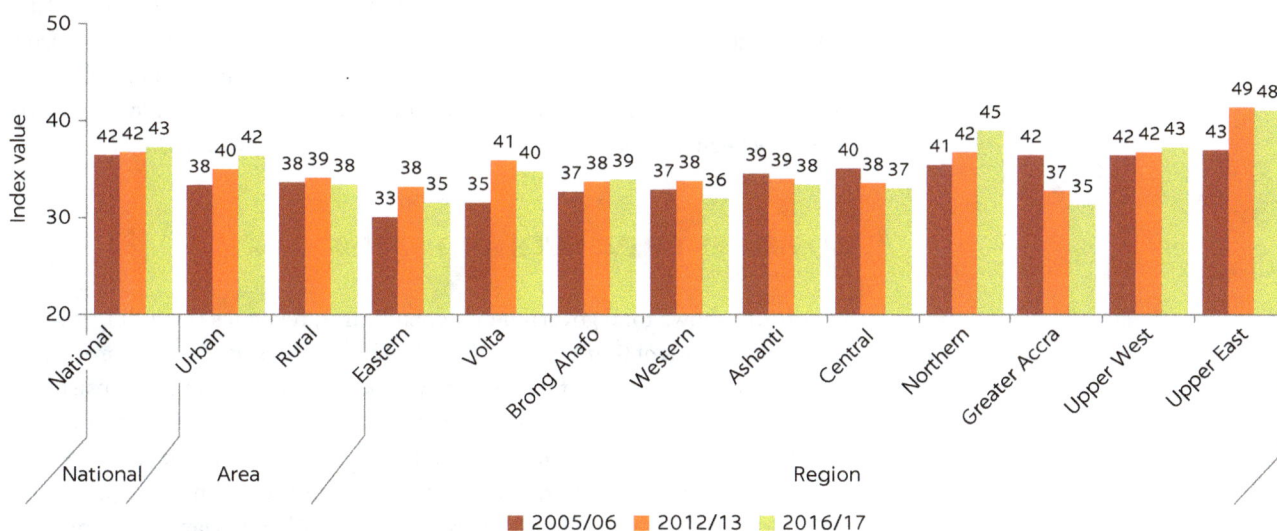

Source: Statistics obtained from GSS 2018.
Note: The trends in inequality in consumption are shown for the country as a whole, by urban versus rural areas, and by region. Classification of regions is per Ghana's 2010 population and housing census (GSS 2012).

The 2020 CFSVA survey report indicates that, overall, around 90 percent of households experienced at least one of the 15 different types of shocks listed. The most common shocks experienced by households were the coronavirus pandemic (63.8 percent of households reported this shock), high food prices (34.1 percent), and delayed rains or drought (21.6 percent). Urban households were more likely than rural households to report pandemic or high food price shocks, while rural households were more likely than urban households to report delayed rain or drought shocks.

The survey report also provides a more detailed analysis of the coronavirus pandemic shock. The pandemic predominantly affected households by keeping members from (fully) pursuing their self- and wage-employment activities. The main, specific factors were curfew and lockdown measures, reduced working time, temporary layoffs, and closed workplaces. The report's analysis of correlates suggests that wealthier households were more likely to report a coronavirus pandemic shock.

ECONOMIC GROWTH AND POVERTY TRENDS DURING THE CORONAVIRUS PANDEMIC

Ghana's pattern of real GDP growth rates over the period of the coronavirus pandemic suggests a V-shaped trajectory. Real GDP grew by 6.2 percent in 2018 and by 6.5 percent in 2019. In 2020, real GDP growth fell sharply to 0.4 percent, before rebounding to 5.4 percent in 2021 and 3.2 percent in 2022 (IMF 2021, 2022, 2023).

The last actual measurement of poverty for Ghana was in 2016/17, based on the Ghana Living Standards Survey. As noted earlier, the estimated poverty rate for that year was 12.7 percent, based on the international poverty line of $1.90 per day in 2011 PPP dollars. Annual poverty rates using the same poverty line and predicted as a function of actual GDP per capita in constant cedis are available for Ghana through 2021 (World Bank 2022). The pattern of evolution in these predicted poverty rates consists of a steady decline through the late 2010s, with a slight increase during the first year of the coronavirus pandemic, from 8.4 percent in 2019 to 9.2 percent in 2020, and then down again (World Bank 2022). Of course, the counterfactual for the effect of the pandemic on poverty may have been a monotonic downward trajectory over the period.

GOVERMENT REVENUES AND EXPENDITURES

Figure 2.12 shows total government expenditures, revenues (including grants), and debt as shares of GDP since 2010; it also shows debt service as a share of total government expenditures for the same period. Expenditures have consistently exceeded revenues, often by large amounts and especially in election years (figure 2.12a).[3] The fiscal deficit averaged 4.8 percent of GDP from 2010 to 2019, then rose sharply to 14.7 percent with the onset of the coronavirus pandemic. In 2021, the deficit declined to 11.4 percent of GDP, still much larger than prepandemic levels. Although smaller than in 2011, the deficit in 2022 remained high compared to the average level in the 2010s.

As a consequence of persistent deficits, the government's debt position worsened steadily throughout the 2010s and dramatically with the coronavirus pandemic. General government debt as a share of GDP rose steadily from 2010 to 2019, although external public debt as a share of GDP stabilized from 2015 to 2019 (figure 2.12b). Instead, the government financed its spending with increasing amounts of domestic debt. The large pandemic-era deficits have been funded, both internally and externally, with Ghana's overall debt level rising to concerning levels in 2022.

A further consequence of Ghana's persistent deficits is a steady rise in debt service. Interest payments as a share of total government expenditure grew by

FIGURE 2.12

Ghana's fiscal position, 2010–22

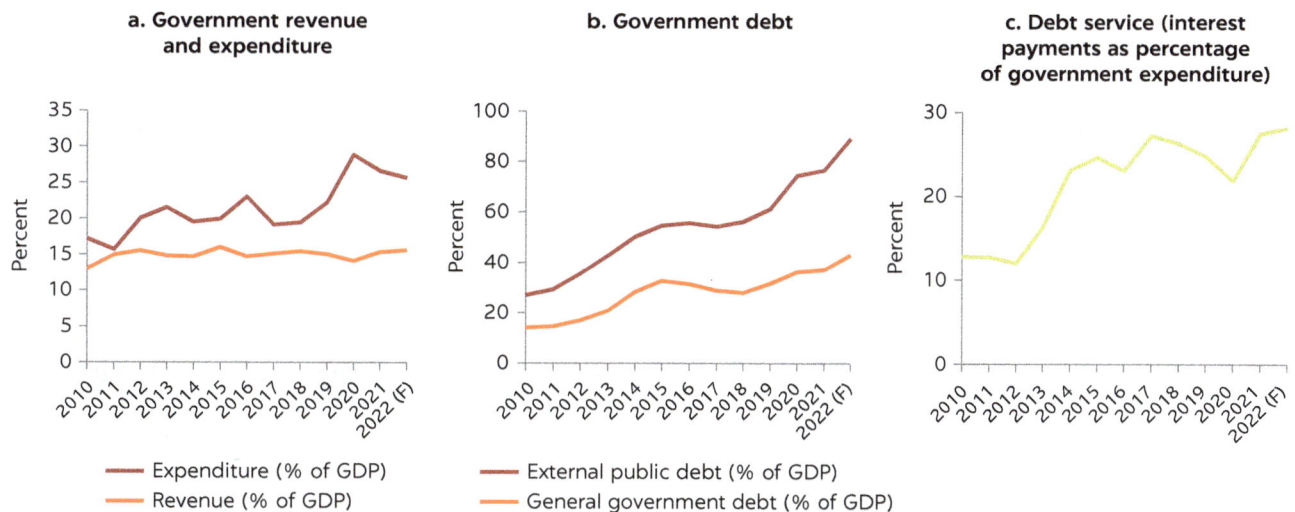

a. Government revenue and expenditure

b. Government debt

c. Debt service (interest payments as percentage of government expenditure)

— Expenditure (% of GDP)
— Revenue (% of GDP)

— External public debt (% of GDP)
— General government debt (% of GDP)

Source: Statistics obtained from the World Bank, Macro Poverty Outlook for Sub-Sahara Africa, Ghana datasheet, April 2023.
Note: Figure shows trends in government revenue, expenditure, and debt as a percentage of gross domestic product; it also shows the trend in government debt service as a percentage of government expenditure. On the x-axis, "F" indicates a forecasted value.

10 percentage points between 2010 and 2014 and were then on a roughly stable trend until the start of the coronavirus pandemic (figure 2.12c). Interest payments rose sharply in 2021 and 2022 in the wake of the heavy pandemic-era borrowing, a development that is expected to reduce the fiscal space for public spending on the social protection programs reviewed in this study.

SOCIAL PROTECTION

The basis for the public provision of social protection derives from the Constitution of the Fourth Republic of Ghana, specifically the Directive Principles of State Policy. Social protection is covered under the National Social Protection Policy (NSPP) introduced in 2015 (MOGCSP 2015). This policy follows the Social Protection Strategy introduced in 2007 and revised in 2012. The policy defines "social protection" to be "a range of actions carried out by the state and other parties in response to vulnerability and poverty, which seek to guarantee relief to those sections of the population who for any reason are not able to provide for themselves."

The NSPP presents the concept of a "social protection floor," which is composed of access to basic health care for all as well as minimum income security to meet the basic needs for children, people of working age, and the elderly. The policy also specifies three (partially overlapping) target groups for its services and programs for individuals who are chronically poor, economically at risk, and socially vulnerable. It also lays out incremental steps the country should take over a 15-year period toward achieving universal social protection. While the policy emphasizes rights protection and social services, followed by social safety net (or social assistance) programs, it gives marginal attention to the social insurance agenda and associated programs.

The NSPP assigns the MOGCSP primary responsibility for implementing the policy and coordinating activities and actors in the social protection space. The MOGCSP was established in 2013, succeeding the Ministry of Women and Children's Affairs. Key government partners for implementing the social protection policy comprise the Ministries of Education; Employment and Labour Relations; Finance; Food and Agriculture; Health; and Local Government, Decentralization, and Rural Development. The policy underscores the need for decentralized delivery of the main social protection programs, with the involvement of the Community Social Protection Committees; District Social Protection Committees; Local Government Service; Metropolitan, Municipal, and District Assemblies; and Regional Coordinating Councils (through Regional Planning Coordinating Units).

The social protection policy acknowledges multiple other policies pertinent to the social protection agenda, including the National Ageing Policy (introduced in 2010), the National Youth Policy (2010), the National Local Economic Development Policy (2013), the National Gender Policy (2014), and the National Employment Policy (2015). The National Labor-Intensive Public Works Policy, introduced in 2016, has substantive links with the national social protection, employment, and local economic development policies (MELR and MLGRD 2016).

The NSPP considers the Livelihood Empowerment Against Poverty (LEAP) program, the Labor-Intensive Public Works (LIPW) program, and the Ghana School Feeding Programme (GSFP) as main (or "flagship") public social protection programs. It also characterizes registration, renewal, and premium payment exemptions for National Health Insurance Scheme (NHIS) participation received by certain population groups, among them "indigent" individuals and pregnant women, as main public social protection measures (not NHIS in its entirety). Finally, the policy denotes "capitation grants," per-student subsidies, provided to government basic schools, as another public main social protection measure. Capitation grants are mainly used to help defray the cost of teaching and learning materials. The policy presents these five interventions as Ghana's social protection "basket."

The Social Security and National Insurance Trust (SSNIT) pension scheme is not classified as a key social protection program, although the NSPP recognizes the program's relevance in the social insurance area. For the purposes of our performance review, along with SSNIT pensions, we examine all the interventions in the NSPP's social protection basket except for capitation grants for basic schools, because we consider this measure as much more of a standard public education intervention than a public social protection approach.

None of the main public social assistance programs—the LEAP program, the LIPW program, orGSFP—is covered by legal provisions. With respect to social insurance and social security, NHIS and SSNIT pensions are covered by legal provisions. Specifically, NHIS was established through the National Health Insurance Act of 2003 (Act 650); the program is currently covered by the National Health Insurance Act of 2012 (Act 852). The current SSNIT pension schemes were established through the National Pensions Act of 2008 (Act 766).

Additionally, the government requires that employers provide for sickness and maternity benefits through the Labor Act of 2003 (Act 651) and the National Health Insurance Act of 2012, respectively. For work-related injuries, the government requires employers to provide, as applicable, disability, medical care, survivor, or funeral benefits. These benefits are mandated through the Workmen's Compensation Act of 1987 (Act 187).

Several international organizations have provided or currently provide technical and financial assistance to the government for its rights protection and social welfare services, as well as for its social protection programs. These organizations include the African Development Bank, the European Union, the International Labour Organization, the United Kingdom Foreign, Commonwealth & Development Office (formerly the United Kingdom Department for International Development), the United Nations Children's Fund, the United Nations Development Programme, the United Nations High Commissioner for Refugees, the United Nations Population Fund, the United States Agency for International Development, the World Bank, and the World Food Programme.

NOTES

1. Households include the homeless population.
2. Ghana holds national elections every 4 years, with the most recent in 2020. See Younger (2016) for a discussion of macroeconomic developments in Ghana, including political business cycles.
3. Younger (2016) discusses political business cycles in Ghana.

REFERENCES

GSS (Ghana Statistical Service). 2012. *2010 Population and Housing Census: Summary Report of Final Results*. Accra: GSS.

GSS (Ghana Statistical Service). 2018. *Poverty Trends in Ghana, 2005–2017*. Accra: GSS.

GSS (Ghana Statistical Service). 2019. *Ghana Living Standards Survey (GLSS) 7: Main Report*. Accra: GSS.

GSS (Ghana Statistical Service). 2021a. *Ghana 2021 Population and Housing Census: General Report. Vol. 3a, Population of Regions and Districts*. Accra: GSS.

GSS (Ghana Statistical Service). 2021b. *Ghana 2021 Population and Housing Census: General Report. Vol. 3b, Age and Sex Profile*. Accra: GSS.

GSS, MOFA, WFP, and FAO (Ghana Statistical Service, Ministry of Food and Agriculture, World Food Programme, and Food and Agriculture Organization). 2021. *2020 Comprehensive Food Security and Vulnerability Analysis*. Accra: GSS, MOFA, WFP, and FAO.

IMF (International Monetary Fund). 2021. *Regional Economic Outlook. Sub-Saharan Africa: One Planet, Two Worlds, Three Stories*. Washington, DC: IMF.

IMF (International Monetary Fund). 2022. *Regional Economic Outlook. Sub-Saharan Africa: Living on the Edge*. Washington, DC: IMF.

IMF (International Monetary Fund). 2023. *Regional Economic Outlook. Sub-Saharan Africa: The Big Funding Squeeze*. Washington, DC: IMF.

MELR and MLGRD (Ministry of Employment and Labour Relations and Ministry of Local Government and Rural Development). 2016. *National Labour-Intensive Public Works Policy: Enhancing Employment Opportunities and Economic Security for the Poor*. Accra: MELR and MLGRD.

MOGCSP (Ministry of Gender, Children, and Social Protection). 2015. *Ghana Social Protection Policy*. Accra: MOGCSP.

Nxumalo, Mpumelelo, and Dhushyanth Raju. 2020. "Structural Transformation and Labor Market Performance in Ghana." Jobs Working Paper 55, World Bank, Washington, DC.

World Bank. 2018. *Ghana Systematic Country Diagnostic: Priorities for Ending Poverty and Boosting Shared Prosperity.* Washington, DC: World Bank.

World Bank. 2020. *Ghana Poverty Assessment.* Washington, DC: World Bank.

World Bank. 2022. Macro Poverty Outlook: Country-by-Country Analysis and Projections for the Developing World, April 2022 . Washington, DC: World Bank.

Younger, Stephen D. 2016. "Ghana's Macroeconomic Crisis: Causes, Consequences, and Policy Responses." *Ghanaian Journal of Economics* 4 (1): 5–34.

3 Programs

INTRODUCTION

In this chapter, we provide an overview of the government of Ghana's main social protection programs: the Livelihood Empowerment Against Poverty (LEAP) program, the Labor-Intensive Public Works (LIPW) program, the Ghana School Feeding Programme (GSFP), Social Security and National Insurance Trust (SSNIT) pension scheme, and the National Health Insurance Scheme (NHIS). The LEAP program, the LIPW program, and GSFP are social assistance programs, while SSNIT pensions and NHIS are social insurance programs. The overview discusses key program design and implementation parameters, as well as findings for the programs from available operational and beneficiary assessments and impact evaluations.

The government also administers an additional social assistance program, the Complementary Livelihood and Asset Support Scheme (CLASS). Targeting LEAP and LIPW program beneficiary households, CLASS provides selected household members (one person per household) training, small capital grants, and post-training mentoring and coaching to help improve the performance of beneficiaries' farm and nonfarm income-generating activities. A pilot of the program was administered between 2014 and 2018, covering around 7,100 individuals in eight districts in the Upper East region.

CLASS was launched in 2020, with the plan to reach different sets of communities in rounds, in five regions in the north (Upper East, Upper West, North East, Northern, and Savannah). The program, currently in its second round of implementation, remains small in scale. It covered about 9,000 individuals in the first round and currently covers some 11,900 individuals in the second round. Given the program's small scale and the absence of relevant data and rigorous research to assess its performance, we do not discuss CLASS in this study.

For the LEAP program, the LIPW program, GSFP, the NHIS, and SSNIT pensions, we discuss recent trends and current patterns in selected key program indicators, specifically for 2017, which overlaps with the reference period for our performance review of the programs based on the Ghana Living Standards Survey (GLSS) 2016–17 (GSS 2019), discussed in chapter 4.

LIVELIHOOD EMPOWERMENT AGAINST POVERTY PROGRAM

Following the recommendation made in the National Social Protection Strategy of 2007, the government introduced the LEAP program in 2008 with the main aim of reducing household poverty and vulnerability. To this end, the program provides unconditional cash transfers to extreme-poor households in impoverished geographic areas.

Overall responsibility for the program currently lies with the LEAP Management Secretariat under the Ministry of Gender, Children, and Social Protection (MOGCSP).[1] Responsibility for ground-level implementation lies with district officials, community leaders and volunteers, and contracted private parties. Key organizational structures and personnel at the ground level include District LEAP Implementation Committees (DLICs), Community LEAP Implementation Committees (CLICs), district social welfare officers, and Beneficiary Welfare Associations.

Several international organizations have provided financial and technical assistance for the conceptualization, design, and implementation of the program at different points in time and for different durations. The main organizations include the European Union (EU), the United Kingdom Foreign, Commonwealth & Development Office (UK FCDO), the United Nations Children's Fund (UNICEF), the United States Agency for International Development (USAID), and the World Bank.

Launched as a pilot in February 2008, the program initially covered 1,700 extreme-poor households with orphans and vulnerable children (orphaned or made vulnerable by HIV/AIDS) ages 0–15 years in 21 districts across all regions in Ghana.[2] In 2009, the program was extended to extreme-poor households with elderly persons (those age 65 or older) without economic support and households with persons who have severe disabilities and no productive capacity. Since then, the program has been incrementally scaled out to cover extreme-poor households with "eligible" members in at least one of three sociodemographic categories: (a) orphans and vulnerable children[3] (younger than age 18), (b) individuals age 65 or older, and (c) individuals with severe disabilities.

In 2015, the MOGCSP introduced a sister cash transfer program, LEAP 1000, with the official aim of financially supporting the health and nutrition status of pregnant and lactating mothers and young children.[4] In that year, the program reached 6,100 extreme-poor households with pregnant women, mothers of children younger than 12 months, and children younger than 12 months in 10 districts in the Northern and Upper East regions. LEAP 1000 was subsumed within the larger LEAP program soon after, in 2016, adding a fourth sociodemographic category to the program.

At the end of 2021, the LEAP program covered 344,000 households in all districts in Ghana, equivalent to 6.6 percent of the national population.[5] Figure 3.1 shows the trend in program household numbers from 2008, when the program was initiated, through 2021. Figure 3.2 maps the distribution of program households across districts between 2016 and 2021. Over the 4 years from 2018 to 2021, more than 50 percent of program households were from districts in 3 of the country's 10 regions (regional classification per the 2010 population and housing census, [GSS 2012]): Northern, Upper East, and Upper West. In 2017, the LEAP program covered 197,000 households, equivalent to 4.1 percent of the national population.

FIGURE 3.1
Number of LEAP program households, 2008–21

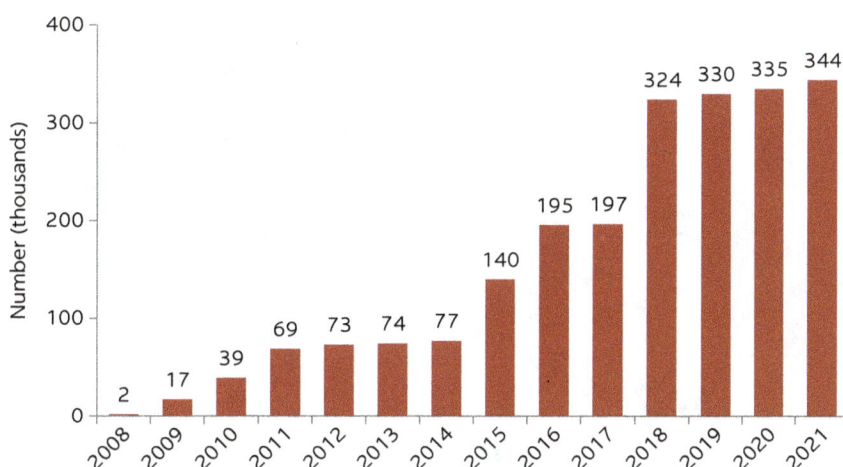

Source: LEAP program administrative data obtained from the Ministry of Gender, Children, and Social Protection.
Note: Figure shows the trend in the number of LEAP program households.
LEAP = Livelihood Empowerment Against Poverty.

Program targeting was based on a four-level process: region, district, community, and household. The targeting rules sought to hone in on the poorest locations in the country. The MOGCSP selected the regions and districts for the program, based on region- and district-level poverty statistics obtained from the Ghana Statistical Service (GSS).

Communities within districts were selected by DLICs following guidelines provided by the MOGCSP. These guidelines called for a qualitative determination of the poverty status of the community using proxy indicators, such as the availability of various infrastructure, amenities, and services; school participation and health outcomes; and dwelling quality of residents. The District LEAP Implementation Committees communicated to the MOGCSP the communities they had selected for the LEAP program.

Within communities selected for the program, the household selection approach has evolved over time. From program inception until 2015, community-based selection was used to identify households for the program. The CLICs identified extreme-poor households that met the categorical criteria for program eligibility. In 2010, the MOGCSP introduced a proxy means test (PMT) criterion for program eligibility, with the aim to better identify extreme-poor households for the program. Using relevant data gathered from community-selected households through a questionnaire, the MOGCSP estimated the household's PMT score.[6] Community-selected households with a PMT score that fell below predefined cutoffs were selected by the MOGCSP for the program, and this information was communicated to DLICs and CLICs. The CLICs then informed and registered the households selected for entry into the program. In October 2015, the MOGCSP launched a national social registry, the Ghana National Household Registry, which is in the process of being rolled out across regions of the country. This national social registry is expected to serve as the main source of data for the PMT (MOGCSP 2019).

FIGURE 3.2

Distribution of LEAP program households, by district, 2016–21

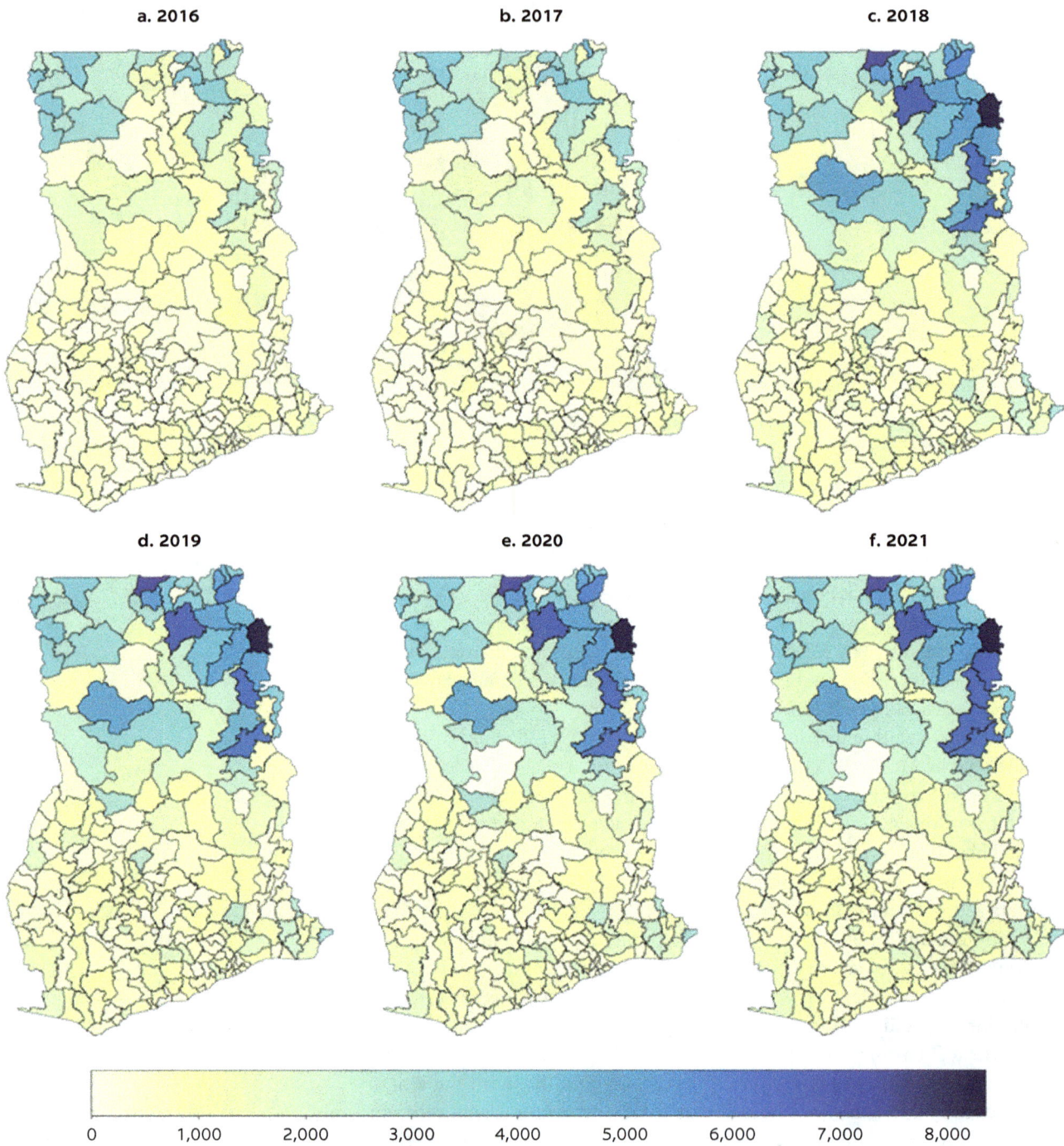

a. 2016 b. 2017 c. 2018

d. 2019 e. 2020 f. 2021

0   1,000   2,000   3,000   4,000   5,000   6,000   7,000   8,000

Source: LEAP program administrative data obtained from the Ministry of Gender, Children, and Social Protection.
Note: The maps show the distribution of LEAP program households across districts in Ghana in each year between 2016 and 2021. The program household numbers correspond to the numbers that were part of the last LEAP program payment round in each year. LEAP = Livelihood Empowerment Against Poverty.

The MOGCSP stipulates that the eligibility status of existing LEAP program households should be reassessed and recertified at least once every 2–4 years (MOGCSP 2019). Program households that no longer meet the PMT score criteria in the reassessment are deemed ineligible, even if the PMT was not originally applied in assessing the household for entry into the program. The MOGCSP recently initiated its first reassessment and recertification exercise for program households.

LEAP program benefit amounts were originally set as a function of eligible members of the household who fall under the sociodemographic categories for program eligibility. Based on the latest benefit amount (last revised in September 2015), households with one eligible member receive GH¢32 per month; two eligible members, GH¢38 per month; three eligible members, GH¢44 per month; and four or more eligible members, GH¢53 per month.

In the past few years, the MOGCSP has dropped the sociodemographic categorical targeting of households for the program. Accordingly, benefit amounts are now set as a function of household members (instead of eligible household members), while all other benefit structure parameters remain unchanged (MOCGSP 2019). To date, there has been no significant intake of new households into the program where this benefit structure has been applied. A significant intake is expected after the first reassessment and recertification exercise is completed.

Benefit amounts are not automatically adjusted for price inflation but are revised upward over time in irregular intervals based on a deliberative process undertaken by the MOGCSP. Since the start of the program through December 2022, benefit amounts have been raised twice: in July 2013 (roughly 5 years after program inception) and in September 2015 (after approximately another 2 years). The government recently announced that the benefit amounts will be doubled starting from fiscal year 2023 (Government of Ghana 2022); the monthly benefit amount will now range between GH¢64 and GH¢106.

Figure 3.3a presents the trend in nominal benefit amounts from program inception (February 2008) through August 2022, whereas figure 3.3b presents the trend in real benefit amounts over the same period. From September 2015 (when benefit levels were last revised) to August 2022, the real value fell by 60 percent.

According to program administrative data, the average annual benefit was GH¢471 in 2021 and 2022. In 2017, the corresponding average was GH¢469.

Between program inception and December 2015, Ghana Post served as the payment service provider for the program, contracted by the former Ministry of Employment and Social Welfare. Ghana Post distributed cash benefits to beneficiaries or their caregivers at payment points in or near LEAP program communities. To receive the benefits at payment points, beneficiaries or their caregivers presented their LEAP program (or other official) identification card and provided their thumbprint for eligibility verification and payment confirmation.

After a short pilot in two phases (in November–December 2013 and January 2014), the benefit payment system was changed in December 2015 to delivery through banks with local branches in LEAP program districts contracted by the Ghana Interbank Payment and Settlement Systems (GhIPSS), a payment service provider.[7] The GhIPSS had been, in turn, contracted by the MOGCSP for the program. Under this current system, program beneficiaries receive biometric smart cards—"e-zwich" cards. Partnering banks adopted the

FIGURE 3.3

Nominal and real changes in stipulated LEAP program benefit levels, 2008–22

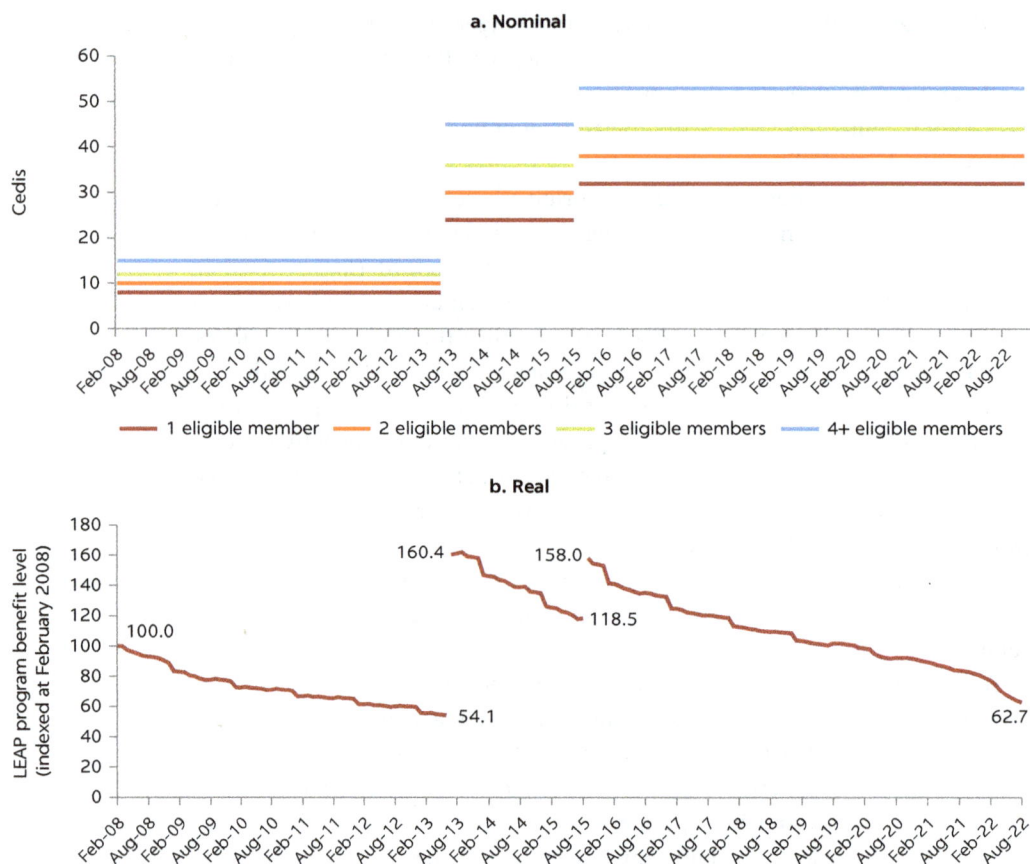

Source: Program administration information obtained from the Ministry of Gender, Children, and Social Protection. Consumer price index statistics obtained from the Ghana Statistical Service.
Note: Figure shows the trend in officially stipulated LEAP program benefit levels, in nominal and real terms. Real benefit levels are calculated using the national consumer price index series. The base month and year is February 2008, when the LEAP program was launched). LEAP = Livelihood Empowerment Against Poverty.

payment points previously used by Ghana Post or established new ones where necessary. Program beneficiaries or their caregivers can collect their benefits at payment points, after verification of eligibility, using their e-zwich cards. Alternatively, program beneficiaries or their caregivers can visit the partnering banks to collect their benefits following the same verification process.

The LEAP program stipulates a benefit payment periodicity of every 2 months (6 payment rounds per year), following a fixed calendar. In each payment round, 2 months' worth of benefits are to be delivered to program households. The transition from Ghana Post to the GhIPSS and partnering banks produced a payment delivery gap spanning several months. Once the new payment system was fully operational at the needed scale, the payment periodicity improved greatly. From 2016 through 2018, the program was able to deliver 6 payment rounds (2 months of benefits per payment round), even if the fixed calendar was not followed perfectly (figure 3.4). However, from late 2019 through 2022, the program began to slip in its payment periodicity; it delivered fewer payment rounds and, at times, compensated by delivering 4 months of benefits in a payment round. The slip in payment periodicity was mainly due to delays in government budgetary releases for the program.

FIGURE 3.4

Periodicity of LEAP payment rounds and number of monthly benefits per payment round, 2016–22

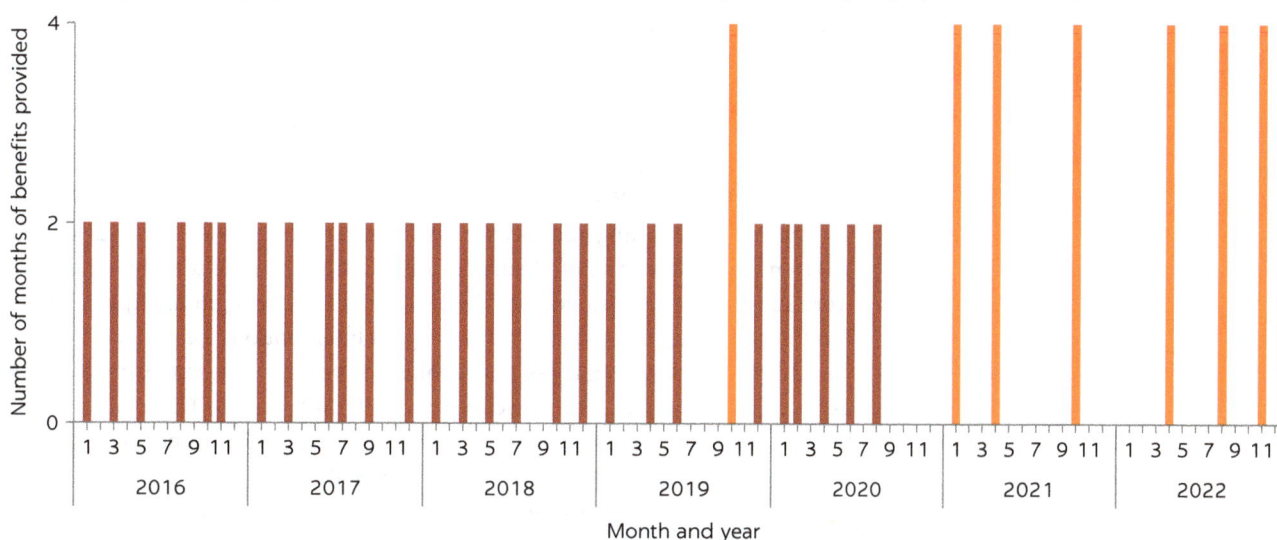

Source: LEAP program administrative data obtained from the Ministry of Gender, Children, and Social Protection.
Note: Figure shows the periodicity of LEAP benefit payment rounds as well as the number of monthly benefits per payment round. Months on the x-axis are denoted numerically (i.e., 1 = January, 11 = November). Red lines = 2 months; orange lines = 4 months. LEAP = Livelihood Empowerment Against Poverty.

While the LEAP program provides cash benefits to households without conditionalities, it encourages certain co-responsibilities. These include, relevant to the program household, enrollment and attendance of children ages 6–15 at local schools; uptake of maternal, newborn, and child health and nutrition services at local health facilities; participation in locally provided financial and nutrition education interventions; and enrollment in NHIS and renewal of membership annually, under membership categories that exempt the household from paying registration or renewal fees and premiums (MOGCSP 2019). The key organizational structures at the district and community levels for the program are expected to facilitate program households in meeting these co-responsibilities.

An impact evaluation of the LEAP program, assessed 2 and 6 years after the baseline measurement, found that the intervention by and large did not have any positive effects on various socioeconomic indicators (Handa et al. 2017). At baseline in 2010, the study matched a sample of prospective LEAP program households in the Brong Ahafo, Central, and Volta regions to similar households interviewed in a separate national survey.[8] The program and counterfactual samples were then tracked over time, with follow-up data collected in 2012 and 2016. Program impacts were estimated based on a difference-in-differences strategy. The researchers argued that the counterfactual group appeared to be weak.

Nevertheless, the evaluation found that welfare improved dramatically over time among sample LEAP program households. Furthermore, consistent with the pattern in payment rounds discussed earlier, the evaluation found that benefit payments became much more regular in the later evaluation period (2012–16) than in the earlier period (2010–12), with the pattern linked to the shift in the benefit payment system from the Ghana Post to the GhIPSS and banks in 2015. However, at the same time, average time to payment points and the likelihood of leakage at payment points increased, while the likelihood of feeling secure at payment points decreased in the later evaluation period compared with the earlier period. The researchers speculated that these issues may have been teething problems with the changeover to the new system.

Another impact evaluation found more favorable results for a certain variant of the program (LEAP 1000 Evaluation Study Team 2018). The researchers examined the pilot LEAP 1000 intervention, which targeted pregnant women and mothers with young infants with cash transfers coupled with fee waivers for NHIS membership. As noted earlier, this pilot program and its beneficiaries were subsequently subsumed within the overall LEAP program. Exploiting the PMT cutoff for household entry into the pilot intervention, the evaluation compared outcomes between those households just below and just above the cutoff, using data collected in 2015 (baseline) and 2017 (follow-up). Those households below the cutoff received the intervention. The evaluation period spanned 13 payment rounds. Program impacts were mixed.

The evaluation found significant positive impacts on multiple individual and household welfare measures but not on several others. Furthermore, most significant positive impacts were modest in size. In terms of consumption and poverty, average program impacts were GH₵9 for monthly overall household consumption per adult equivalent (in August 2017 prices), GH₵7 for monthly household food consumption per adult equivalent, –2.1 percentage points for the poverty rate, and –2.6 percentage points for the poverty gap.[9] The impacts were found over a period when consumption fell and poverty increased in the overall evaluation sample. The researchers, however, noted that program impacts were expected to be modest because the evaluation looked at the LEAP program households near the PMT cutoff (that is, relatively more well-off LEAP program participants) and not the more typical LEAP program household.

On the basis of the same identification strategy and data noted earlier, studies have examined the impacts of the pilot LEAP 1000 intervention (cash transfers combined with fee waivers for NHIS membership) on intimate partner violence (Peterman, Valli, and Palermo 2022) and NHIS membership (Palermo et al. 2019), with the latter study finding significant, large positive impacts.

Several other quantitative and qualitative studies have examined samples of LEAP program households (for example, FAO 2013; CDD-Ghana 2016). Their findings on levels and changes in outcomes are consistent with the corresponding findings for LEAP program households from more rigorous evaluations (that is, those that incorporate a reasonable counterfactual group). Beneficiary feedback assessments indicate high satisfaction rates among LEAP program households (for example, P&OD Consult 2018). The introduction of the smart card payment system for beneficiaries appears to be an important factor behind this result. Interviews with program beneficiaries and administrators suggest that program implementation rules and procedures are generally well defined, but their application can fall short because of insufficient knowledge, competency, and capacity of local program administrators. A careful operational assessment conducted in 2012 indicates no widespread or severe issue with program implementation across the delivery chain (Handa et al. 2012). Beneficiary feedback and operational assessments also have identified the need for greatly improved communication and awareness-raising efforts targeted toward program households, communities, and local program administrators on various aspects of program design and implementation.

LABOR-INTENSIVE PUBLIC WORKS PROGRAM

The main aim of the LIPW program is to reduce poverty and vulnerability by offering rural, poor households temporary labor-earning opportunities during the agricultural off-season. These opportunities are engendered through public works employment activities that result in the creation, rehabilitation, or maintenance of public or community infrastructure (referred to as "community "assets" by the authorities). The agricultural lean season runs from November to March or April. Typical public works activities (referred to as "subprojects" by the authorities) involve feeder roads, basic water resources infrastructure (small earth dams and dugouts), and soil and land conservation (seedling and plant nurseries and community tree planting).

The LIPW program is covered under the National Labor-Intensive Public Works Policy (Ministry of Employment and Labour Relations and Ministry of Local Government and Rural Development 2016). The government approved the policy in August 2016, and it took effect in January 2017. Overall current responsibility for administering the program lies with the Rural Development Coordination Unit (RDCU) under the Ministry of Local Government, Decentralization, and Rural Development (MLGDRD). Current responsibility for administering the program on the ground lies with the District Assemblies (DAs) with support from zonal coordinating officers of the RDCU and local community facilitators. Subprojects are fully managed by communities, or DAs contract private contractors to manage them. Private contractors are usually contracted to manage road or water resources infrastructure subprojects. The program is fully financed by the World Bank.

The LIPW program was launched in 40 districts across all regions in 2011. Figure 3.5 plots the number of participants and subprojects per year from inception through 2021, whereas figure 3.6 charts the distribution of participants across districts for each year between 2016 and 2021. Individuals and subprojects are not necessarily unique across consecutive pairs of years, as the works activity can span 2 years. In 2018, the program was implemented (that is, it engaged participants) for only part of the year; in 2019, it did not engage any participants; and in 2020, program implementation with the engagement of participants restarted. The hiatus in the engagement of participants was connected to interrupted donor financing.[10] The program supported 30,000 participants engaged in 352 subprojects in 80 districts across all regions in 2021 and 32,900 participants engaged in 321 subprojects in 80 districts across all regions in 2017.

Program targeting for each agricultural off-season follows a three-level process. First, the MLGDRD selects districts with the worst levels of poverty based on data provided by the GSS. Second, the poorest communities within the selected districts are identified jointly by DAs and the RDCU using information from the GSS, District Medium-Term Development Plans, and other sources. In selecting communities, DAs and the RDCU prioritize existing LEAP program communities, assess the willingness and interest of the community to participate in the LIPW program, and evaluate whether a subproject proposed by the

Number of LIPW program beneficiaries and subprojects, 2011–21

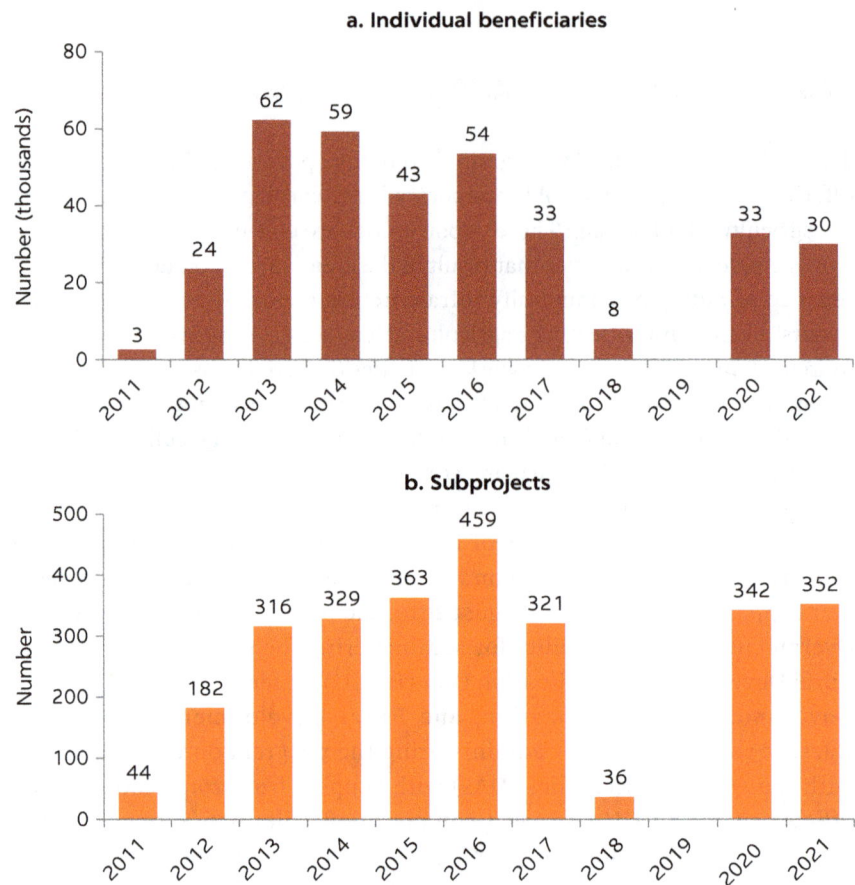

a. Individual beneficiaries

b. Subprojects

Source: LIPW program administrative data obtained from the Ministry of Local Government, Decentralization, and Rural Development.
Note: Figure shows the trend in the number of LIPW program beneficiary individuals and LIPW subprojects. The LIPW program was only partly active in 2018 and fully inactive in 2019 due to an interruption in donor financing. Program beneficiary individuals and subprojects are not necessarily unique across consecutive year pairs. LIPW = Labor-Intensive Public Works.

community qualifies. For a subproject to ultimately qualify, among other criteria, the percentage of the subproject's total budget for labor costs must exceed the stipulated minimum, which varies by the nature of the subproject. The selected subproject should also preferably last for two agricultural off-seasons.

Third, within a selected community, a combination of individual self-selection and community selection is used to identify participants for the LIPW program. DAs and community facilitators for the program make households aware of the program along with expectations and rules for participation. Individuals ages 18–65 (adults) can seek to participate in a subproject by registering with the community facilitator. If the number of registered individuals exceeds the labor needs for the subproject, guidelines indicate that the poorest individuals among those registered are to be selected by the community, led by the community facilitator and two community leaders; this means starting off with selecting registered participants from LEAP program households. The list of selected participants for the subproject is to be made publicly

FIGURE 3.6

Distribution of LIPW program individuals, by district, 2016–21

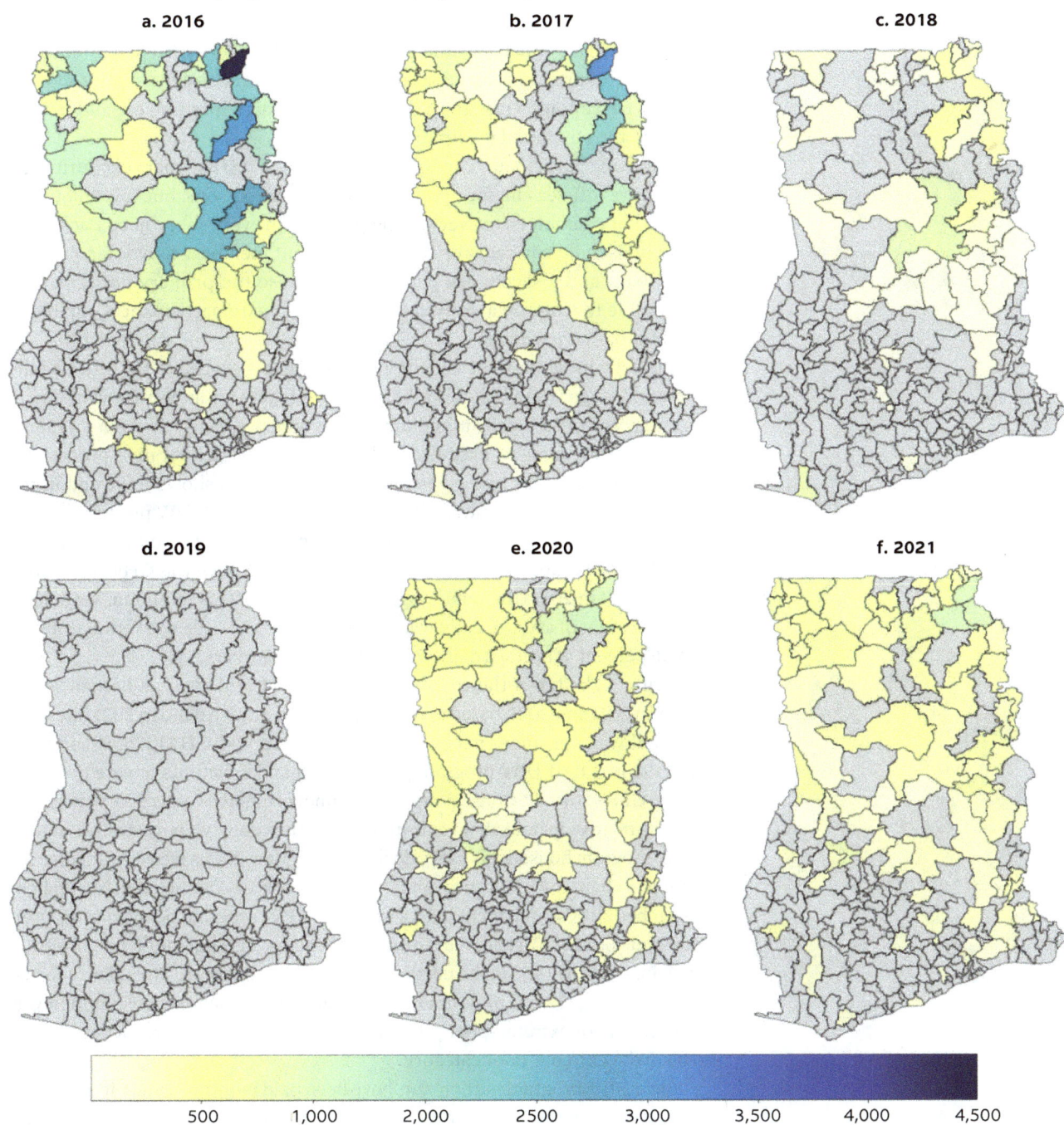

Source: LIPW program administrative data obtained from the Ministry of Local Government, Decentralization, and Rural Development.
Note: The maps show the distribution of LIPW program beneficiary individuals across districts in Ghana in various years. The map for 2019 is blank because there were no LIPW program beneficiary individuals in 2019 due to the lack of program financing. LIPW = Labor-Intensive Public Works.

available at common gathering places in the community, and complaints can be voiced on the selection process or outcome through several channels. Program guidelines call for at least 60 percent of program participants selected by DAs and community facilitators to be women, a goal to be achieved through community sensitization; outreach; and conducive work activities, working conditions, hours, and amenities.

Administrative data on a sample of individual LIPW program participants in 2016 and 2017 indicate that 57 percent were women. The average age of participants was roughly 39 years, with the average age of women slightly lower than that for men, by less than a year. While the stipulated minimum age of 18 years for program participation appears to have been consistently applied, a small percentage (less than 5 percent) of participants were older than 65 years, the stipulated maximum age.

Qualifying participants can work a maximum of 200 days per year during the agricultural off-season, for up to two consecutive seasons, but this amount of work is not guaranteed to every participant and in every subproject. Each qualifying household can register two capable adult members to work, a primary participant and a secondary participant, in case the primary participant is unavailable to work on a given day. Only the primary participant is eligible to collect program payments.

The daily program wage benefit in a given year is pegged to the official daily minimum wage (rounded up to the nearest integer) for an 8-hour workday in that year. The official daily minimum wage is adjusted yearly through a national tripartite (government, organized labor, employers) deliberative process for considering increases in the cost of living. Figure 3.7a shows the trend in the stipulated daily minimum wage between 2011 and 2022. LIPW program beneficiaries are, however, required to work only a maximum of 6 hours per day (but are paid for an 8-hour workday). The daily minimum wage was GH¢13.5 in 2022 and GH¢8.8 in 2017 (the same wage for both sexes). This minimum wage level was 21 percent of average daily wage earnings for rural male workers ages 18–65 and 56 percent of average daily wages for female workers.[11]

Figure 3.7b shows the trends in nominal and real average benefit levels between 2011 and 2021, based on program administrative data. In 2021, the average total wage payment per program participant was GH¢1,176; it had been GH¢498 in 2017. LIPW program participation and benefit data were not gathered in GLSS 2016–17. Consequently, we cannot estimate average LIPW program benefits relative to household consumption or the country's poverty lines among LIPW program households as we do for the other programs (see the "Incidence" section in chapter 4). However, on the basis of a survey conducted in November–December 2015, which included a sample of LIPW program beneficiaries, Osei-Akoto et al. (2016) reported an average total wage payment per program participant of GH¢455 in the north and GH¢828 in the south. They also reported that the average LIPW program benefit relative to household consumption was 25.9 percent for extreme-poor program households, with 87 percent determined to be in the extreme-poor category.

Since 2016, program participants have been paid monthly using the same payment system as the LEAP program.[12] The RDCU has contracted the GhIPSS which, in turn, has contracted financial institutions to administer payment points in or near LIPW program communities. Biometric smart cards were provided to primary program participants to use at payment points. The authorized payment amount is based on information on the number of days worked by the participant captured in the program's DASH (Daily Attendance Sheet) system and transmitted by DAs to the GhIPSS via the RDCU.

Figure 3.8 shows the results of LIPW works subprojects by year. Between 2011 and 2020, the LIPW program yielded 1,603 kilometers of rural roads, 37.3 million cubic meters of dam and dugout volume, and 4,616 hectares of afforestation and reforestation.

FIGURE 3.7

Stipulated minimum wage and average LIPW program wage payment levels, 2011–22

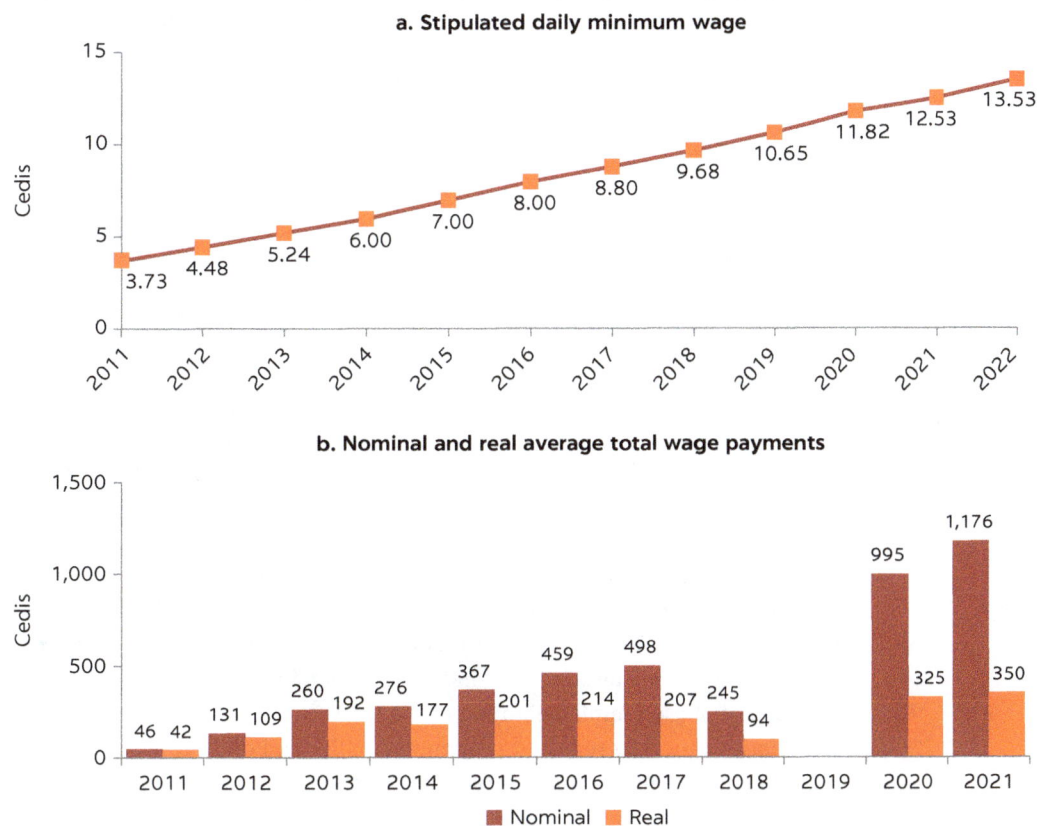

a. Stipulated daily minimum wage

b. Nominal and real average total wage payments

Source: LIPW program administrative information obtained from the Ministry of Local Government, Decentralization, and Rural Development. Annual national consumer price index data obtained from the World Bank, World Development Indicators database.
Note: Figure shows the trend in the officially stipulated daily minimum wage and in the nominal and real average total wage payments received by LIPW program beneficiary individuals. The LIPW program was only partly active in 2018 and fully inactive in 2019 due to an interruption in donor financing. Real average wage payments were calculated by using annual national consumer price index data (base year = 2010). LIPW = Labor-Intensive Public Works.

The effects of the LIPW program on individual and household outcomes have been evaluated (Osei-Akoto et al. 2016) based on a randomized phase-in design, in which works subprojects were randomly assigned to two implementation phases, with the first phase in 2015 and the second in 2016. LIPW program beneficiary households in a sample of phase 1 program communities (stratified by the type of subproject) were compared with statistically matched households in a sample of phase 2 communities after the completion of the first phase of implementation. Based on a cross-sectional analysis using follow-up household survey data in November–December 2015, the study found that the program increased individual employment and earnings outcomes, measured variously. These results are consistent across the different types of subprojects. Depending on the type of subproject and outcome indicator, the study also found mixed evidence that the program influenced household crop output and sales; nonfarm enterprise activity; borrowing, lending, and savings; migration; income and consumption; and the use of health and education services.

FIGURE 3.8

Civil and environmental works results from LIPW program subprojects, 2011–20

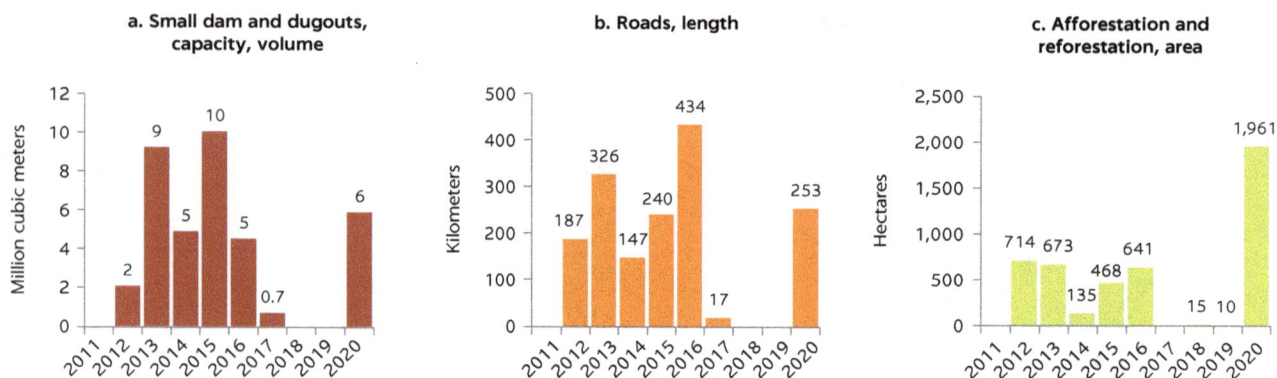

Source: LIPW program administrative data obtained from the Ministry of Local Government, Decentralization, and Rural Development.
Note: Figure shows the trends in the civil, conservation, and environmental works results of LIPW subprojects, by type of subproject. The LIPW program was only partly active in 2018 and fully inactive in 2019 due to an interruption in donor financing. LIPW = Labor-Intensive Public Works.

The evaluation data also have been used to conduct an operational review and an assessment of beneficiary satisfaction (Osei-Akoto et al. 2016). For this, the follow-up survey in November–December 2015 was complemented by information from focus group discussions conducted earlier, in July–August 2015, closer to the end of phase 1 implementation of the LIPW works subprojects. Program beneficiaries generally reported program activities and other aspects—such as awareness raising, registration, household selection, wait time from registration to actual participation, and payment mode—to be satisfactory. Large shares of households, however, indicated delays in benefit payments (the stipulated payment period being every 2 weeks during the period of the study data) and conflicts between days and hours (within a day) for LIPW works activities and agricultural activities. (LIPW works activities are supposed to be restricted to the agricultural off-months.)

GHANA SCHOOL FEEDING PROGRAMME

According to Ghana's National School Feeding Policy (approved in and effective since 2016), the GSFP primarily seeks to increase school enrollment, attendance, and retention in poor, rural communities; improve the nutrition status of young, school-age children; encourage local food production and consumption; and increase rural income (MOGCSP 2016).

Specifically, the program aims to provide one cooked, nutritious meal every school day to each student in public preprimary, primary, and special education schools in poor, rural communities covered by the program. Meals are to be provided by local private caterers contracted by the government for the program. Caterers are expected to purchase most of their foodstuff for the program from local farmers.

GSFP was launched in late 2005. From 2005 to 2014, primary overall responsibility of the program lay with the former Ministry of Local Government and Rural Development (now MLGDRD) through its National School Feeding Secretariat. In 2015, this responsibility was assumed by the MOGCSP through the establishment of its own National School Feeding Secretariat by the same name.

The main actors engaged in implementation are Regional Coordination Offices, DAs, District Implementation Committees (DICs), School Implementation Committees (SICs), caterers, and cooks. RCOs are expected to perform a liaison function for the GSFP between the National School Feeding Secretariat and the DAs and also have reporting and monitoring functions. DAs, through their DICs, have primary responsibility for ground-level implementation of the program. Program implementation in communities and schools is supported by SICs, composed of local community members and school staff. Importantly, adopting a "caterer model" for the program, DAs contract private services to procure food, prepare meals, and serve students at program schools. These private caterers typically come from the program communities, and they hire cooks from the program communities.

Various international organizations have provided financial and technical assistance to the program at different points during conceptualization and implementation. These organizations, importantly, include the Food and Agriculture Organization, the embassy of the Netherlands in Accra, the Partnership for Child Development, the SNV Netherlands Development Organisation, UNICEF, USAID, the World Food Programme (WFP), and the World Bank. Several civil society organizations have also supported DICs, SICs, schools, and caterers to perform their roles. Since 2011, the program has been fully financed by the government through general revenues.

The program was launched as a pilot in 2005, covering approximately 1,900 students in 10 schools, one in each region (region classification per Ghana's 2010 population and housing census [GSS 2012]). Since then, the program has been rapidly scaled up. In academic year 2016/17 (which overlapped with the fielding of the GLSS 2016–17), the program covered 1.67 million students in 5,682 schools served by 4,975 caterers across all regions. In academic year 2018/19 (the most recent year before the coronavirus pandemic disrupted program implementation), the program covered 2.94 million students in 9,162 schools served by 9,561 caterers.

Figure 3.9 maps the distribution of program students across regions for academic years 2016/17 through 2018/19. The Ashanti region is a positive outlier in terms of the share of program schools and students.

Program targeting is at the community level. DAs have primary responsibility for assessing and selecting public schools and communities covered under the program. Community selection for the program is expected to be based on criteria stipulated by the MOGCSP. These criteria include low levels of schooling, high gender disparities in schooling, low adult literacy levels, high poverty levels, and low levels of access to potable water. The assessment also includes such criteria as strong intracommunity relations and management capacity in the prospective community, willingness of the prospective community to provide cash or in-kind contributions for basic amenities for the program (for example, use of a kitchen or storeroom), and the absence of any other feeding program in prospective schools. Student enrollment numbers for the program are transmitted by the schools and the DAs to the National School Feeding Secretariat (Dunaev and Corona 2019).

Caterers contracted by the DAs are required to follow menus designed by the National School Feeding Secretariat in consultation with the DAs. The meals under these menus are formulated to provide at least 30 percent of the recommended dietary allowance of essential nutrients on a daily basis (Dunaev and Corona 2019).

FIGURE 3.9
Distribution of GSFP beneficiaries, by region, 2016/17 to 2018/19

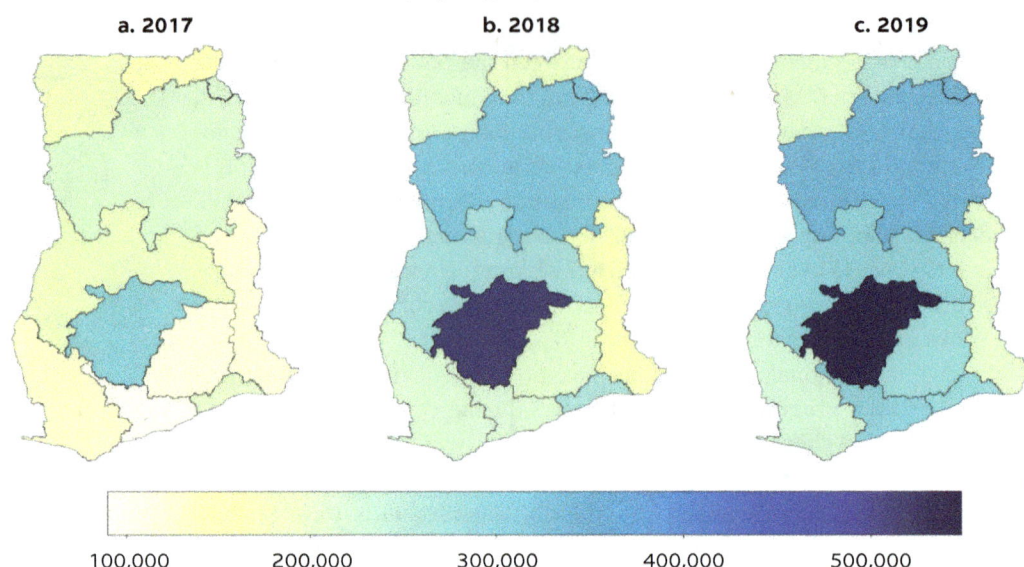

Source: Program administrative data obtained from the Ministry of Gender, Children, and Social Protection.
Note: Maps show the distribution of GSFP individuals across regions in various academic years. For these statistics, the academic year runs from September through July. The classification of regions is per Ghana's 2010 population and housing census (GSS 2012). GSFP = Ghana School Feeding Programme.

To cover the costs of food procurement, preparation, and service, caterers receive a payment amount per student per meal. This payment amount is not automatically adjusted over time for price inflation. In academic years 2015/16 and 2016/17, caterers were paid GH¢0.8 per student per meal. Starting in the second term of the academic year 2017/18, the payment amount was raised to GH¢1. The government recently announced that the payment amount will be increased starting from the 2023 academic year (Government of Ghana 2022).[13]

For the caterer to earn any profit, the actual per-student expense would have to be lower than the payment amount received. However, independent costing of the menus using local prices indicates that school meals would cost more than the payment amounts received if caterers strictly adhered to the menus. Indeed, many caterers report that their expenses exceed their payments. The contract that caterers sign stipulates that they should spend at least 60 percent of their payment amount on expenses. Available evidence suggests that the purchase of food accounts for on average 80 percent of total expenses by caterers, while transportation of food, payment of the salaries of cooks, and the purchase of water and cooking fuel make up the remainder (Dunaev and Corona 2019).

Available evidence also suggests caterers often face chronic and long delays in receiving their payments. Caterers are contractually obligated to prefinance meals for one academic term, but the delays tend to extend for several months into the subsequent term and even multiple subsequent terms. The low payment amount (compared with caterers' expenses) and the long delay in receiving payments appear to have led caterers to reduce the frequency, size, and nutritional value of meals (Dunaev and Corona 2019).

GSFP has been rigorously evaluated (Aurino et al. 2023; Gelli et al. 2019). Under this research, from a sample of 58 districts, 2 communities in each district were randomly assigned to either program status or nonprogram status. Assessed in 2016, more than 2 academic years after the baseline measurement in 2013, the researchers found that GSFP improved academic achievement among girls, children from poor households, and children from the northern regions (which had better program implementation than others). They also found that the program improved nutritional status (specifically, standardized height for age) among girls, younger children, and younger children from poor households. These positive program impacts occurred despite significant implementation deficiencies due to delayed and insufficient payments from the government to caterers, as pointed out in the research.

SOCIAL SECURITY AND NATIONAL INSURANCE TRUST PENSION SCHEME

Since 2010, Ghana has had a three-tiered pension scheme. The first tier is the National Social Security Scheme, a defined pension benefit program that is the focus of this discussion. The second tier is a defined contribution pension scheme managed by various private trustees. The third tier includes all other pension and provident funds. The first two tiers are mandatory for almost all workers in the formal sector and voluntary for those in the informal sector. The third tier is voluntary for all.

SSNIT is a public trust whose main purpose is to manage the first tier of the pension scheme. SSNIT is governed by a board of directors that includes representatives from the President's Office, organized labor, the Ghana Employers' Association, the National Pensioners' Association, the Ministry of Finance, and the security services (excluding the military). Operations are managed by an executive committee comprised of full-time SSNIT employees. International organizations that have provided technical assistance for SSNIT pensions include the International Labour Organization and the World Bank.

All workers in Ghana are eligible to join SSNIT. In the formal sector, employers are required to register their employees and make the stipulated contributions on their behalf. In the informal sector, registration is voluntary and rare, as we discuss later.

Some workers are exempt from joining SSNIT if they belong to other pension schemes in its stead, including employees in the armed forces, police, the Prisons Service, the National Fire Service, and a few senior civil servants stipulated in the Constitution.

Figure 3.10 shows the total number of active contributors to SSNIT between 2005 and 2020, as well as the total number of active contributors as a share of the total labor force. Over this period, the number of active contributors increased from 0.9 million to 1.6 million, with an average annual growth of 4 percent and a cumulative growth of 82 percent. The program participation share of the total labor force increased, from 8–9 percent during the earlier years of the period to 10–12 percent during the latter years. Notwithstanding, the shares are low because the formal sector is small in Ghana.[14]

The service sector has the overwhelming majority of active contributors. In 2020, 86 percent of active contributors were involved in services. The percentage of active contributors from the services sector had increased steadily

FIGURE 3.10

SSNIT active contributors, 2005–20

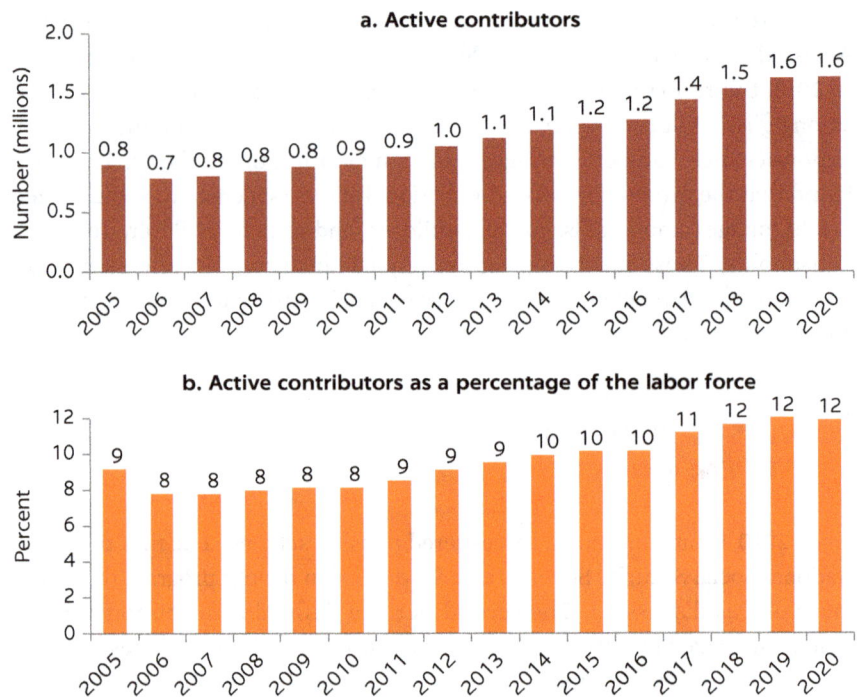

Source: Program administrative statistics obtained from the Social Security and National Insurance Trust. Labor force estimates obtained from the World Bank, World Development Indicators database.
Note: Figure shows the trend in the number of active contributors to the SSNIT pension scheme and in the share of active contributors in the overall labor force.
SSNIT = Social Security and National Insurance Trust.

between 2009 and 2020 from the low 70s in the earlier years of the period. Most active members are also from the formal private sector. In 2020, 64 percent were from the formal private sector, 35 percent were from the public sector, and less than 1 percent were from the informal private sector. The distribution largely remained stable between 2009 and 2020.

Workers contribute 5.5 percent of their basic salary (withheld by the employer), while employers contribute the equivalent of 13 percent of each worker's salary. The self-employed must contribute the entire 18.5 percent. Of this 18.5 percent, 11 percent goes to SSNIT, 5 percent goes to the defined contribution pension scheme in tier 2, and 2.5 percent goes to NHIS as premia for SSNIT members (contributors and pensioners) who are automatically enrolled in NHIS.

SSNIT offers four types of benefits: (a) retirement pensions, (b) invalidity pensions, (c) survivor's pension (paid as a lump sum), and (d) an emigration benefit for retirees leaving Ghana.

To qualify for a retirement pension, the member must be age 60 or older and have made contributions for 15 years if they joined SSNIT after 2008 and 20 years if they joined before. The amount of the monthly pension, payable until death, is the average of the employee's best 36 months of salary times a "pension right." For those who joined the system before 2008, the pension right is 37.5 percent for the first (required) 180 months of contributions and an additional 1.125 percent for each additional year of contributions. For those who joined after, the pension right is 2.5 percent per year for the first 15 years of contributions and 1.125 percent for each additional year, up to a maximum of 60 percent. There is an early retirement option for those ages 55–60. The requirements are the same, including the minimum number of contributions, but the amount of the monthly pension is reduced by 60 percent for those age 55 and is reduced up to 90 percent for those age 59. For a member who does not qualify for a retirement pension, their contributions are refunded with interest at retirement.

To qualify for an invalidity pension, a member must have made contributions in at least 12 of the 36 months preceding their invalidity and must be permanently incapable of any normal gainful employment. The disability status must be confirmed by a medical officer and certified by a regional medical board that includes a SSNIT medical officer. The amount of the monthly pension, payable until death, is calculated in the same way as the retirement pension, but a minimum age limit is not enforced. For those who have not made the minimum 15 years of contributions, the pension right is 37.5 percent.

The survivors' pension is paid to a member's dependents on their death before age 75, whether or not the member is working at the time of death. If the member has made 12 contributions in the 36 months preceding death, the survivor's pension is a lump sum equal to the present value of 15 years' pension as calculated earlier. When the member is already retired, the lump sum is the present value of the unexpired pension payments up to age 75.

The emigration benefit is for non-Ghanaians only and only for those who will leave Ghana permanently. It is a lump-sum payment of whatever benefit is due to the member. For those who qualify for a pension, this is the present value of the member's pension payments. For those who do not qualify for a pension, their contributions are returned with interest.

Pension benefits are not indexed to inflation but are adjusted at irregular intervals through a deliberative process undertaken by SSNIT linked in part to considerations around the availability of current and predicted future funds.

Figure 3.11 shows the number of pensioners over the past decade. The number has increased steadily from 99,000 in 2009 to 227,000 in 2020, a growth of 8 percent per year and a cumulative growth of 131 percent over the period. In 2017, the number of pensioners was 190,000.

Figure 3.11 also shows the average pension payment (monthly and lump-sum payments combined) in nominal and real terms over the past decade. Both the nominal and real values increased steadily between 2009 and 2020, for a cumulative increase of 542 percent and 89 percent, respectively. The average nominal pension payment was GH¢14,524 in 2020; it had been GH¢11,551 in 2017.

Because of the relative youth of the labor force, Ghana has many more working-age contributors (more than 1.6 million in 2020) than pensioners (227,000 in 2020), so an important aspect of SSNIT's activities is to invest the accumulated difference between contributions collected and pensions paid to guarantee SSNIT's ability to pay pensions in the future. These investments include government debt, equity in listed and unlisted firms, real estate, and hospitals and health care centers. Figure 3.12 shows the real rate of return on SSNIT's portfolio over the past decade. While very strong until 2014, real returns have become more volatile and generally lower since, threatening SSNIT's financial sustainability. An external actuarial review conducted in 2017 indicates that the "SSNIT scheme is not financially sustainable over the period covered by the projections from the report" (SSNIT 2019, 38). Nevertheless, the same review

FIGURE 3.11

SSNIT pensioner beneficiaries and average pension benefits, 2009–20

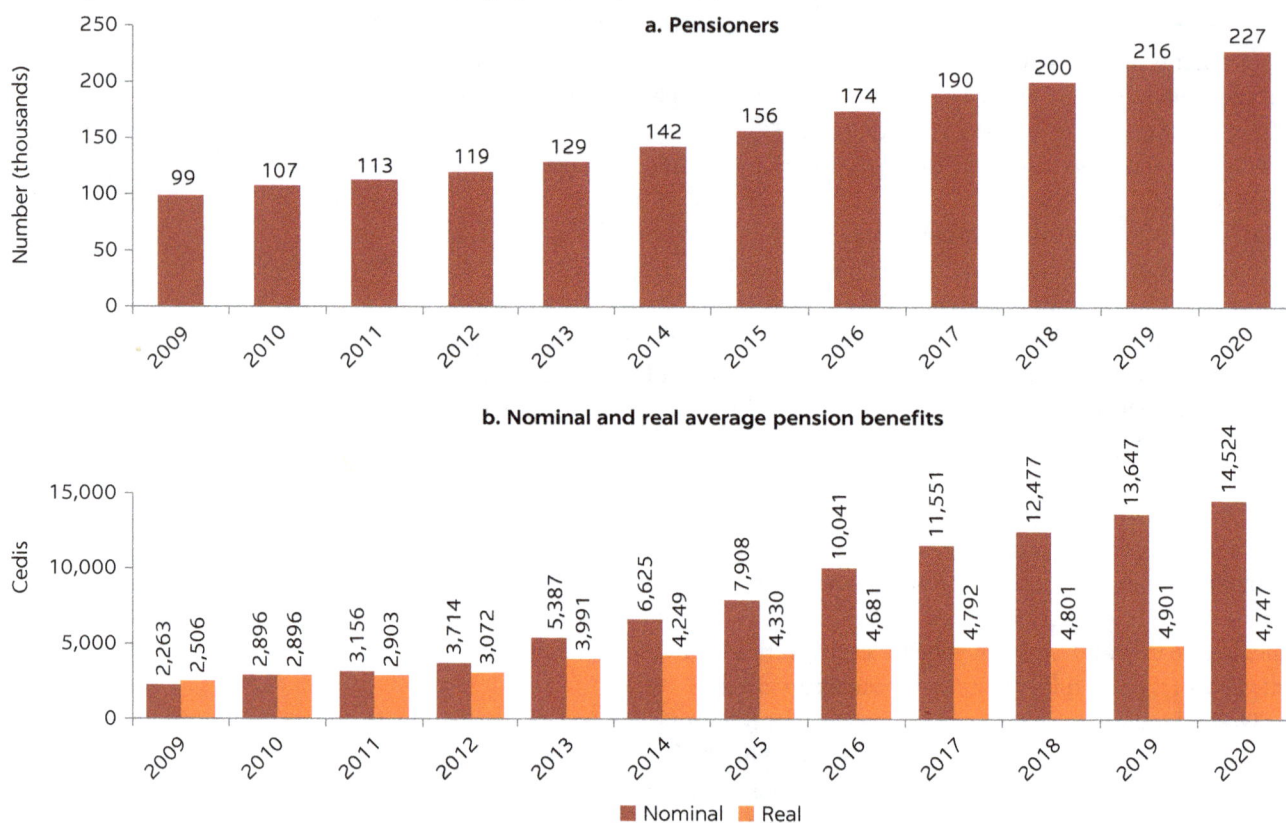

a. Pensioners

Year	Number (thousands)
2009	99
2010	107
2011	113
2012	119
2013	129
2014	142
2015	156
2016	174
2017	190
2018	200
2019	216
2020	227

b. Nominal and real average pension benefits

Year	Nominal (Cedis)	Real (Cedis)
2009	2,263	2,506
2010	2,896	2,896
2011	3,156	2,903
2012	3,714	3,072
2013	5,387	3,991
2014	6,625	4,249
2015	7,908	4,330
2016	10,041	4,681
2017	11,551	4,792
2018	12,477	4,801
2019	13,647	4,901
2020	14,524	4,747

Nominal ■ Real ■

Source: Program administrative statistics obtained from the Social Security and National Insurance Trust. Consumer price index statistics obtained from the World Bank, World Development Indicators database.
Note: Figure shows the trend in the number of SSNIT pensioners and the average pension benefits received by pensioners, in nominal and real terms. Real benefit levels are calculated by using the national consumer price index series (base year = 2010). SSNIT = Social Security and National Insurance Trust.

reports that at a hypothetical real rate of return of 4.25 percent (less than the past decade's average real return), SSNIT has funds sufficient to last until 2038.

Dorfman (2015) has provided a general review of pension systems in Sub-Saharan Africa, which allows for a comparison of the SSNIT pension scheme to other pension schemes. Schwarz (2016) provided a critical review of Ghana's pension system, including SSNIT pensions. Both studies show that the contribution rates of the SSNIT pension scheme are among the highest in Sub-Saharan Africa. Schwarz concluded that the SSNIT pension scheme has little room to further increase contribution rates. This is important because an external actuarial analysis performed in 2017 shows that the SSNIT pension scheme is not sustainable in the long run (SSNIT 2019), a conclusion reached by several earlier actuarial analyses of the scheme as well.

SNNIT pensions are based on only the best 36 months of salary. Schwarz (2016) argued that this feature gives employers strong incentive to underreport salaries until an employee's last 3 years of work, showing how sharply reported salaries rise during employees' final years of work. Increasing the number of years of salary that serve as the basis for pensions would reduce this incentive for underreporting and thus allow the SSNIT pension scheme to raise contribution revenue without increasing contribution rates.

FIGURE 3.12

SSNIT pension fund investment performance, actual real return, 2009–20

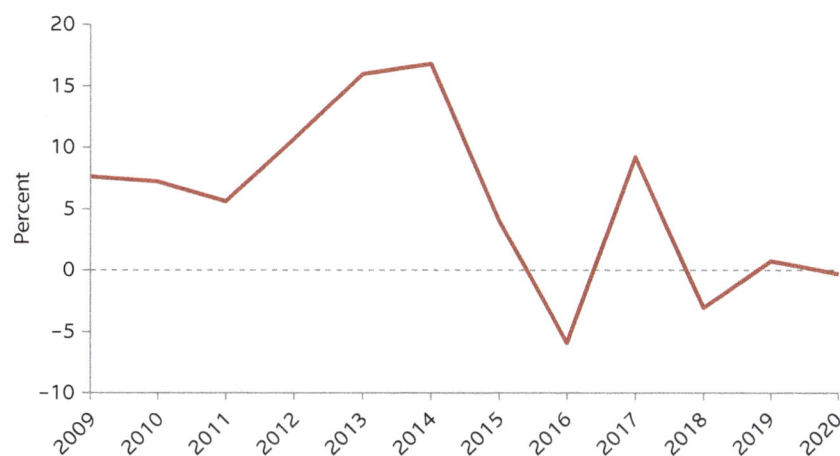

Source: Program administrative statistics obtained from the Social Security and National Insurance Trust.
Note: Figure shows the trend in actual real returns from SSNIT's investments of pension funds. SSNIT = Social Security and National Insurance Trust.

NATIONAL HEALTH INSURANCE SCHEME

NHIS was passed into law in 2003 and rolled out across the country in 2005/06. The program allows for members to receive free health care services at participating facilities.

NHIS is managed by the National Health Insurance Authority (NHIA), a public agency charged with overseeing both NHIS and private insurance schemes, but the latter are rare in Ghana. The Ministry of Health sets broad policy guidelines for NHIS, but the NHIA is responsible for their implementation. The NHIA maintains regional, district, and metropolitan offices where members can register, health care providers can seek accreditation and file claims, and both can file complaints.

Several international organizations have provided or currently provide technical and financial assistance to NHIS: Agence Française de Développement, FCDO, the Global Fund, the International Labour Organization, the Japan International Cooperation Agency, Marie Stopes International, USAID, and the World Bank.

NHIS membership is, in practice, voluntary.[15] Figure 3.13 shows active membership size (measured at the end of each year) between 2010 and 2020. Active membership has increased (unevenly), from 7.4 million individuals in 2010 to 11.8 million individuals in 2020, a cumulative growth of 58 percent. Figure 3.13 also shows active membership as a share of population. Over the period, active membership has ranged between 30 percent and 40 percent of the national population. In 2017, active membership was 10.7 million individuals, equivalent to 35.3 percent of the national population.

To obtain membership, individuals must pay a registration fee, which is currently GH¢8, or an annual renewal fee of GH¢5, as well as an annual premium of GH¢7 in rural areas and GH¢48 in urban areas. The premium is waived for several selected groups, including those younger than age 18, those age 70 or older, indigent individuals, SSNIT contributors and

FIGURE 3.13

NHIS individual beneficiaries, 2010–20

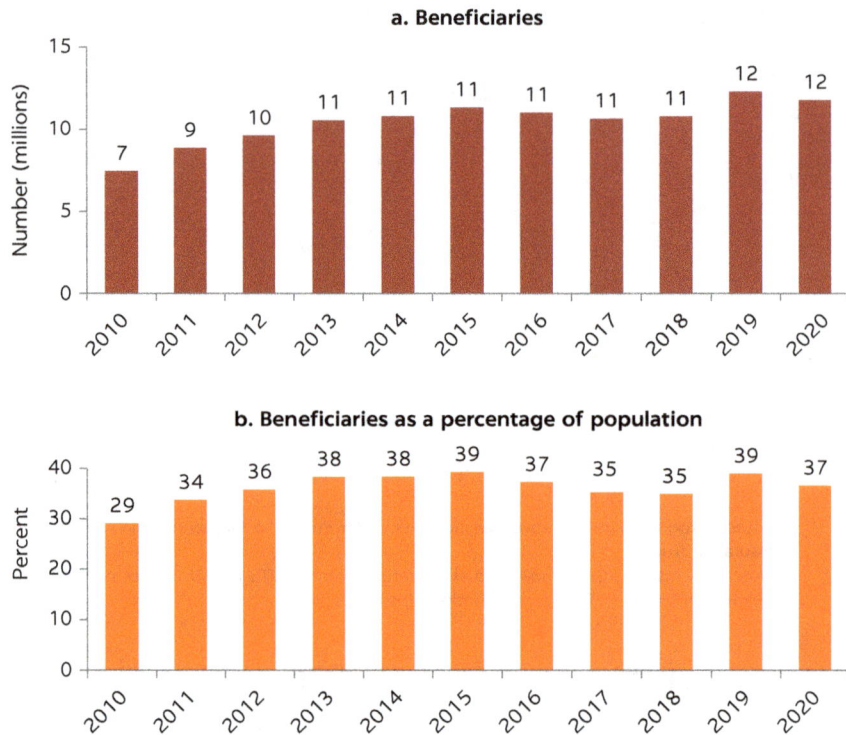

a. Beneficiaries

b. Beneficiaries as a percentage of population

Source: Program administrative statistics obtained from the National Health Insurance Authority. Population estimates obtained from the World Bank, World Development Indicators database.
Note: Figure shows the trend in the number of NHIS beneficiary individuals and the share of beneficiary individuals in the overall population. Beneficiary individual numbers correspond to end-of-year active membership numbers. NHIS = National Health Insurance Scheme.

pensioners, and pregnant women and women with infants younger than 3 months and their infants. The indigent, pregnant women, and women with young infants also do not have to pay the registration or renewal fee. The NHIA defines indigent as an individual who "does not have any visible source of income," "does not have a fixed place of residence," "does not live with a person who is employed and has [a] fixed place of residence," and "does not have a consistent source of support from another person." The NHIA currently relies on the MOGCSP to identify indigent persons.

Looking at end-of-year active membership for 2019, 34 percent were non-exempt members. Around 46 percent of members were in the group younger than age 18. The other exempted groups each constituted 5 percent of total membership. There were large swings between 2006 and 2019 in member numbers (and hence the membership distributional shares) of exempt groups, including indigent individuals and pregnant women and women with infants.

Figure 3.14 shows average nominal and real benefit levels over the past decade. For each year, average benefits were obtained by dividing reported annual expenditures on claims by the number of active members at the end of the year. Average nominal benefits rose (unevenly), from GH₵58 in 2010 to

FIGURE 3.14

Nominal and real average NHIS benefits for individuals

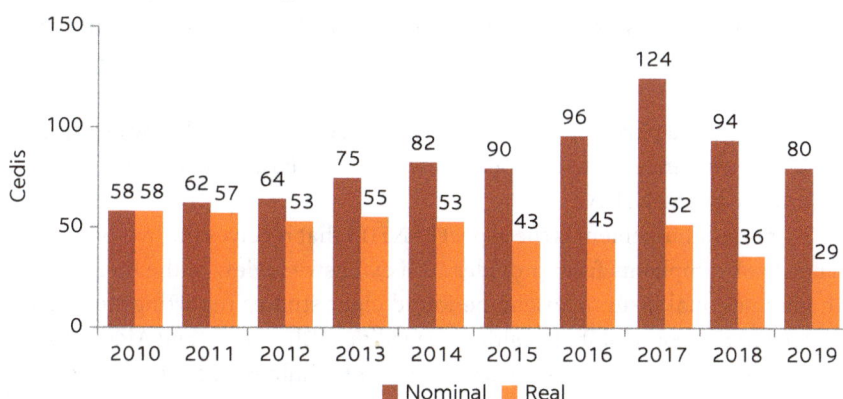

Source: Program administrative statistics obtained from the National Health Insurance Authority. Annual national consumer price index statistics obtained from the World Bank, World Development Indicators database.
Note: Figure shows the trend in average NHIS benefits received by beneficiary individuals, in nominal and real terms. For each year, the benefit level is calculated by dividing expenditures on claims by active membership at the end of the year. Real benefit levels are calculated by using the annual national consumer price index series (base year = 2010). NHIS = National Health Insurance Scheme.

GH¢80 in 2019, a cumulative increase of 38 percent over the period. On the other hand, real benefits decreased over the period, in a cumulative decline of 51 percent. In 2017, the average nominal benefit was GH¢124.

NHIS covers only health care services provided by participating hospitals, clinics, health care centers, and pharmacies. To participate, providers must register with the NHIA, giving proof that they are in good standing with the appropriate regulatory authority (the Health Facilities Regulatory Authority or the Pharmacy Council) and providing documentation to show that the professional staff are in good standing with the appropriate regulatory authorities. Providers may be public, private, or mission facilities. For providers whose staff are not paid by government through other mechanisms, NHIS reimbursements are somewhat higher, although these facilities complain that the additional amounts they receive are insufficient to cover their staff costs (Laar, Asare, and Dalinjong 2021).[16]

In 2020, Ghana had 4,793 NHIS-accredited facilities, of which 69 percent were government run, 26 percent were privately run, and 5 percent were run by missions. In 2017, there were 4,010 facilities, with roughly similar proportions of government-, private-, and mission-run facilities.

NHIS members are not required to make a copayment when they receive services, including medicine. Instead, health care providers must file a claim with the NHIA to be paid for the service provided. Originally, such claims were made on a fee-for-service basis, but this led to concerns that providers were overbilling the NHIA. In 2012, for all payments except medicine, the NHIA switched to a diagnosis-related group·approach, providing payment based on a standard set of diagnoses stipulated by the NHIA in cooperation with the providers. Medicine continues to be reimbursed on a fee-for-service basis.

The same act of Parliament that allowed for diagnosis-related groupings also allowed for capitation payments as a means to control costs.[17] The NHIA piloted a capitation scheme in the Ashanti region in 2012, but the pilot was politically contentious, never expanded, and eventually abandoned (Abiiro, Alatinga, and Yamey 2021).

NHIS fees and payment rates for health care services provided by health care facilities are not indexed to inflation but adjusted based on a deliberative process undertaken by the NHIA.

Claims reimbursement is the aspect of NHIS that receives the overwhelming majority of complaints from providers. An extensive review of the literature on Ghana's national insurance scheme found eight studies reporting slow reimbursement as a complaint of health care facilities (Christmals and Aidem 2020), and another study recorded slow or nonexistent reimbursement for medicine in interviews with key informants (Agyepong et al. 2016). Anecdotal evidence suggests that this problem is so severe that some participating facilities turn away NHIS members or charge them for services, even though members should not have copays. Raju and Younger (2021) found quantitative support for this observation, based on GLSS 2016–17 data.

The NHIS is an unusual insurance scheme in that the fees and premia charged to members, even with increases in recent years, are far short of what would be actuarially fair. Instead, NHIS receives the bulk of its funding—roughly three-fourths—from a special 2.5 percent addition to the value added tax (VAT), the National Health Insurance Levy (NHIL). A further one-fifth of its funding comes from SSNIT, which pays NHIS fees for its members (Wang , Otoo, and Dsane-Selby 2017). The NHIL, SSNIT contributions, registration and renewal fees, and premia are all pooled in the National Health Insurance Fund (NHIF), which is managed by the NHIA to pay provider claims and the operating expenses of the NHIA.

Despite the large share of VAT revenue earmarked for NHIS, there have long been concerns that it is not financially sustainable as currently operated (Aikens et al. 2021; Wang, Otoo, and Dsane-Selby 2017).

NHIS is meant to cover all Ghanaians, but as we have seen, coverage only reaches 30–40 percent of the national population. Given that the insurance scheme covers 95 percent of diagnosed conditions found in Ghana and that there are no copays, it may seem surprising that so few Ghanaians enroll in NHIS.

Figure 3.15, based on GLSS 2016–17 data, shows the responses of the overall and poor populations to the question "Why have you never been registered with any health insurance scheme?" Almost half of the overall population reported financial inability to pay for membership (or, inversely, the high cost of membership), and 70 percent of the poor population reported the same. Sizable percentages of the overall population also indicated that they did not need health insurance or did not have confidence in the NHIS. The GLSS 2016–17 also asked respondents who formerly had NHIS membership "If you are no longer covered, why?" Figure 3.15 shows the distribution of the responses to this question for the overall and poor population as well. The results are similar to those for the "never" question, although financial inability to pay is more likely here as a response.

In the operational literature on issues with NHIS, the greatest concern is with claims reimbursement. As we have noted, anecdotal and qualitative evidence suggests that this problem is so severe that participating providers sometimes turn away NHIS members or insist that they pay for services that should be free. GLSS 2016–17 respondents, however, often did not select a reason for not

FIGURE 3.15

Surveyed reasons for never or no longer being an NHIS member

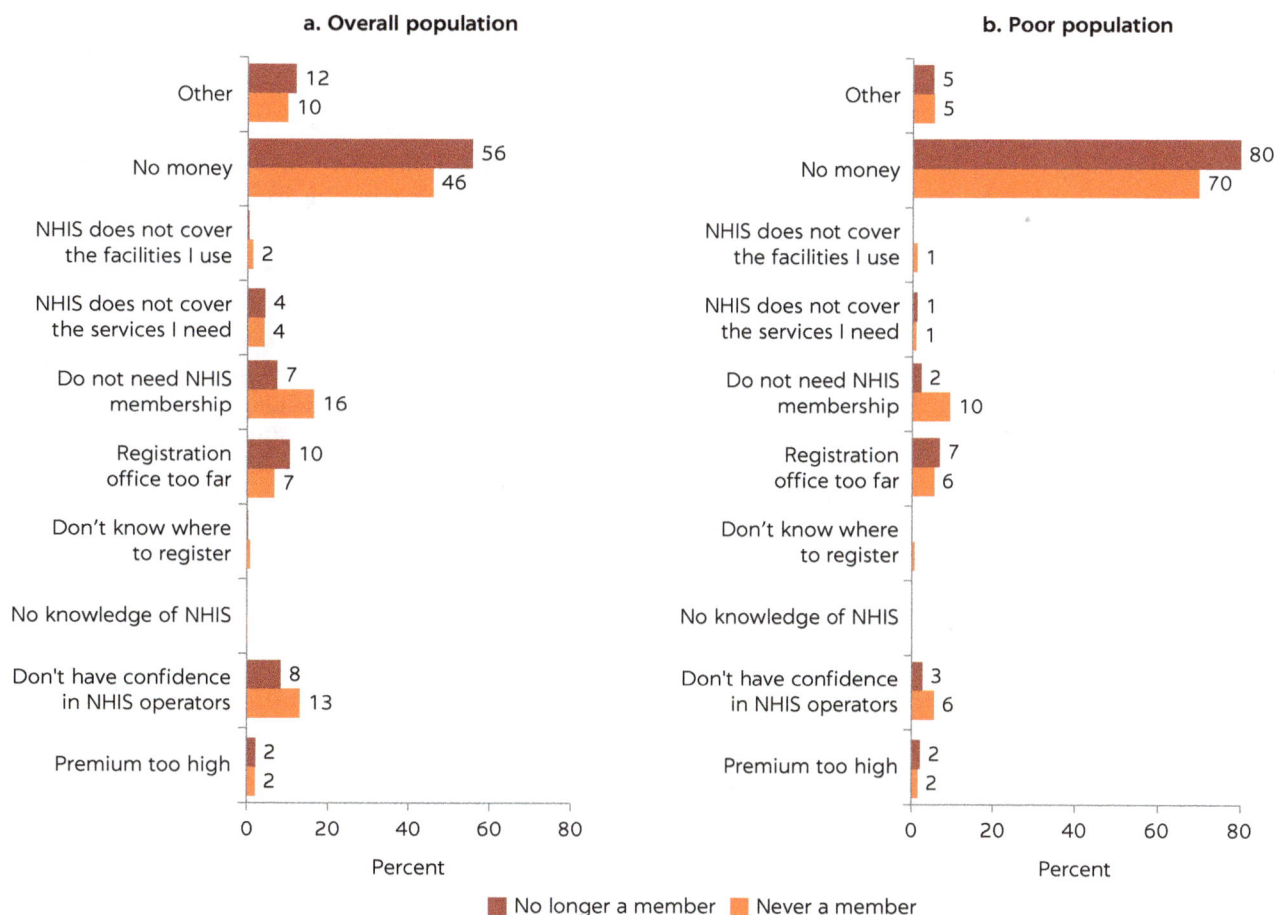

a. Overall population

Other	12 / 10
No money	56 / 46
NHIS does not cover the facilities I use	2
NHIS does not cover the services I need	4 / 4
Do not need NHIS membership	7 / 16
Registration office too far	10 / 7
Don't know where to register	
No knowledge of NHIS	
Don't have confidence in NHIS operators	8 / 13
Premium too high	2 / 2

Percent

b. Poor population

Other	5 / 5
No money	80 / 70
NHIS does not cover the facilities I use	1
NHIS does not cover the services I need	1 / 1
Do not need NHIS membership	2 / 10
Registration office too far	7 / 6
Don't know where to register	
No knowledge of NHIS	
Don't have confidence in NHIS operators	3 / 6
Premium too high	2 / 2

Percent

■ No longer a member   ■ Never a member

Source: Original estimates based on data from the Ghana Living Standards Survey 2016–17.
Note: Figure shows the distribution of responses as to why the individual no longer is, or never was, an NHIS member for the overall and poor population. In the figures, bars reflecting values less than 1 percent are not labeled. NHIS = National Health Insurance Scheme.

registering or renewing that is consistent with that argument.[18] Instead, the upfront registration, renewal, and premium fees seemed to be the main deterrents to membership enrollment and continuation.

The academic literature on the impact of NHIS on health care usage, health status, and out-of-pocket expenditures is quite large, perhaps because NHIS was one of the first attempts to provide universal health insurance in Africa. Blanchet and Acheampong (2013), Degroote, Ridde, and De Allegri (2020), and Okoroh et al. (2018) have provided useful literature reviews. There is a clear consensus on the following across studies using a variety of methods:

- NHIS membership increased utilization of health care services;
- NHIS members had lower out-of-pocket health care expenditures than did nonmembers;
- NHIS members had lower "catastrophic" health care expenditures, variously defined; and
- NHIS members usually did not have better health outcomes than did nonmembers.

While we do not pretend to review all these studies, our interest in describing the distributional consequences of social assistance programs leads us to summarize three studies that examine the impact of the NHIS on out-of-pocket health care expenditures, as this directly affects beneficiaries' disposable income (net of health care costs).

Powell-Jackson et al. (2014) investigated a randomized allocation of free health care in one district of Ghana, Dangme West, in 2004, just before the advent of the NHIS. They found that this comprehensive insurance reduced out-of-pocket health care expenditures by 27 percent on average and that the reduction was higher at the upper end of the health care expenditure distribution, suggesting that those faced with the largest health care expenditures benefited the most from the insurance.[19]

García-Mandicó, Reichert, and Strupat (2021) used data from the Ghana Living Standards Survey (GLSS) 2005–06, whose fielding straddled the rollout of NHIS at that time. Thus, they were able to use a difference-in-differences estimator to compare survey respondents in the same districts, some of whom gained access to NHIS during the survey fielding period and some of whom did not. These researchers found a mean decrease in out-of-pocket health care expenditures of 18 percent and a 29 percent decrease for households that experienced "more illness."[20] They also reported small but statistically significant reductions in the probability of catastrophic health care expenditures, defined as out-of-pocket expenditures of more than 10 percent of the total household expenditures.

Aryeetey and colleagues (2016) used instrumental variable methods to estimate the impact of NHIS membership on out-of-pocket and catastrophic expenditures. To instrumentalize NHIS membership, these researchers used the data and results of a cluster randomized control trial meant to study the effect of a "multistakeholder problem-solving program" on NHIS enrollment. Comparing the difference between insured and uninsured households before the intervention and after, they found that NHIS coverage reduced out-of-pocket expenditures for outpatient care by GH¢20 on average, as compared to an average expenditure in both samples of GH¢32. This is a much larger percentage reduction in out-of-pocket expenditure than that found in Powell-Jackson et al. (2014), but with a small cedi amount, perhaps because it considered only out-of-pocket expenditures for outpatient services.[21] The study also estimated the impact of NHIS membership on catastrophic health care expenditures, defined as 40 percent or more of nonfood consumption. The researchers found a 4-percentage-point reduction in the number of households experiencing catastrophic expenditures, on average, as compared with an average of 23 percent across the two samples.

NOTES

1. The LEAP Management Secretariat was established in 2015. Before that, overall responsibility for the program lay with a unit within the Department of Social Welfare under the former Ministry of Employment and Social Welfare.
2. The program started off by targeting needy households with orphans and vulnerable children because of a preexisting program in the pilot districts by the Ministry of Employment and Social Welfare, under which premiums for participation in the National Health Insurance Scheme were waived for orphans and vulnerable children.

3. A child in a needy household has to be classified as both an orphan (the death of one or both parents) *and* vulnerable to be considered eligible.

4. The name of the program refers to the first 1,000 days of life, a period considered critical for health and nutrition-enhancing inputs for the child's long-term growth and development. The design and introduction of LEAP 1000 was supported by UNICEF and USAID.

5. To convert the number of households to number of individuals, GLSS 2016–17 data were used to estimate an average household size of 6.3 members in LEAP program households.

6. The original PMT model used by the MOGCSP was constructed based on GLSS 2005–06 data. The PMT model currently in use is based on GLSS 2016–17 data.

7. The GhIPSS is a subsidiary of the Bank of Ghana.

8. Matching was performed based on propensity scores.

9. The average baseline values for the comparison group were GH¢120 for monthly overall household consumption per adult equivalent, GH¢90 for monthly household food consumption per adult equivalent, 91 percent for the poverty rate, and 49 percent for the poverty gap.

10. Donor financing was interrupted by a protracted design period for the World Bank–supported Ghana Productive Safety Net Project, which became effective in June 2019, following the closing of the World Bank–supported Ghana Social Opportunities Project in May 2018.

11. Average daily wage earnings are estimated based on GLSS 2016–17 data.

12. See the discussion of the GhIPSS and e-zwich cards in the "LEAP Program" section.

13. The academic year was changed from September–July to January–December, starting from 2021.

14. Based on GLSS 2016–17 data, of the 25 percent of workers who were wage employed, 44 percent had a written contract, and 35 percent had employer-provided social security (Nxumalo and Raju 2020). Using these conditions (written contract, social security coverage) as indicators of formal employment status, roughly 10 percent of workers were formally employed in Ghana.

15. Since 2012, membership has technically been mandatory, but this is not enforced except for formal sector employees, whose employers are required to ensure that they are enrolled.

16. Staff costs at public facilities and some quasi-public facilities, such as the Christian Health Association of Ghana, are paid by the central government through a separate mechanism, not through the NHIA. Thus, for anyone seeking care at a public facility, the staff costs are "insured" by the central government whether they are an NHIS member or not. This implies that at public facilities, NHIS only covers nonstaff (and noncapital) costs, mostly medicine and diagnostic services.

17. Capitation payments pay providers a fixed annual amount for each member who enrolls with that provider as their "preferred primary provider."

18. "Don't have confidence in operators of scheme" and "Health insurance does not cover the services I need" are the two responses most consistent with the proposition that providers are not providing the services that should be free of charge.

19. They do not, however, estimate the impact on catastrophic health care expenditures as usually defined.

20. This is defined as being above the sample median for the total number of days ill for adults in the household divided by the total number of adults in the household times 14 days.

21. Their results for inpatient services actually suggest that NHIS *increases* out-of-pocket expenditures.

REFERENCES

Abiiro, Gilbert Abotisem, Kennedy A. Alatinga, and Gavin Yamey. 2021. "Why Did Ghana's National Health Insurance Capitation Payment Model Fall Off the Policy Agenda? A Regional Level Policy Analysis." *Health Policy and Planning* 36 (6): 869–80.

Agyepong, Irene Akua, Daniel Nana Yaw Abankwah, Angela Abroso, ChangBae Chun, Joseph Nii Otoe Dodoo, Shinye Lee, Sylvester A. Mensah, Mariam Musah, Adwoa Twum, Juwhan Oh, Jinha Park, DoogHoon Yang, Kijong Yoon, Nathaniel Otoo, and Francis Asenso-Boadi.

2016. "The 'Universal' in UHC and Ghana's National Health Insurance Scheme: Policy and Implementation Challenges and Dilemmas of a Lower Middle-Income Country." *BMC Health Services Research* 16: 504.

Aikens, Moses, Philip Teg-Nefaah Tabong, Paola Salari, Frabizio Tediosi, Francis M. Asenso-Boadi, and Patricia Akweongo. 2021. "Positioning the National Health Insurance for Financial Sustainability and Universal Health Coverage in Ghana: A Qualitative Study among Key Stakeholders." *PLoS One*. https://doi.org/10.1371/journal.pone.0253109.

Aryeetey, Genevieve Cecilia, Judith Westeneng, Ernst Spaan, Caroline Jehu-Appiah, Irene Akua Agyepong, and Rob Baltussen. 2016. "Can Health Insurance Protect against Out-of-Pocket and Catastrophic Expenditures and Also Support Poverty Reduction? Evidence from Ghana's National Health Insurance Scheme." *International Journal for Equity in Health* 15: 116.

Aurino, Elisabetta, Aulo Gelli, Clement Adamba, Isaac Osei-Akoto, and Harold Alderman. 2023. "Food for Thought? Experimental Evidence on the Learning Impacts of a Large-Scale School Feeding Program." *Journal of Human Resources* 58 (1): 74–111.

Blanchet, Nathan, and Osei B. Acheampong. 2013. *Building on Community-Based Health Insurance to Expand National Coverage: The Case of Ghana*. Bethesda, MD: Abt Associates.

CDD-Ghana (Ghana Center for Democratic Development). 2016. *Report on Vulnerability and Social Protection in Ghana: The Case of Livelihood Empowerment Against Poverty Program (LEAP) Survey*. Accra: CDD-Ghana.

Christmals, Christmal Dela, and Kizito Aidem. 2020. "Implementation of the National Health Insurance Scheme (NHIS) in Ghana: Lessons for South Africa and Low- and Middle-Income Countries." *Risk Management and Healthcare Policy* 13: 1879–904.

Degroote, Stéphanie, Valery Ridde, and Manuel De Allegri. 2020. "Health Insurance in Sub-Saharan Africa: A Scoping Review of the Methods Used to Evaluate Its Impact." *Applied Health Economics and Health Policy* 18 (6): 825–40.

Dorfman, Mark. 2015. "Pension Patterns in Sub-Saharan Africa." Social Protection and Labor Discussion Paper 1503. Washington, DC: World Bank.

Dunaev, Alexander, and Federica Corona. 2019. *School Feeding in Ghana: Investment Case: Cost Benefit Analysis Report*. Accra: World Food Programme.

FAO (Food and Agriculture Organization). 2013. *Qualitative Research and Analyses of the Economic Impacts of Cash Transfer Programs in Sub-Saharan Africa: Ghana Country Case Study Report*. Rome: FAO.

García-Mandicó, Sílvia, Arndt Reichert, and Christoph Strupat. 2021. "The Social Value of Health Insurance: Results from Ghana." *Journal of Public Economics* 194: 104314.

Gelli, Aulo, Elisabetta Aurino, Gloria Folson, Daniel Arhinful, Clement Adamba, Issac Osei-Akoto, Edoardo Masset, Kristie Watkins, Meena Fernandes, Lesley Drake, and Harold Alderman. 2019. "A School Meals Program Implemented at Scale in Ghana Increases Height-for-Age during Mid-Childhood in Girls and in Children from Poor Households: A Cluster Randomized Trial." *Journal of Nutrition* 149 (8): 1434–42.

Government of Ghana. 2022. *Draft*: 2023 *Budget Speech*. https://mofep.gov.gh/sites/default/files/budget-statements/2023-Budget-Speech.pdf.

GSS (Ghana Statistical Service). 2019. *Ghana Living Standards Survey (GLSS) 7: Main Report*. Accra: GSS.

GSS (Ghana Statistical Service). 2012. 2010 *Population and Housing Census: Summary Report of Final Results*. Accra: GSS.

Handa, Sudhanshu, Michael Park, Robert Darko Osei, and Isaac Osei-Akoto. 2012. *Livelihood Empowerment Against Poverty Program: Assessment of LEAP Operations*. Chapel Hill: Carolina Population Center, University of North Carolina at Chapel Hill.

Handa, Sudhanshu, et al. 2017. *Livelihood Empowerment Against Poverty Programme: Endline Impact Evaluation Report*. Chapel Hill: Carolina Population Center, University of North Carolina at Chapel Hill.

Laar, Alexander Suuk, Michael Asare, and Philip Ayizem Dalinjong. 2021. "What Alternative and Innovative Sources of Healthcare Finance Can Be Explored for the Sustainability of the

National Health Insurance Scheme of Ghana? Perspectives of Health Managers." *Cost Effective and Resource Allocation* 19: 69.

LEAP 1000 Evaluation Study Team. 2018. *Ghana LEAP 1000 Programme: Endline Evaluation Report*. Chapel Hill: University of North Carolina Population Center, University of North Carolina at Chapel Hill. https://transfer.cpc.unc.edu/wp-content/uploads/2021/04/LEAP1000_Report_Final-2019-for-dissemination.pdf.

MELR and MLGRD (Ministry of Employment and Labour Relations and Ministry of Local Government and Rural Development). 2016. *National Labour-Intensive Public Works Policy: Enhancing Employment Opportunities and Economic Security for the Poor*. Accra: MELR and MLGRD.

MOGCSP (Ministry of Gender, Children, and Social Protection). 2016. *National School Feeding Policy*. Accra: MOGCSP.

MOGCSP (Ministry of Gender, Children, and Social Protection). 2019. *Ghana Productive Social Net Project: Project Operational Manual: . Vol. 3, Livelihood Empowerment Against Poverty (LEAP) Programme Operational Manual*. Accra: MOGCSP.

Nxumalo, Mpumelelo, and Dhushyanth Raju. 2020. "Structural Transformation and Labor Market Performance in Ghana." Jobs Working Paper 55, World Bank, Washington, DC.

Okoroh, Juliet, Samuel Essoun, Anthony Seddoh, Hobart Harris, Joel S. Weissman, Lydia Dsane-Selby, and Robert Riviello. 2018. "Evaluating the Impact of the National Health Insurance Scheme of Ghana on Out of Pocket Expenditures: A Systematic Review." *BMC Health Services Research* 18 (1): 426.

Osei-Akoto, Isaac, Simon Bawakyillenuo, George Owusu, Felix Essilfie, and Innocent Agbelie. 2016. *Short Term Impact Evaluation Report: Labour Intensive Public Works (LIPW) of Ghana Social Opportunities Project (GSOP)*. Accra: Institute of Statistical, Social, and Economic Research.

Palermo, Tia M., Elsa Valli, Gustavo Ángeles-Tagliaferro, Marlous de Milliano, Clement Adamba, Tayllor Renee Spadafora, Clare Barrington, and LEAP 1000 Evaluation Team. 2019. "Impact Evaluation of a Social Protection Paid with Fee Waivers on Enrolment in Ghana's National Health Insurance Scheme." *BMJ Open* 9 (11): e028726.

P&OD Consult. 2018. *Beneficiary Assessment of the Livelihood Empowerment Against Poverty Program*. Accra: P&OD Consult.

Peterman, Amber, Elsa Valli, and Tia Palermo. 2022. "Government Antipoverty Programming and Intimate Partner Violence in Ghana." *Economic Development and Cultural Change* 70 (2): 529–66.

Powell-Jackson, Timothy, Kara Hanson, Christopher J. M. Whitty, and Evelyn K. Ansah. 2014. "Who Benefits from Free Healthcare? Evidence from a Randomized Experiment in Ghana." *Journal of Development Economics* 107: 305–19.

Raju, Dhushyanth, and Stephen D. Younger. 2021. "Social Assistance Programs and Household Welfare in Eswatini." Social Protection and Jobs Working Paper 2106, World Bank, Washington, DC.

Schwarz, Anita M. 2016. *The Ghanaian Pension System: An Evaluation with Suggestions for Reform*. Washington, DC: World Bank.

SSNIT (Social Security and National Insurance Trust). 2019. *Annual Report 2019*. Accra: SSNIT.

Wang, Huihui, Nathaniel Otoo, and Lydia Dsane-Selby. 2017. *Ghana National Health Insurance Scheme: Improving Financial Sustainability Based on Expenditure Review*. Washington, DC: World Bank.

4 Performance Analysis

INTRODUCTION

In this chapter, we discuss findings from our analysis of the performance of the selected social protection programs in six main parts. In the first section, we examine the levels of, and patterns and trends in, spending on programs. In the second through fifth sections, we discuss findings for program coverage, incidence, and effectiveness, as well as the hypothetical results on program incidence and outlay from simulating reforms in coverage and benefit levels for the Livelihood Empowerment Against Poverty (LEAP) program. In the last section, we analyze the findings from investigating the association between shocks and social assistance program participation.

The findings throughout are based on government administrative data on programs, Ghana Living Standards Survey (GLSS) 2016–17 data, high-resolution climate map data, and government administrative data on programs. As data on Labor-Intensive Public Works (LIPW) program participation were not gathered in the GLSS 2016–17, we omit coverage, incidence, and effectiveness for this program.

SPENDING

How much expenditure went toward benefits under the government's main social protection programs, that is, the LEAP program, the LIPW program, the Ghana School Feeding Programme (GSFP), Social Security and National Insurance Trust (SSNIT) pensions, and the National Health Insurance Scheme (NHIS)? For each program, we specifically discuss the level of benefit spending in 2017, which mostly overlaps with the period for our ensuing performance analysis based on the GLSS 2016–17, and we examine the level of benefit spending in the most recent year for which we have data. We examine the level of benefit spending relative to gross domestic product (GDP) and overall government spending across years, bounded by 2021, the latest year for which we have actual (instead of forecasted) GDP and overall government spending statistics for Ghana. The periods for our benefit spending data differ from program to program. All program benefit spending data were obtained directly from the relevant program implementing agencies. In pooling relevant programs, we also analyze patterns and trends in benefit spending for social assistance (namely, the LEAP program, the LIPW program, and GSFP), social insurance (namely, SSNIT pensions and NHIS), and social protection (social assistance and social insurance combined) programs.

For this study, we attempted to obtain data on spending on program administration, but they were either not shared by the program-implementing agencies (SSNIT and the National Health Insurance Authority [NHIA]), or the data shared were potentially problematic because the program-implementing agencies shared administrative arrangements and personnel across multiple programs and initiatives (the Ministry of Local Government, Decentralization, and Rural Development and the Ministry of Gender, Children, and Social Protection [MOGCSP]).

For all programs apart from SSNIT pensions, a fair amount of the yearly fluctuation in benefit spending is explained by delays in the internal flow of required funds to program-implementing agencies. In the case of the LIPW program, the fluctuation is also attributable to the availability of donor financing. Across programs, periods of an uptrend in benefit spending in the data are largely explained by increases in the numbers of beneficiaries. In the case of SSNIT pensions, they are also attributable to nominal increases in the value of pension payments.

We obtained data on benefit spending for the LEAP program for the period 2016 to 2022 and for GSFP from 2016 to 2019. Over the time span of the data, the LEAP program was partly financed through donor financing channeled through the government, whereas GSFP was financed by the government through general revenues.

In 2017, LEAP program benefit spending was GH¢93 million, equivalent to 0.035 percent of GDP and 0.19 percent of overall government spending (figure 4.1). In 2022, total program benefit spending was GH¢162 million.

In 2017, GSFP benefit spending was GH¢259 million, equivalent to 0.10 percent of GDP and 0.5 percent of overall government spending (figure 4.2). In 2019, the latest year for which we have data and also the year before implementation of the program was interrupted by public school closures resulting from the coronavirus pandemic, total program benefit spending was GH¢445 million, equivalent to 0.12 percent of GDP and 0.6 percent of overall government spending.

We obtained LIPW program benefit spending data for the period 2011 to 2021. The LIPW program is fully financed by donor funds channeled through the government. There was little spending in 2011, when the program was launched (so we exclude this year from our examination), and little to no spending in 2018 and 2019, when donor financing was unavailable (we retain these years in our examination). Except for the years when donor financing was unavailable, program benefit spending generally increased over time (figure 4.3). Program benefit spending is divided between labor payments and payments for nonlabor components of the small civil works. Across years with significant program scale and spending, labor payments ranged from a low of 41.6 percent of total benefit spending (in 2017) to a high of 70.1 percent (in 2021). In 2017, total benefit spending under the LIPW program was GH¢39 million, equivalent to 0.015 percent of GDP and 0.079 percent of overall government spending. In 2021, total benefit spending under the program was GH¢50 million, equivalent to 0.011 percent of GDP and 0.029 percent of overall government spending.

FIGURE 4.1

Spending on the LEAP program, 2016–22

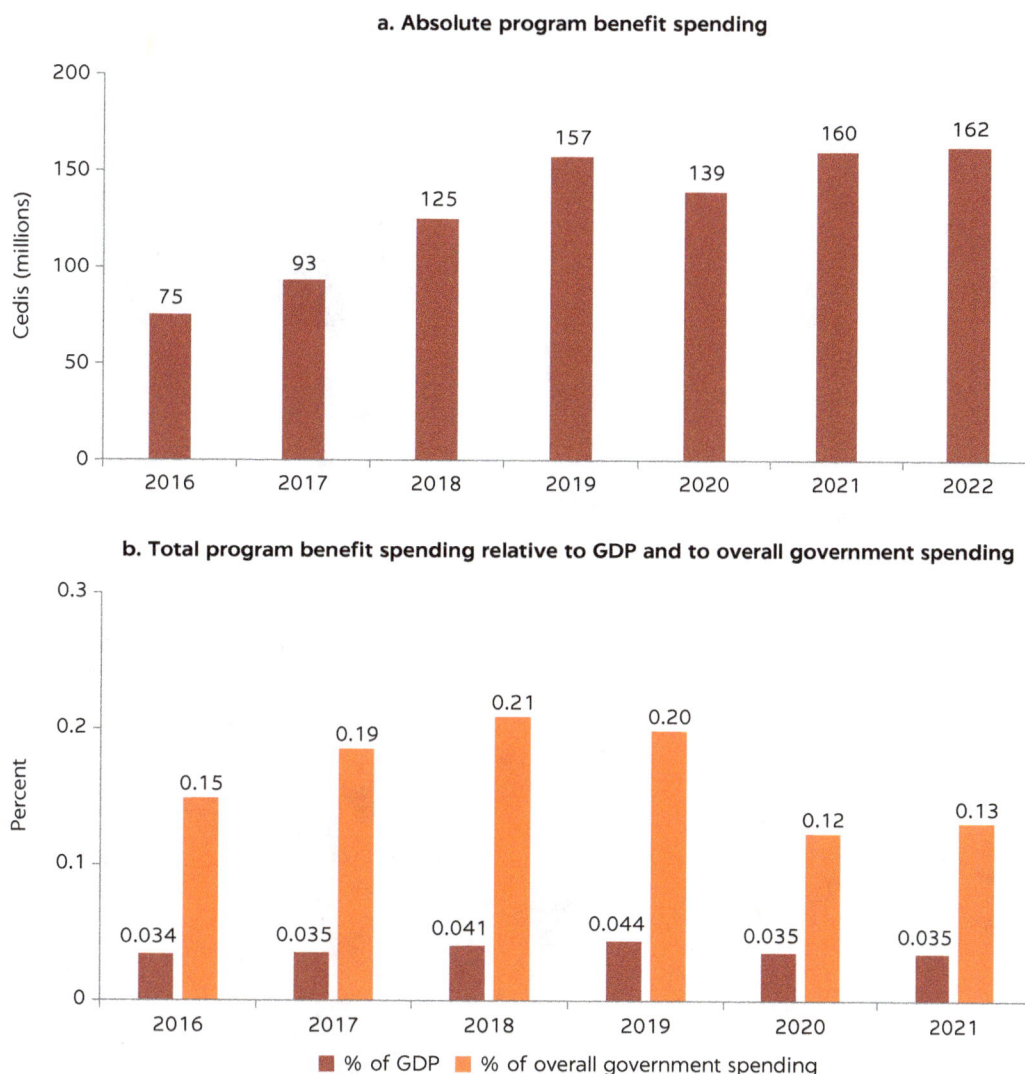

a. Absolute program benefit spending

b. Total program benefit spending relative to GDP and to overall government spending

■ % of GDP ■ % of overall government spending

Source: Original estimates based on program administrative data from the Ministry of Gender, Children, and Social Protection and on GDP and overall government expenditure statistics from the World Bank, Macro Poverty Outlook for Sub-Sahara Africa, Ghana datasheet, April 2023.
Note: Figure shows the trend in absolute benefit spending as well as in benefit spending relative to GDP and to overall government spending for the LEAP program. Panel (b) does not report statistics for 2022 because actual GDP and overall government spending information was unavailable. GDP = gross domestic product; LEAP = Livelihood Empowerment Against Poverty.

The SSNIT pension benefit spending data cover the period between 2010 and 2020. In 2017, total spending on pension benefits was GH¢2,189 million, of which monthly pension benefits accounted for 84.6 percent and lump-sum payments for 13.4 percent (figure 4.4a). This level of spending on pension benefits was equivalent to 0.83 percent of GDP and 4.4 percent of overall government spending (figure 4.4b). The benchmarking of program benefit spending to overall government spending should not be interpreted as reflecting how much the government spends on the program benefits. SSNIT pensions are financed by contributions from employers and workers provided to SSNIT and returns from

FIGURE 4.2

Spending on GSFP, 2016–19

a. Absolute program benefit spending

b. Total program benefit spending relative to GDP and to overall government spending

■ % of GDP ■ % of overall government spending

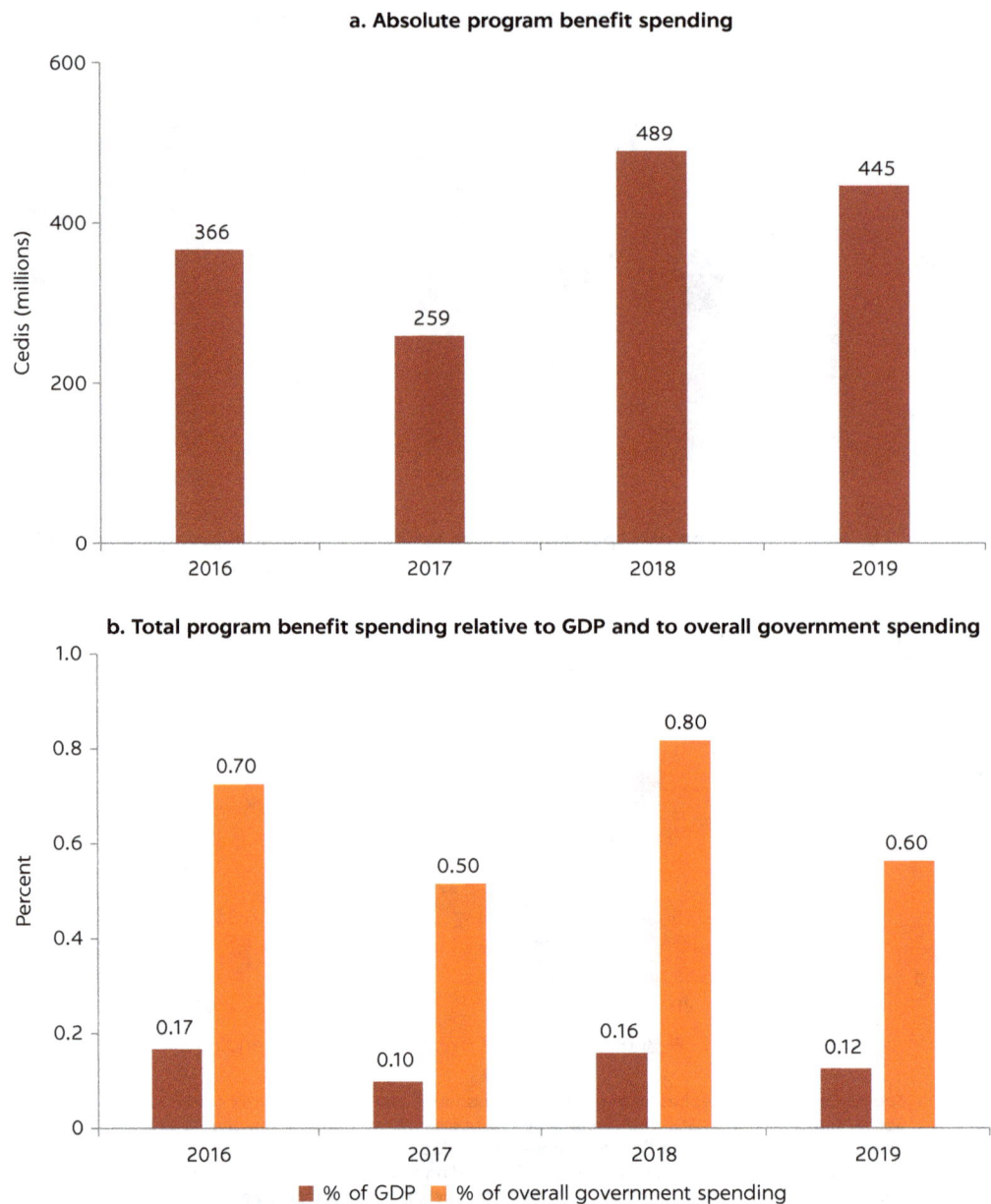

Source: Original estimates based on program administrative data from the Ministry of Gender, Children, and Social Protection and on GDP and overall government expenditure statistics from the World Bank, Macro Poverty Outlook for Sub-Sahara Africa, Ghana datasheet, April 2023.
Note: Figure shows the trend in absolute benefit spending and in benefit spending relative to GDP and to overall government spending for GSFP. GDP = gross domestic product; GSFP = Ghana School Feeding Programme.

investments of contribution funds by SSNIT. Government spending on program benefits applies to the extent that the government pays contributions on behalf of its employees to SSNIT. In 2020, the latest year of our data, total spending on pension benefits was GH¢3,303 million, equivalent to 0.84 percent of GDP and 2.9 percent of overall government spending.

NHIS benefit spending data (that is, NHIS spending on claims) are for 2010 to 2019. Program spending is almost fully financed by earmarked taxes and NHIS

FIGURE 4.3

Spending on the LIPW program, 2012–21

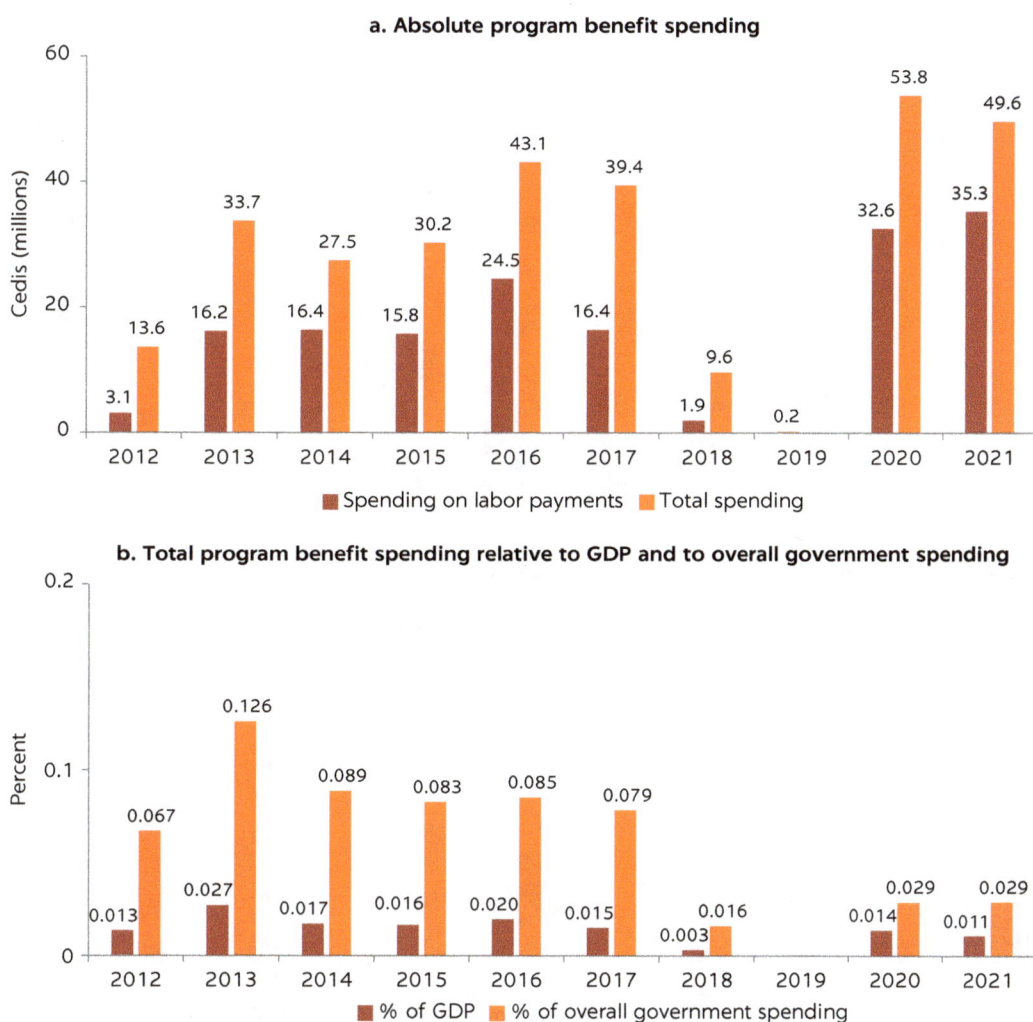

a. Absolute program benefit spending

Spending on labor payments ■ Total spending

b. Total program benefit spending relative to GDP and to overall government spending

■ % of GDP ■ % of overall government spending

Source: Original estimates based on program administrative data from the Ministry of Local Government, Decentralization, and Rural Development and on GDP and overall government expenditure statistics from the World Bank, Macro Poverty Outlook for Sub-Sahara Africa, Ghana datasheet, April 2023.
Note: Figure shows the trend in absolute benefit spending and in benefit spending relative to GDP and to overall government spending for the LIPW program. GDP = gross domestic product; LIPW = Labor-Intensive Public Works. Benefit spending = labor and nonlabor payments.

premium payments by SSNIT on behalf of its contributors and pensioners. Across the years, earmarked taxes have tended to account for roughly three-quarters of funds received by the NHIA for the program.

In 2017, total NHIS benefit spending was GH¢1,325 million, equivalent to 0.50 percent of GDP and 2.6 percent of overall government spending. In 2019, the latest year of our data, total program benefit spending was GH¢979 million, equivalent to 0.27 percent of GDP and 1.6 percent of overall government spending (figure 4.5). The caveat for our benchmarking against overall government spending that we mentioned in relation to SSNIT pensions applies to this program as well, albeit to a much lesser degree given that the bulk of funds for NHIS comes from earmarked taxes (that is, government financing).

FIGURE 4.4

Spending on SSNIT pensions, 2010–20

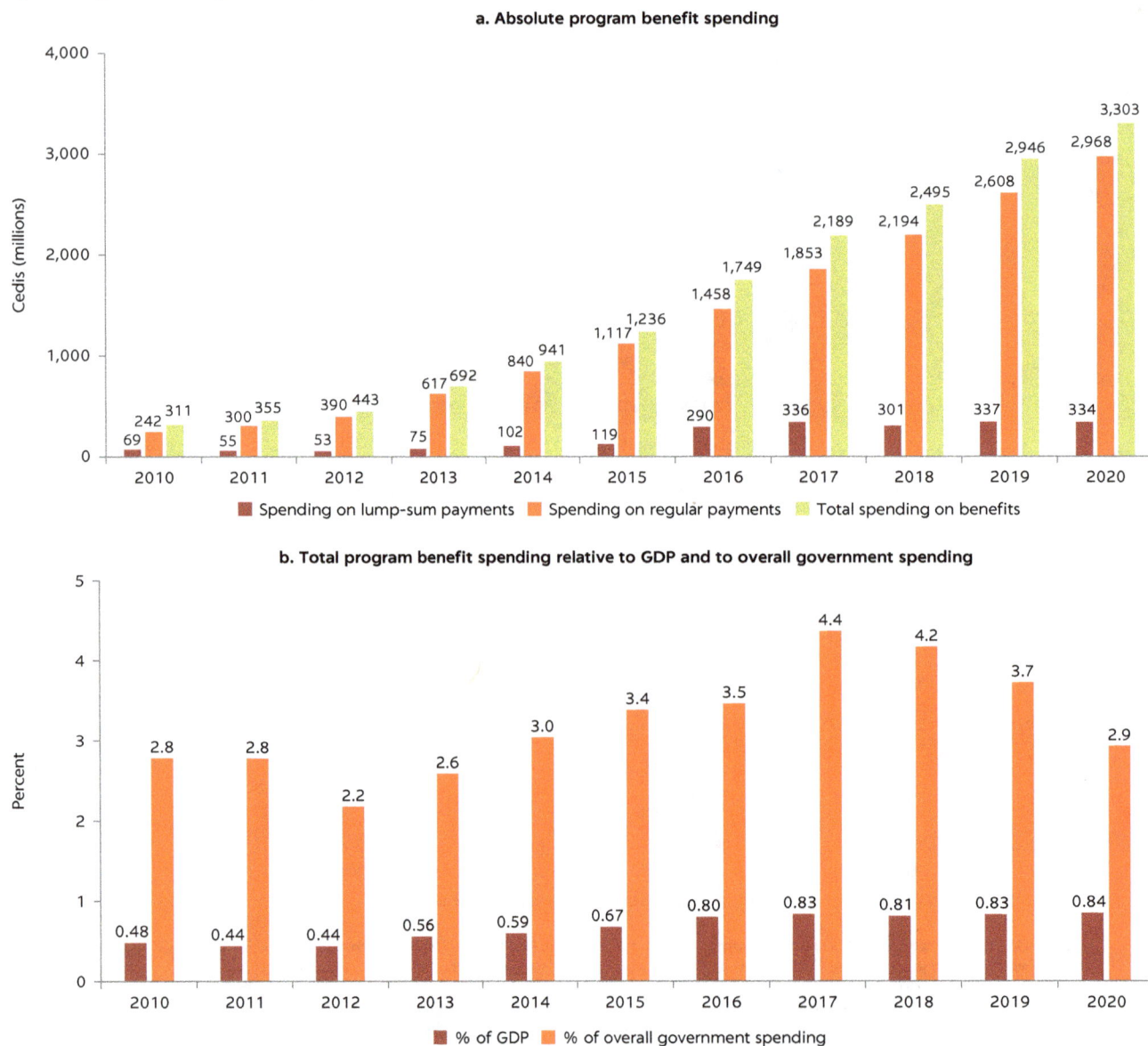

a. Absolute program benefit spending

■ Spending on lump-sum payments ■ Spending on regular payments ■ Total spending on benefits

b. Total program benefit spending relative to GDP and to overall government spending

■ % of GDP ■ % of overall government spending

Source: Original estimates based on program administrative data from the Social Security and National Insurance Trust and on GDP and overall government expenditure statistics from the World Bank, Macro Poverty Outlook for Sub-Sahara Africa, Ghana datasheet, April 2023.
Note: Figure shows the trend in absolute benefit spending and in benefit spending relative to GDP and to overall government spending for SSNIT pensions. GDP = gross domestic product; SSNIT = Social Security and National Insurance Trust.

Combining benefit spending under the LEAP program, the LIPW program, and GSFP, we examined total benefit spending under social assistance programs between 2016 and 2019, a period that subsumes our program performance analysis subperiod of 2016/17. GSFP benefit spending accounts for at least two-thirds of total benefit spending under social assistance programs (figure 4.6). Social assistance program spending is equivalent to 0.15–0.2 percent of GDP and 0.8–1.0 percent of overall government spending. This level of spending relative to GDP is far below the corresponding average levels of social assistance programs in Sub-Saharan African countries and in low- and middle-income

FIGURE 4.5

Spending on NHIS, 2010–19

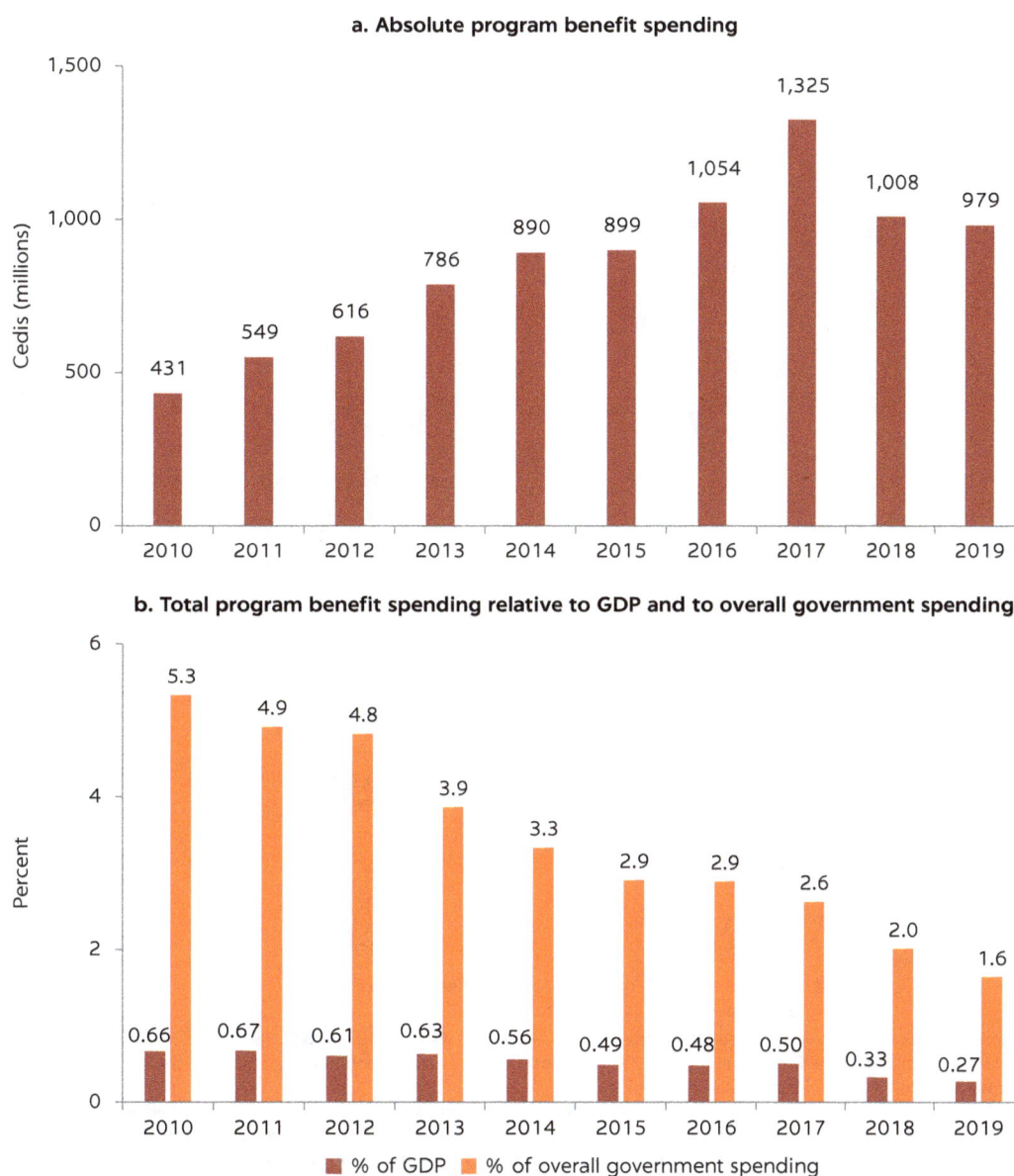

a. Absolute program benefit spending

b. Total program benefit spending relative to GDP and to overall government spending

■ % of GDP ■ % of overall government spending

Source: Original estimates based on program administrative data from the National Health Insurance Authority and on GDP and overall government expenditure statistics from the World Bank, Macro Poverty Outlook for Sub-Sahara Africa, Ghana datasheet, April 2023.
Note: Figure shows the trend in absolute benefit spending and in benefit spending relative to GDP and to overall government spending for NHIS. GDP = gross domestic product; NHIS = National Health Insurance Scheme. Benefit spending = spending on claims.

countries more generally, for which we have estimates of social assistance program spending based on national household sample survey data (figure 4.7). The average level of social assistance program spending in these two groups of countries is 1.55 percent of GDP.[1]

We also examined total social protection program benefit spending, combining benefit spending under social assistance programs with benefit spending under social insurance programs (the latter composed of NHIS and SSNIT pensions) between 2016 and 2019. Benefit spending under social insurance programs

FIGURE 4.6

Government spending across social assistance programs, 2016–19

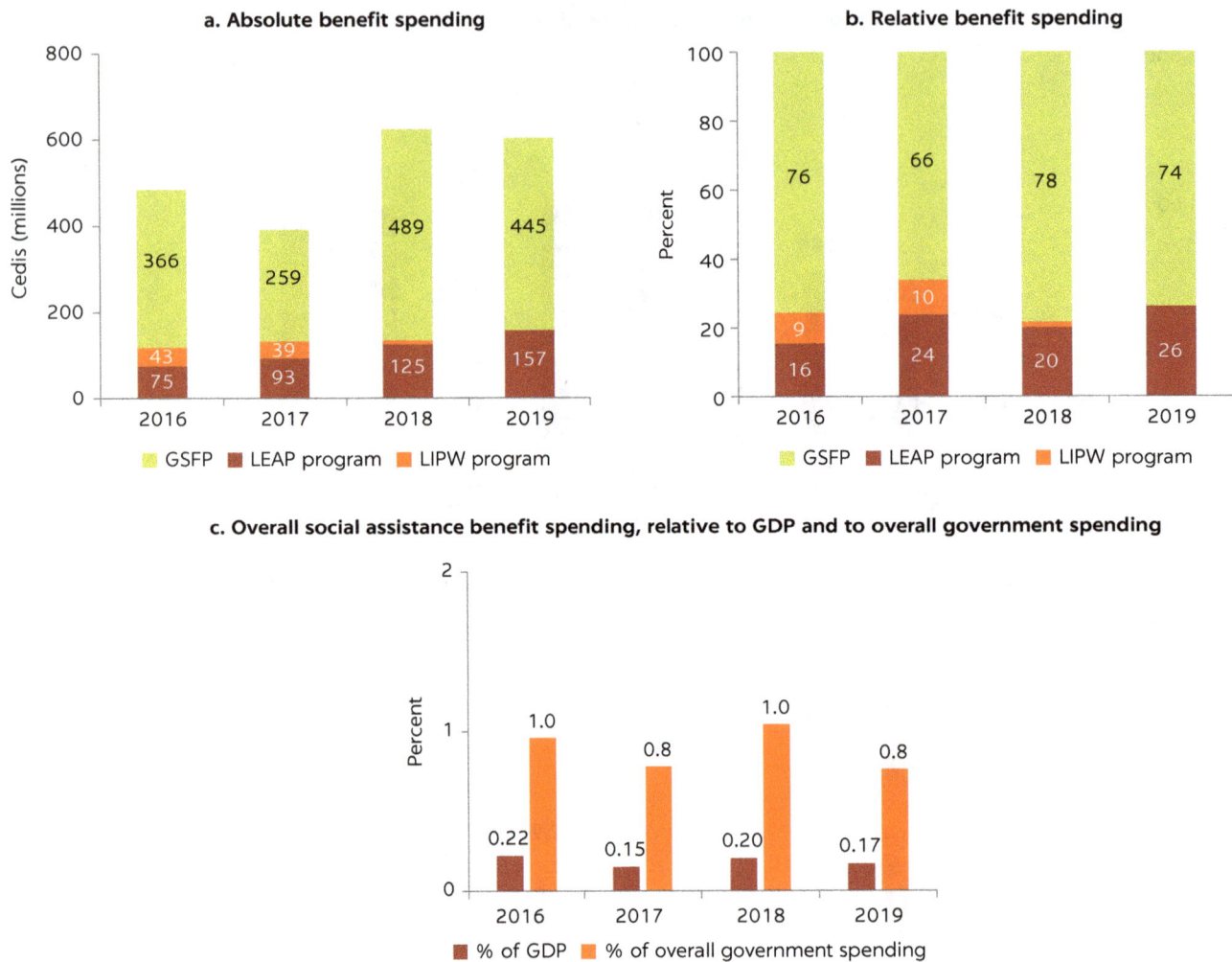

a. Absolute benefit spending

b. Relative benefit spending

c. Overall social assistance benefit spending, relative to GDP and to overall government spending

Source: Original estimates based on program administrative data from the Ministry of Gender, Children, and Social Protection; the Ministry of Local Government, Decentralization, and Rural Development; and GDP and overall government expenditure statistics from the World Bank, Macro Poverty Outlook for Sub-Sahara Africa, Ghana datasheet, April 2023.
Note: Figure shows the trends in benefit spending for the LEAP program, the LIPW program, and GSFP, in absolute and relative terms; the figure also shows the trend in overall social assistance benefit spending relative to GDP and to overall government spending. GDP = gross domestic product; GSFP = Ghana School Feeding Programme; LEAP = Livelihood Empowerment Against Poverty; LIPW = Labor-Intensive Public Works. Social assistance = LEAP program, LIPW program, and GSFP.

accounted for at least four-fifths of total social protection program benefit spending (figure 4.8). Social protection program benefit spending was equivalent to 1.3–1.5 percent of GDP and 6–8 percent of overall government spending.

As discussed before in relation to benefit spending levels of NHIS and SSNIT pensions, the noted percentage of overall government spending should be interpreted with caution given the important nongovernment sources of financing of NHIS and SSNIT pensions.

COVERAGE

What is the extent of coverage of individuals and households by Ghana's main government-provided social protection programs? The GLSS 2016–17 captured

FIGURE 4.7

Comparative social assistance program spending: International comparison with Ghana

Cumulative distribution of annual social assistance program spending as a percentage of GDP

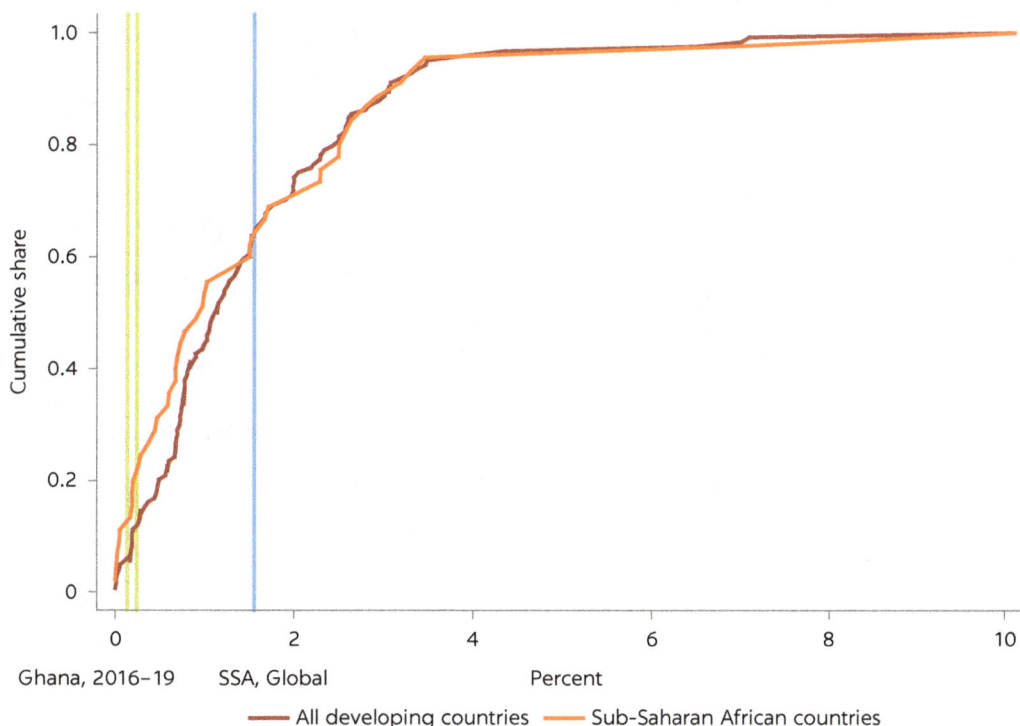

Source: Global data from the World Bank, Atlas of Social Protection Indicators of Resilience and Equity (ASPIRE) database (accessed May 19, 2020), http://datatopics.worldbank.org/aspire/home. Statistic for Ghana is based on the government's administrative data for the LEAP program, the LIPW program, and GSFP and on GDP statistics from the World Bank, World Development Indicators database.
Note: Figure shows the cumulative distribution functions for annual social assistance spending as a percentage of GDP for all developing countries and Sub-Saharan African countries, respectively, with the levels for Ghana for 2016–2019 and the mean levels for two country samples specified. For the global data, the mean year was 2014. The sample size for all developing countries is 124; the sample size for Sub-Saharan African countries is 45. The blue vertical line labeled "SSA, Global" indicates the mean value for all developing countries and for Sub-Saharan African countries. (The mean values for the two country samples are roughly the same, so they are treated as identical for the sake of graphing.) The olive vertical lines labeled "Ghana, 2016–19" reflect the band for values for Ghana between 2016 and 2019. For the purposes of this figure, social assistance programs in Ghana comprise the LEAP program, the LIPW program, and GSFP. GDP = gross domestic product; global = developing countries; GSFP = Ghana School Feeding Programme; LEAP = Livelihood Empowerment Against Poverty; LIPW = Labor-Intensive Public Works; SSA = Sub-Saharan Africa.

information on program participation at the individual level for GSFP, NHIS, and SSNIT pensions. The survey also gathered information on participation at the household level for the LEAP program. For details on the construction of the program participation variables, see appendix A.

Across the programs, table A.1 in appendix A reports survey estimates of beneficiary numbers and compares these estimates with beneficiary numbers from government administrative data. Under the assumption that the government administrative data are accurate, survey-based beneficiary numbers generally fall short. The shortfall is largest for the LEAP program, but these shortfalls are a concern for all programs we examine here. As an important caveat, this suggests that coverage rates for the programs are likely to be underestimated by a significant amount in the survey data. While we have no a priori reason to believe that the likelihood of underreporting in the GLSS 2016–17 correlates with any of

FIGURE 4.8

Social protection spending: Social assistance versus social insurance, 2016–19

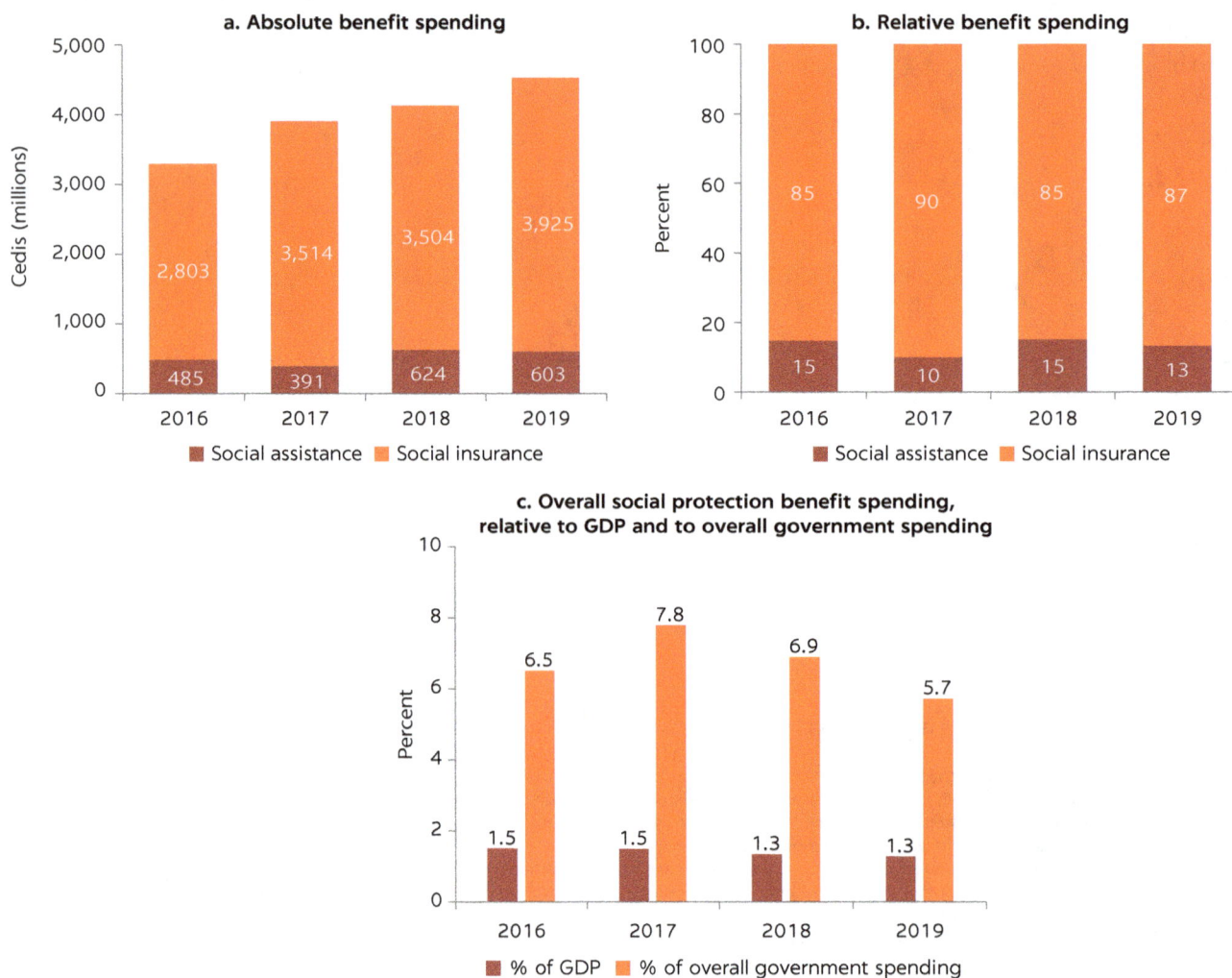

a. Absolute benefit spending

b. Relative benefit spending

c. Overall social protection benefit spending, relative to GDP and to overall government spending

Source: Original estimates based on program administrative data from the various agencies and on GDP and overall government expenditure statistics from the World Bank, Macro Poverty Outlook for Sub-Sahara Africa, Ghana datasheet, April 2023.
Note: Figure shows the trend in benefit spending on social assistance and social insurance programs, in absolute and relative terms; the figure also shows the trend in overall social protection benefit spending relative to GDP and to overall government spending. Social protection = LEAP program, LIPW program, GSFP, NHIS, and SSNIT pensions. Social assistance = LEAP program, LIPW program, and GSFP. Social insurance = NHIS and SSNIT pensions. GDP = gross domestic product; GSFP = Ghana School Feeding Programme; LEAP = Livelihood Empowerment Against Poverty; LIPW = Labor-Intensive Public Works; NHIS = National Health Insurance Scheme; SSNIT = Social Security and National Insurance Trust.

the individual and household characteristics we examine in our subgroup analysis of coverage rates, if it is in fact correlated, it will bias our results.

We examine program coverage rates for individuals (including "presumed eligible" or "target" individuals, based on applying some of the eligibility criteria for program benefit receipt to the GLSS 2016–17 data) and for households. For the definition of the coverage rate, see appendix B. We examine coverage rates separately by poverty group: extreme poor, moderate poor, near poor, and other nonpoor. The extreme-poor population has consumption (per adult equivalent) below the extreme poverty line, the moderate-poor population has consumption between the extreme and overall poverty lines, the near-poor population has consumption between 1 and 1.5 times the overall poverty line, and the other-nonpoor population has consumption above 1.5 times the overall poverty line. At the national level, 8.2 percent of the population are in the extreme-poor group, 15.2 percent are in the moderate-poor group, 17.1 percent are in the near-poor group, and 59.5 percent are in the other-nonpoor group.

To allow for international comparisons, we estimate program coverage rates separately by household consumption quintiles, reported in tables C.1 and C.2 in appendix C. We also estimate program coverage rates for rural and urban areas, reported in the same tables.

The discussion that follows focuses on program coverage rates at the national level for individuals and households, disaggregated by poverty group. For NHIS and SSNIT pensions, which are available to the national population more generally, we also discuss individual coverage rates across regions.

NHIS reaches 34 percent of Ghana's population (figure 4.9a). The other programs reach far fewer Ghanaians. GSFP reaches 4 percent of the national population, the LEAP program reaches 1.5 percent, and SSNIT pensions reach 0.4 percent. The LEAP program and GSFP have pro-poor coverage (figure 4.9b). NHIS coverage rates are roughly similar across poverty groups. Coverage by SSNIT pensions is essentially 0, except for the other-nonpoor, at 0.6 percent.

We also examine the extent of GSFP and SSNIT pension coverage of their respective target groups. GSFP covers 25 percent of public preprimary and primary school students across Ghana, as well as 61 percent of public preprimary and primary school students in GSFP areas (that is, those primary sampling units in the GLSS 2016–17 where there is at least one GSFP beneficiary) (figure 4.10). For GSFP's target group, the progressiveness of program coverage falls when we shift from looking at the country as a whole to looking at GSFP areas within the country, indicating that, like for the LEAP program, GSFP's progressiveness is driven by its geographic targeting of poor areas. SSNIT pensions cover 5 percent of those age 60 or older. For this target group, the program's coverage rate is 8 percent for the other-nonpoor group and between 0.5 and 2 percent for the other poverty groups.

As noted earlier, NHIS covers 34 percent of the national population. However, coverage rates vary widely across regions, from 22 percent in the Central region to 49 percent in the Upper East region (a spread of 27 percentage points) (figure 4.11). SSNIT pension coverage rates range from a low of virtually 0 percent in the Northern region to about 1 percent in the Greater Accra region (figure 4.12a). When limiting the examination to those age 60 or older, coverage rates of SSNIT pensions across regions of course increase: They range from 0.2 percent in the Northern region to 14 percent in the Greater Accra region (figure 4.12b).

We also estimate program coverage rates for households.[2] In the case of individual-level benefits, such as for GSFP, NHIS, and SSNIT pensions, a household is classified as a beneficiary if at least one member receives the program benefit. NHIS covers 48.5 percent of households nationally, followed by GSFP at 7.9 percent, SSNIT pensions at 1.4 percent, and the LEAP program at 0.9 percent (figure 4.13).

For GSFP, NHIS, and SSNIT pensions, coverage rates for households are somewhat higher than are those for individuals. This difference is because, in beneficiary households, some members directly receive the individual-level benefits, while others do not. For the LEAP program, the coverage rate for households is a little lower than is that for individuals. This difference is

FIGURE 4.9

Coverage rates of individuals, by program

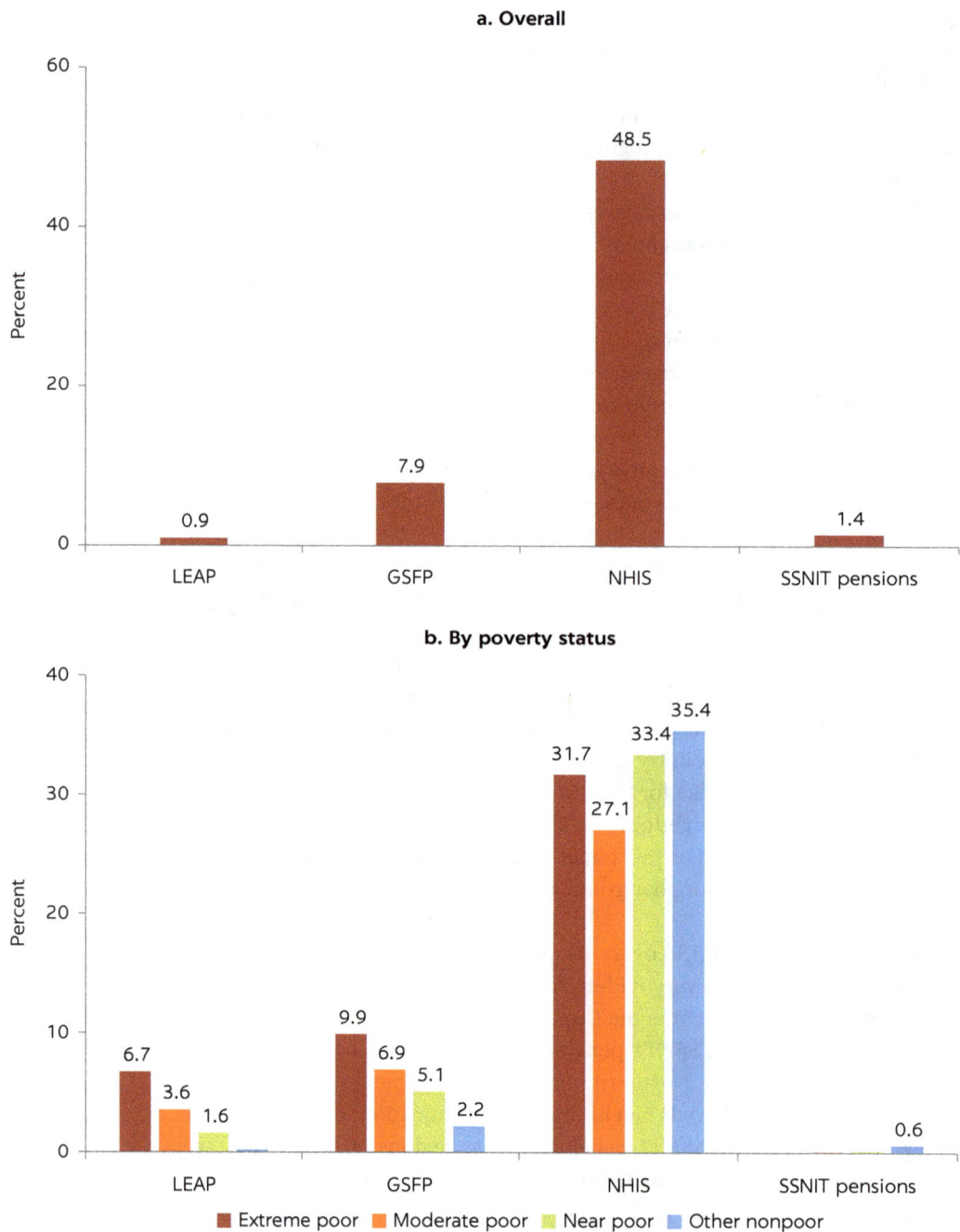

a. Overall

b. By poverty status

Extreme poor ■ Moderate poor ■ Near poor ■ Other nonpoor

Source: Original estimates based on data from the Ghana Living Standards Survey 2016–17.
Note: Figure shows individual coverage rates by program. These coverage rates are also estimated by poverty status (extreme poor, moderate poor, near poor, and other nonpoor); for definitions of the poverty statuses, see appendix A. The LEAP program benefit is treated as a household benefit; given this, all members in LEAP program households are considered beneficiaries. Bars with values lower than 0.5 percent are not labeled. GSFP = Ghana School Feeding Programme; LEAP = Livelihood Empowerment Against Poverty; NHIS = National Health Insurance Scheme; SSNIT = Social Security and National Insurance Trust.

FIGURE 4.10

GSFP and SSNIT coverage rates of individuals in target categories

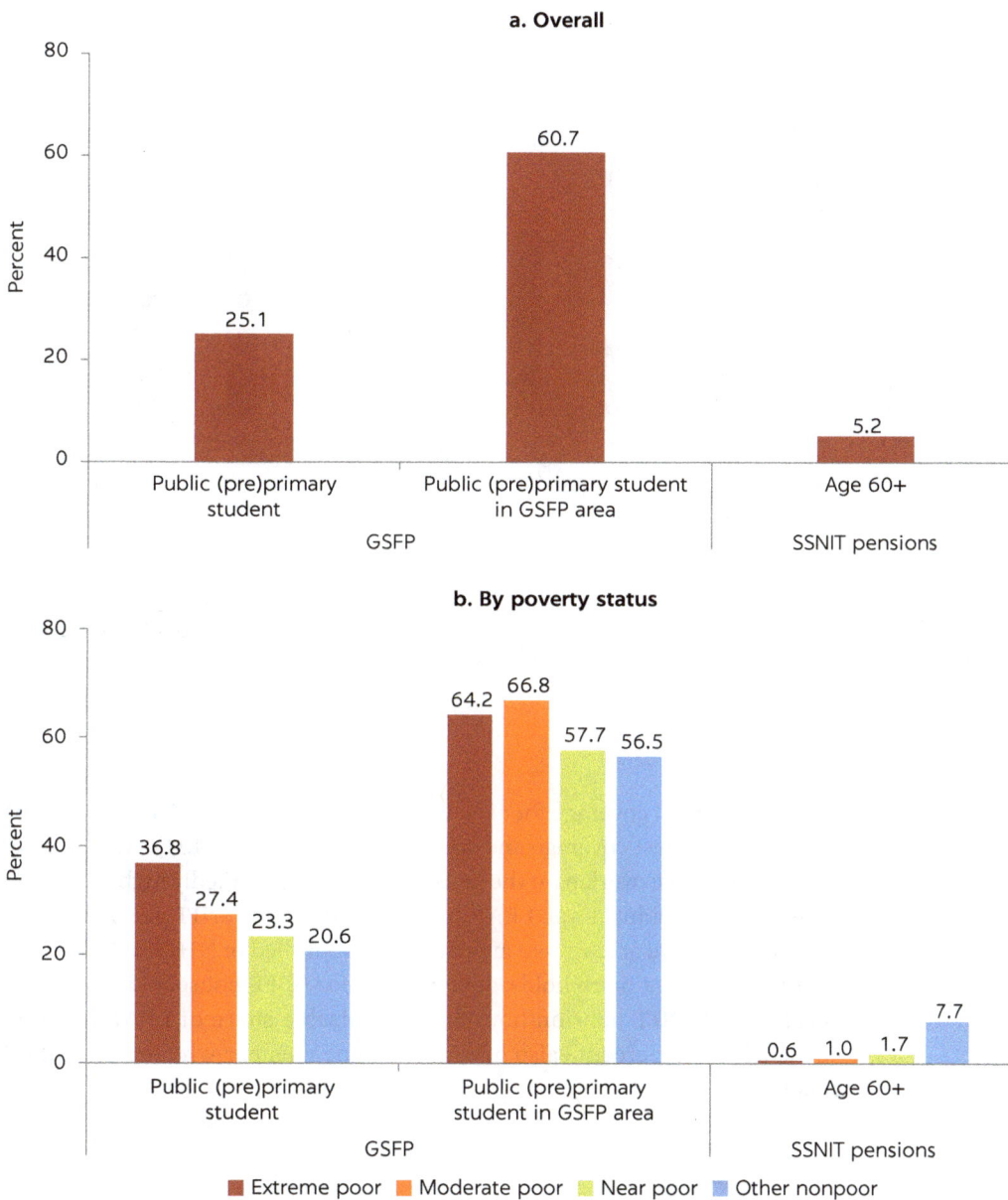

a. Overall

b. By poverty status

■ Extreme poor ■ Moderate poor ■ Near poor ■ Other nonpoor

Source: Original estimates based on data from the Ghana Living Standards Survey 2016–17.
Note: Figure shows individual coverage rates for GSFP and SSNIT pensions in target categories (where target categories are defined in the data by the authors). The coverage rate for GSFP is also estimated in the primary sampling units of the Ghana Living Standards Survey 2016–17 where at least one GSFP household was present, that is, GSFP areas. For definitions of the poverty statuses, see appendix A. GSFP = Ghana School Feeding Programme; SSNIT = Social Security and National Insurance Trust.

because LEAP program households tend to be larger in size and so count more heavily in the individual-level coverage estimates.[3] Program coverage rates for households have patterns similar to program coverage rates for individuals across poverty groups.

Finally, we examine coverage overlaps across programs at the individual and household beneficiary levels. The extent of overlaps correlates positively

FIGURE 4.11

NHIS coverage rates of individuals, by region

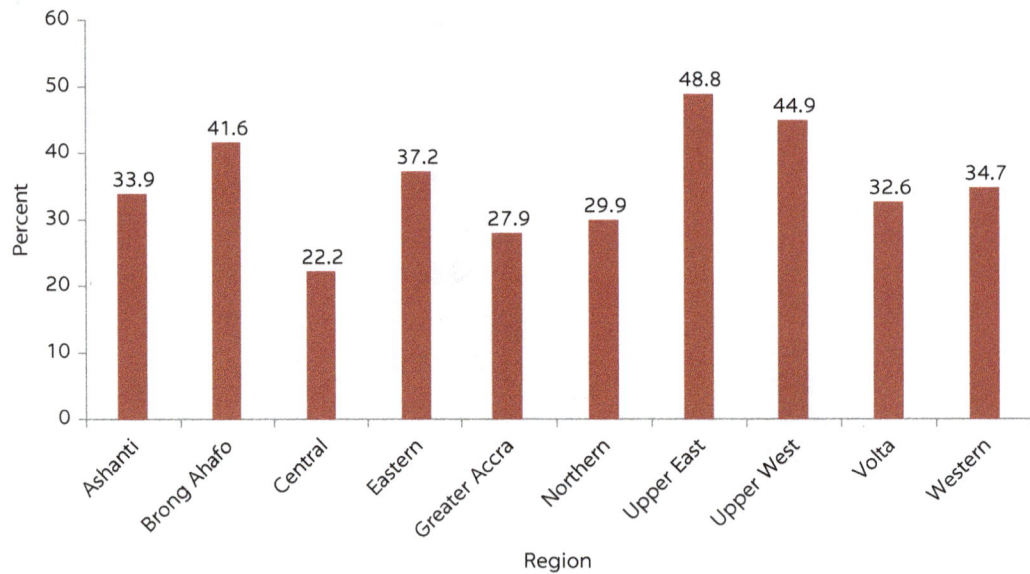

Source: Original estimates based on data from the Ghana Living Standards Survey 2016–17.
Note: Figure shows NHIS coverage rates for the overall populations of the regions. Classification of regions is per Ghana's 2010 population and housing census (GSS 2012). NHIS = National Health Insurance Scheme.

with the extent of coverage for each individual program, with SSNIT pensions having the smallest coverage and NHIS the largest (figure 4.14). As expected, program coverage overlaps at the household level are markedly higher than are those at the individual level. LEAP program, GSFP, and SSNIT pension households tend to have at least one member who is enrolled in NHIS, at 75 percent for LEAP program households, at 65 percent for GSFP households, and at 68 percent for SSNIT pension households. A sizable share of LEAP program households—46 percent—also have at least one member who receives GSFP benefits.

INCIDENCE

Program incidence for the poor population is measured by accounting for who receives a social assistance program benefit and the value of the benefit. For details on the construction of the program benefit variables, see appendix A.

Before discussing our incidence results, we touch on program benefit levels. Based on our construction, the average LEAP program benefit received by LEAP program households is GH¢469. Analogously for the other programs, the benefits are GH¢313 for GSFP households, GH¢291 for NHIS households, and GH¢7,734 for SSNIT pension households.

How large are these program benefits in relative terms? We examine this question based on two measures. The first measure is total benefits from a given program as a percentage of total household consumption averaged over households in that program (average percentage of consumption, for short). This average percentage of consumption is lowest for NHIS, at 3.6 percent, and highest for

FIGURE 4.12

SSNIT pensions coverage rates of individuals, by region

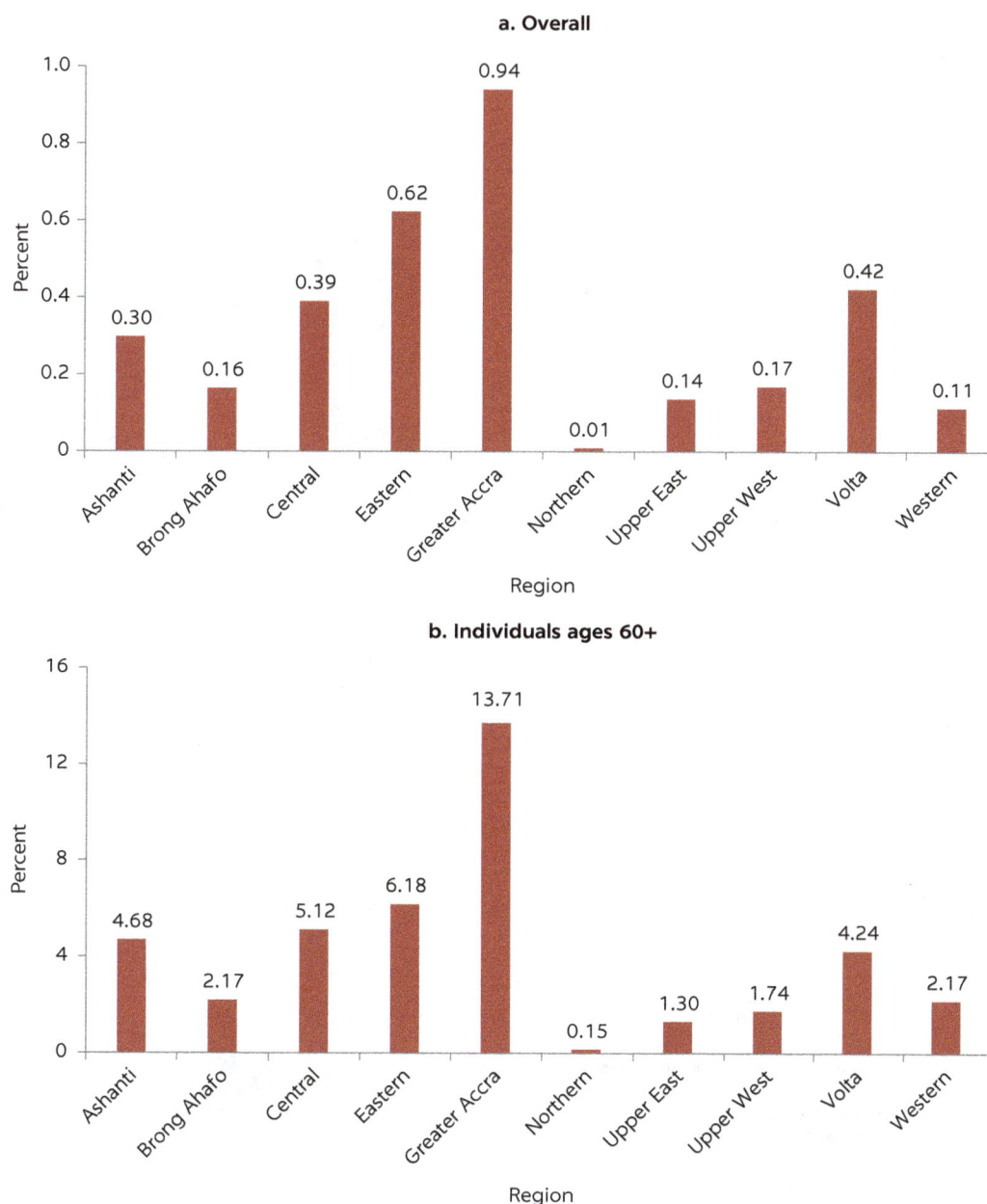

a. Overall

b. Individuals ages 60+

Source: Original estimates based on data from the Ghana Living Standards Survey 2016–17.
Note: Figure shows SSNIT pension coverage rates of individuals by region, for the overall population and for those aged 60 or older. Classification of regions is per Ghana's 2010 population and housing census (GSS 2012). SSNIT = Social Security and National Insurance Trust.

SSNIT pensions, at 60.3 percent (figure 4.15a). For the LEAP program and GSFP, the average is 12.8 percent and 5.2 percent, respectively.[4]

Further breaking down the numbers for the LEAP program and GSFP, if the sample is restricted to poor LEAP program households, the average percentage of consumption for LEAP program benefits is 15.1 percent, whereas it is 20.9 percent if restricted to extreme-poor LEAP program households. Likewise, if the sample is restricted to poor GSFP households, the average for GSFP program

FIGURE 4.13

Coverage rates of households, by program

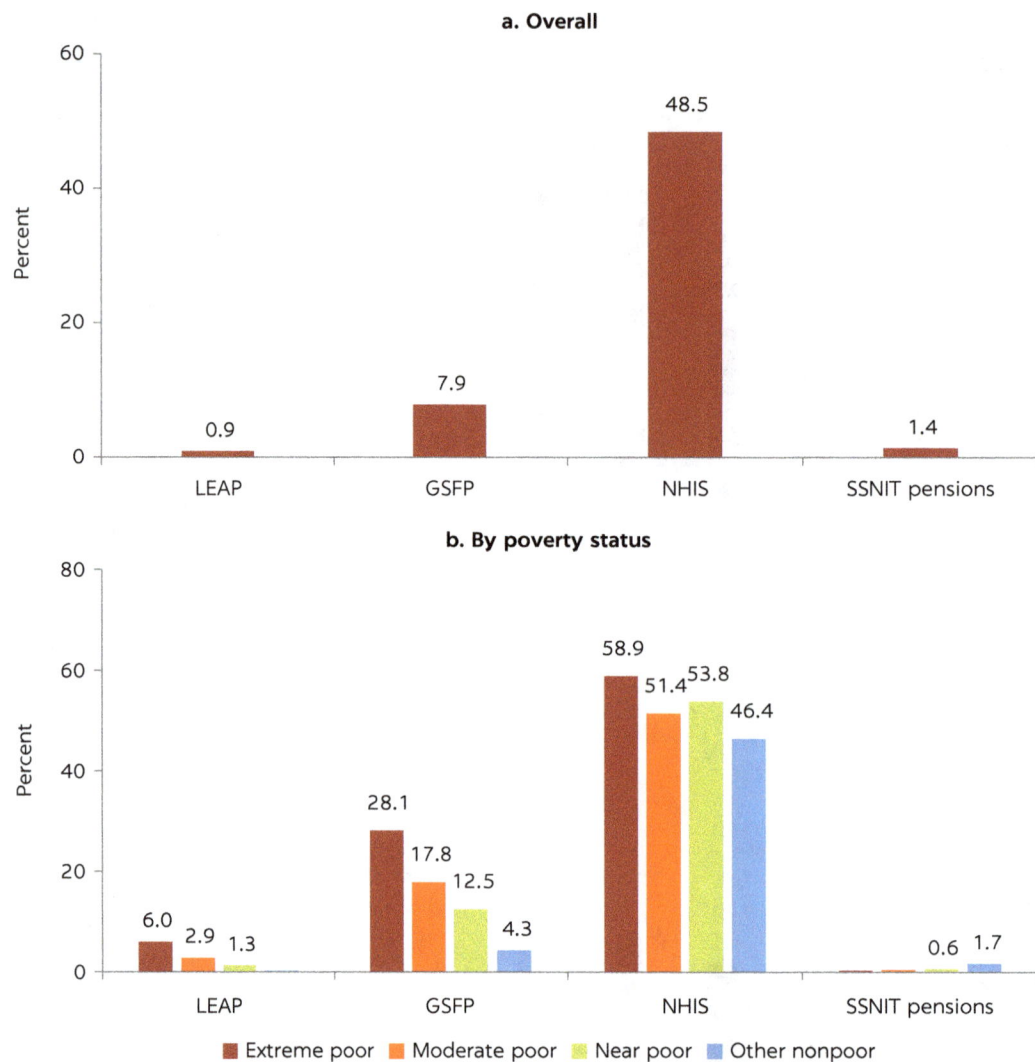

a. Overall

b. By poverty status

■ Extreme poor ■ Moderate poor ■ Near poor ■ Other nonpoor

Source: Original estimates based on data from the Ghana Living Standards Survey 2016–17.
Note: Figure shows coverage rates of households by program. These coverage rates are also estimated by poverty status (extreme poor, moderate poor, near poor, and other nonpoor); for definitions of the poverty statuses, see appendix A. A household is assigned as a beneficiary of a program if any member receives the benefit from the program. Bars with values lower than 0.5 percent are not labeled. GSFP = Ghana School Feeding Programme; LEAP = Livelihood Empowerment Against Poverty; NHIS = National Health Insurance Scheme; SSNIT = Social Security and National Insurance Trust.

benefits is 9.5 percent, whereas it is 14.5 percent if restricted to extreme-poor GSFP households.

The second measure is total benefits from a given program as a percentage of the poverty line calculated at the household level, averaged over households in that program (average percentage of the poverty line, for short). We estimated this measure separately with respect to the overall and extreme poverty lines.[5] The LEAP program, GSFP, and NHIS have averages that are low, specifically between 4 and 18 percent, depending on the program and the poverty line (overall or extreme) (figure 4.15b). SSNIT pensions' average is 226 percent of the overall poverty line and 404 percent of the extreme poverty line.

FIGURE 4.14

Overlapping household- and individual-level coverage across programs

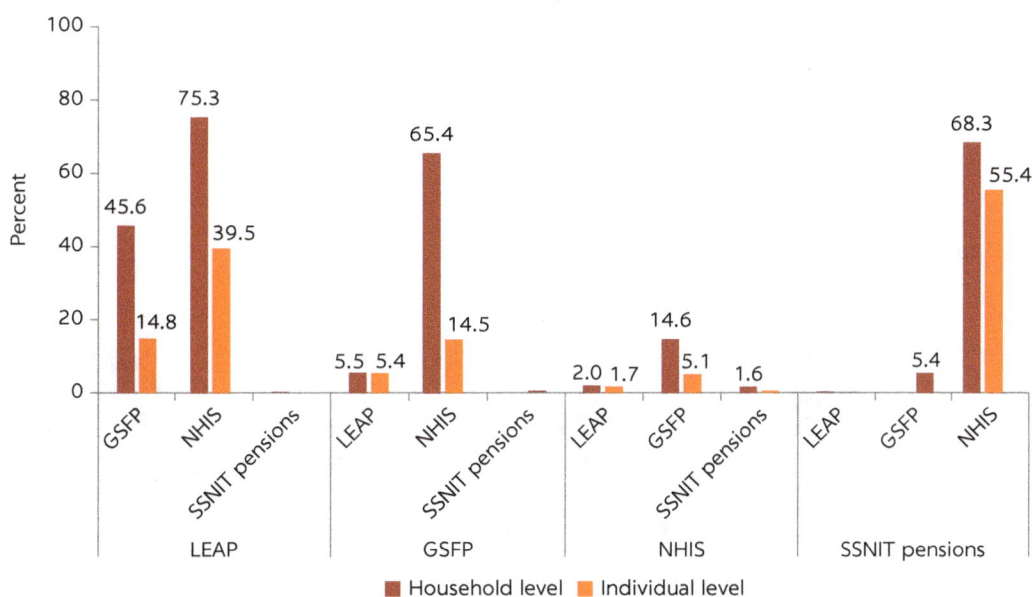

Source: Original estimates based on data from the Ghana Living Standards Survey 2016–17.
Note: Figure shows the rates of individual and household coverage overlap across programs. For the examination of coverage overlap among households, the household is considered a beneficiary of a program if any member of the household receives the benefit from the program. Even in the examination of coverage overlap among individuals, the LEAP program benefit is treated as a household benefit; as such, all members in LEAP program households are considered beneficiaries. Bars with values lower than 1 percent are not labeled. GSFP = Ghana School Feeding Programme; LEAP = Livelihood Empowerment Against Poverty; NHIS = National Health Insurance Scheme; SSNIT = Social Security and National Insurance Trust.

As a first way to assess program incidence, we examine the distributions of program beneficiaries and program benefits by poverty status. Starting with the analysis of the distribution of program beneficiaries by poverty status, LEAP program beneficiaries are disproportionately concentrated among the extreme- and moderate-poor population (figure 4.16a). A total of 74 percent of LEAP program beneficiaries are in the extreme- or moderate-poor group. In comparison, 23.4 percent of the population in general are in either the extreme- or moderate-poor group. Notwithstanding, 17.9 percent of beneficiaries are in the near-poor group, and another 8.1 percent of beneficiaries are in the other-nonpoor group. GSFP beneficiaries are also disproportionately concentrated among the poor population (46.1 percent of beneficiaries are in either the extreme- or moderate-poor group). SSNIT pension beneficiaries are almost entirely in the nonpoor group (96.6 percent of beneficiaries). Of SSNIT pension beneficiaries, 91.1 percent are in the other-nonpoor group.

NHIS beneficiaries are also mostly in the nonpoor group—17.0 percent of beneficiaries are in the near-poor group, and 63.0 percent are in the other-nonpoor group. Looking at the distribution across poverty statuses of NHIS beneficiaries by membership category, while beneficiaries categorized as indigent are more likely to be in the poor group (45.7 percent of indigent beneficiaries are in either the extreme- or moderate-poor group) compared with the population in general (23.4 percent), 42.2 percent of indigent

FIGURE 4.15

Relative benefit levels of program households, by program

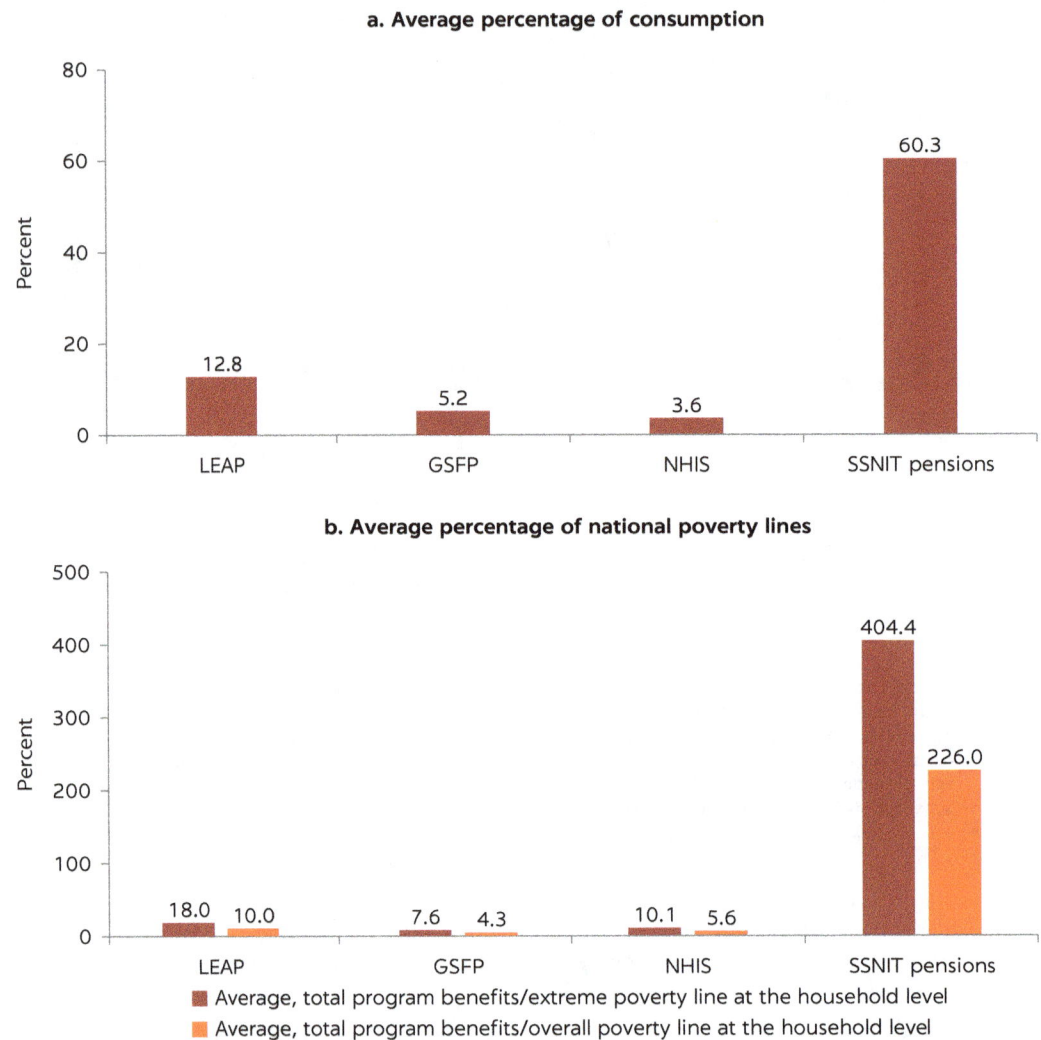

a. Average percentage of consumption

b. Average percentage of national poverty lines

■ Average, total program benefits/extreme poverty line at the household level
■ Average, total program benefits/overall poverty line at the household level

Source: Original estimates based on data from the Ghana Living Standards Survey 2016–17.
Note: Figure shows total program benefits as a percentage of total household consumption averaged across program households, for each program; it also shows total program benefits as a percentage of the overall and extreme poverty lines at the household level averaged across program households, for each program.
GSFP = Ghana School Feeding Programme; LEAP = Livelihood Empowerment Against Poverty; NHIS = National Health Insurance Scheme; SSNIT = Social Security and National Insurance Trust.

beneficiaries are in the other-nonpoor group (figure 4.16b). NHIS beneficiaries in the below age 18, age 70+, and free maternal care membership categories are all distributed (with respect to poverty status) similarly to the population in general. NHIS beneficiaries in the employer-paid and SSNIT-paid categories are much less likely to be in the poor group: 89.3 percent of employer-paid beneficiaries and 95.5 percent of SSNIT-paid beneficiaries are in the other-nonpoor group.

The results from the analysis of the distribution of program benefits by poverty status are qualitatively similar to those from the analysis of the distribution of program beneficiaries by poverty status (figure 4.17). Additionally, one consistent pattern is that, across programs and across NHIS membership categories, the share of benefits that go to the other-nonpoor population exceeds the share

FIGURE 4.16

Distribution of program beneficiaries, by poverty status

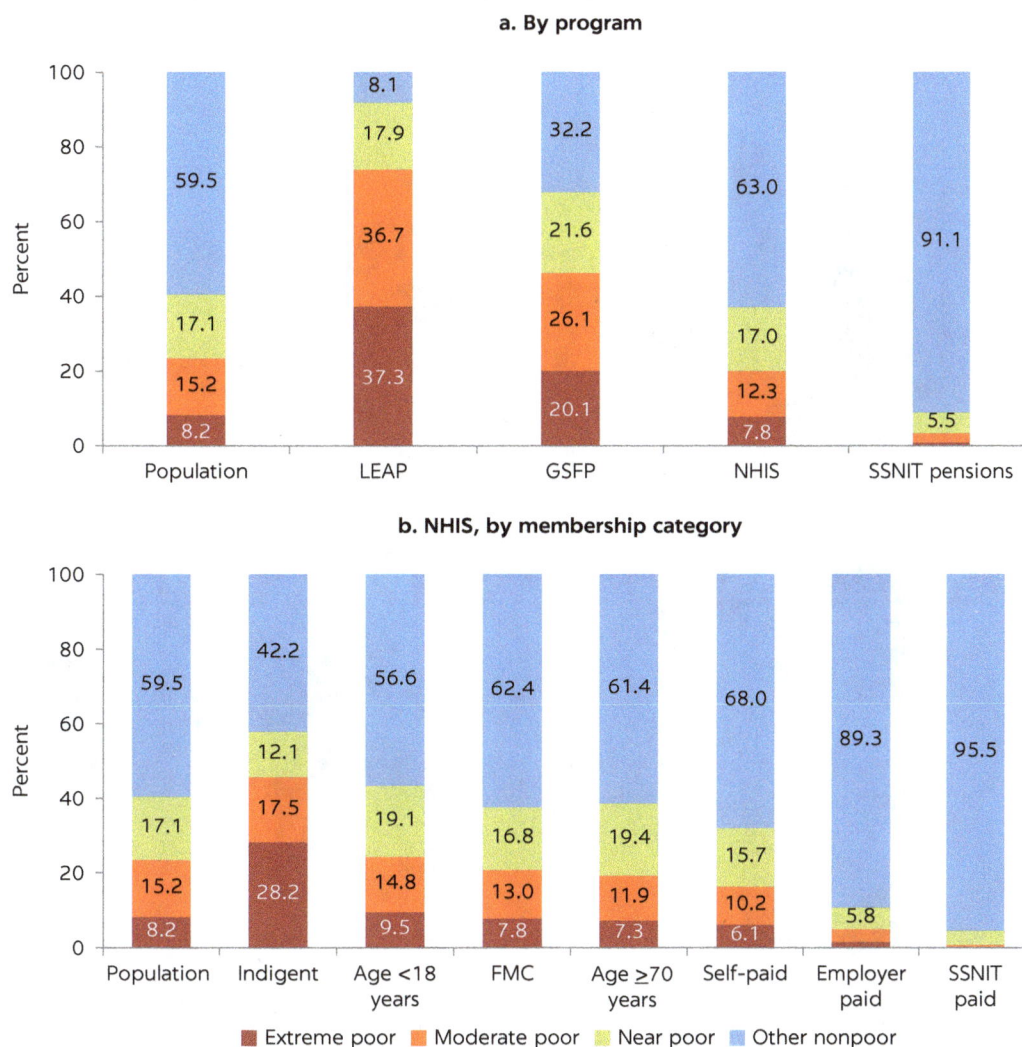

a. By program

b. NHIS, by membership category

■ Extreme poor ■ Moderate poor ■ Near poor ■ Other nonpoor

Source: Original estimates based on data from the Ghana Living Standards Survey 2016–17.
Note: Panel (a) shows the distribution of beneficiaries across poverty status (extreme poor, moderate poor, near poor, and other nonpoor), by program; for definitions of the poverty statuses, see appendix A. Panel (b) shows the distribution of NHIS beneficiaries across poverty status, by category of beneficiary. Bars with values lower than 5 percent are not labeled. FMC = free maternal health care; GSFP = Ghana School Feeding Programme; LEAP = Livelihood Empowerment Against Poverty; NHIS = National Health Insurance Scheme; SSNIT = Social Security and National Insurance Trust.

of beneficiaries in this poverty category, indicating that average program benefits are lower for beneficiaries in the extreme-, moderate-, or near-poor groups (as a collective group).

To allow for a finer division than the poverty statuses we discuss here, figures C.1 and C.2 in appendix C present the distribution of program beneficiaries and program benefits by consumption deciles.

Concentration coefficients offer another way to assess program incidence.[6] A coefficient value closer to –1 indicates that the benefits from a program are more concentrated among poorer households, while a value closer to 1 indicates that they are more concentrated among richer households. LEAP program

FIGURE 4.17

Distribution of program benefits, by poverty status

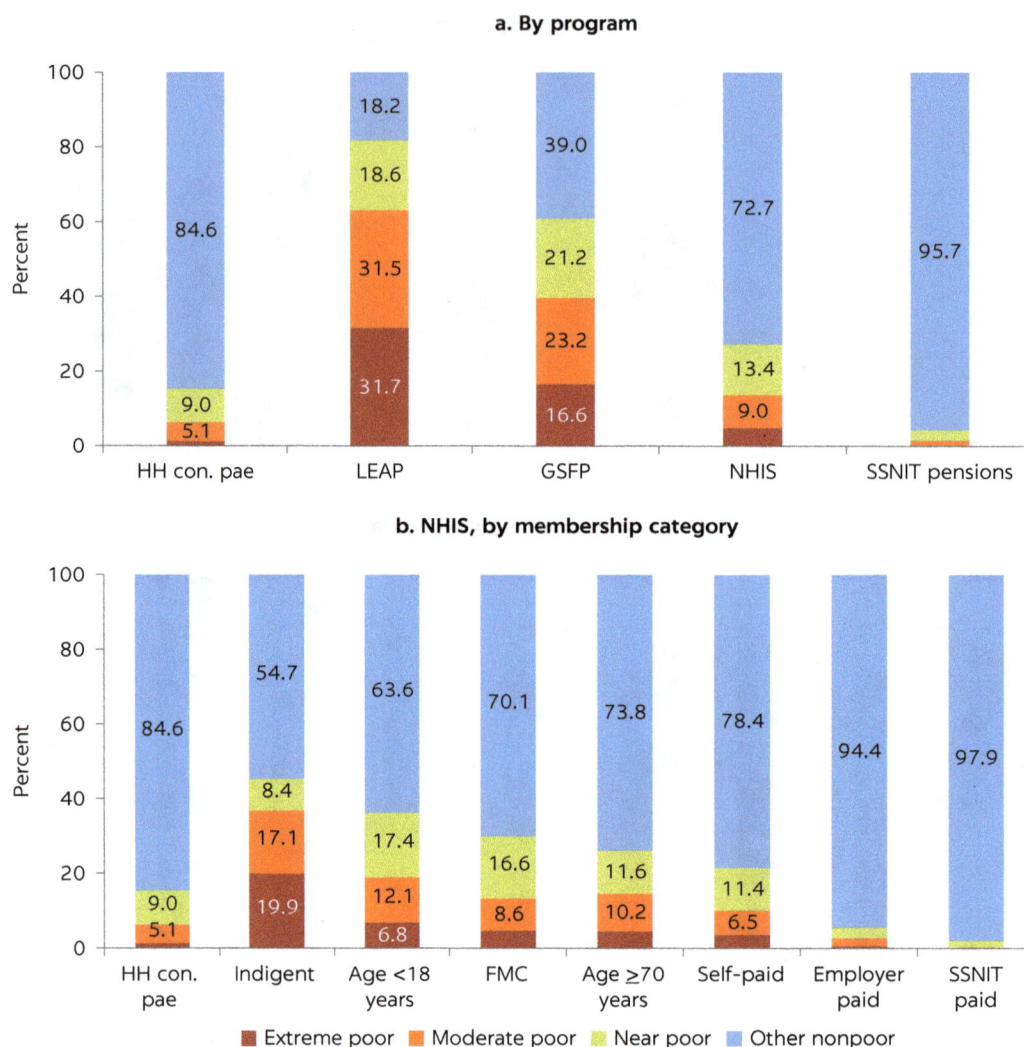

a. By program

b. NHIS, by membership category

Source: Original estimates based on data from the Ghana Living Standards Survey 2016–17.
Note: Panel (a) shows the distribution of total benefits across poverty status (extreme poor, moderate poor, near poor, and other nonpoor), by program; for definitions of the poverty statuses, see appendix A. Panel (b) shows the distribution of total NHIS benefits across poverty status, by category of beneficiary. Bars with values lower than 5 percent are not labeled. FMC = free maternal health care; GSFP = Ghana School Feeding Programme; HH con. pae = household consumption per adult equivalent; LEAP = Livelihood Empowerment Against Poverty; NHIS = National Health Insurance Scheme; SSNIT = Social Security and National Insurance Trust.

benefits are strongly concentrated among poor households (figure 4.18). The program's concentration coefficient of –0.529 compares favorably with similar cash transfer programs in a large set of low- and middle-income countries.[7] GSFP benefits are also concentrated among poor households but are less so than the LEAP program. SSNIT pension benefits, on the other hand, are strongly concentrated among the richest households. The program's concentration coefficient of 0.736 far exceeds the Gini coefficient for household consumption per adult equivalent, at 0.417.

For GSFP and especially for the LEAP program, the concentration coefficient in program areas is less negative than it is for the country as a whole, indicating that benefits from these programs are less well targeted in program areas than

FIGURE 4.18

Program concentration coefficients

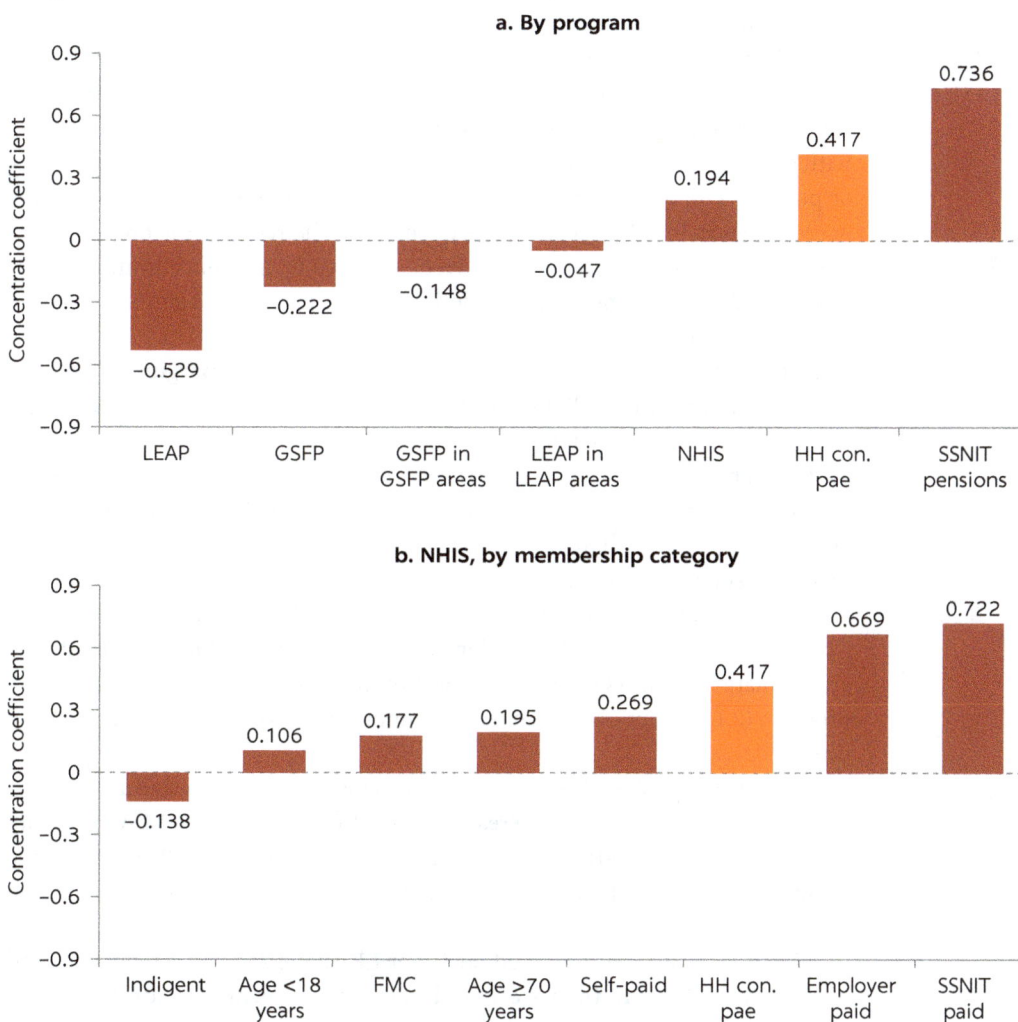

a. By program

b. NHIS, by membership category

Source: Original estimates based on data from the Ghana Living Standards Survey 2016–17.
Note: Panel (a) shows concentration coefficients, by program. Panel (b) shows concentration coefficients for NHIS, by category of beneficiary. FMC = free maternal health care; GSFP = Ghana School Feeding Programme; HH con. pae = household consumption per adult equivalent; LEAP = Livelihood Empowerment Against Poverty; NHIS = National Health Insurance Scheme; SSNIT = Social Security and National Insurance Trust.

they are nationally, although even in program areas, poor households still benefit disproportionately. Nevertheless, much of the success of these programs, especially the LEAP program, is accounted for by good geographic targeting (that is, the identification of program areas).

Overall, benefits of NHIS membership are moderately concentrated among nonpoor households (0.194) but are less concentrated than household consumption per adult equivalent. Disaggregated by membership status, as to be expected, NHIS benefits to indigent individuals are concentrated among poor households (−0.138) but less so than either the LEAP program or GSFP benefits.[8] Benefits for all other NHIS membership categories are not concentrated among poor households.[9] Furthermore, benefits to members who participate in NHIS through the payment of premiums by employers or by SSNIT are concentrated among the richest households, with their concentration coefficients (0.669 and 0.722, respectively) far exceeding the Gini coefficient for household consumption per adult equivalent.

Still another way to assess a program's incidence is through its marginal effects on inequality and poverty.[10] These effects are defined as the change that each program produces in the Gini index, the poverty rate, or the poverty gap, with the sign reversed so that a positive value indicates a *reduction* in inequality or poverty. The poverty rate and the poverty gap are measured using Ghana's overall poverty line. Marginal effects depend on who receives the program benefit and the value of the benefit received, reflected by the concentration coefficient and the size of the program, defined as the program benefits divided by household consumption averaged across households.

At the national level, the base levels for evaluating the marginal effects are 23.4 percent for the overall poverty rate, 8.4 percent for the overall poverty gap, and 41.7 percent for the Gini index.

The marginal effects of the LEAP program, GSFP, NHIS, and SSNIT pensions nationally on inequality and poverty are uniformly small: Virtually all the marginal effects are less than one-fifth of a percentage point (table 4.1). The estimates are small because the sizes of the programs are small.

The marginal effects of the LEAP program in LEAP program areas on inequality and poverty are at least an order of magnitude larger than the LEAP program's marginal effects nationally. This is entirely because the size of the LEAP program (2.1 percent of household consumption on average) is much larger in program areas.

Restricting GSFP to GSFP areas yields changes in program size and in marginal effects similar to when we restricted the LEAP program to LEAP program areas, but the changes are less pronounced. Compared with GSFP nationally, the program size and the marginal effects of GSFP in GSFP areas roughly triple in magnitude.

As noted earlier, we estimated far fewer LEAP program beneficiaries based on the GLSS 2016–17 than we found based on government administrative records. This could be because the survey was not designed to produce a representative sample of LEAP program beneficiaries and just happened to miss the areas where this program is available. Also, it could occur because survey respondents did not report themselves as program beneficiaries. To adjust for this, we predicted an additional set of LEAP program households that reported are similar to those receiving LEAP program benefits in the survey but that they do not receive them. For details on the prediction exercise, see appendix E. We added the predicted LEAP program households to the set of actual LEAP program households until we reach, the administrative number of LEAP program households in January 2017 (roughly 198,000). We refer to this augmented set of program households as "LEAP+."

Compared with the marginal effects for the actual LEAP program nationally, the marginal effects on inequality and poverty are roughly triple for LEAP+. Nevertheless, the effects remain small.

We also estimated marginal effects on poverty and inequality for NHIS, disaggregating by NHIS membership category (table 4.1). Those who are members because they are younger than age 18 and those who paid their own premium account for almost all these effects because they are the only groups with nontrivial NHIS benefit transfers relative to household consumption, but all the effects remain small.

TABLE 4.1 Program marginal effects

	MARGINAL EFFECTS (PERCENTAGE POINTS)			PROGRAM SIZE (PERCENT)
	INEQUALITY (GINI INDEX)	POVERTY RATE	POVERTY GAP	
	(1)	(2)	(3)	(4)
By program				
LEAP	0.03	0.06	0.05	0.14
LEAP, in LEAP areas	0.53	0.82	0.83	2.08
LEAP+	0.11	0.13	0.17	0.51
GSFP	0.03	0.08	0.04	0.11
GSFP, in GSFP areas	0.08	0.27	0.11	0.33
NHIS	0.06	0.21	0.10	0.45
SSNIT pensions	0.00	0.03	0.18	0.22
NHIS, by membership category				
Indigent	0.00	0.00	0.00	0.00
FMC	0.00	0.01	0.00	0.02
Age <18 years	0.05	0.13	0.06	0.23
Age ≥70 years	0.01	0.02	0.02	0.05
SSNIT paid	0.00	0.00	0.00	0.01
Self-paid	0.01	0.06	0.03	0.14
Employer paid	0.00	0.00	0.00	0.00

Source: Original estimates based on data from the Ghana Living Standards Survey 2016–17.
Note: Table reports marginal effects on inequality (measured by the Gini index), the poverty rate, the poverty gap, and program size, by program and by NHIS membership category. At the national level, the base levels for evaluating the marginal effects are 23.4 percent for the overall poverty rate, 8.4 percent for the overall poverty gap, and 41.7 percent for the Gini index. All poverty-related measures are estimated based on the overall poverty line. Program size = program benefits divided by household consumption averaged across households, estimated based on GLSS 2016–17 data. LEAP areas are primary sampling units of the GLSS 2016–17 with at least one LEAP program household. GSFP areas are primary sampling units of the GLSS 2016–17 with at least one GSFP household. LEAP+ refers to actual LEAP program households plus predicted LEAP program households, capped at the administrative statistic for the number of program households in January 2017. FMC = free maternal health care; GLSS = Ghana Living Standard Survey; GSFP = Ghana School Feeding Programme; LEAP = Livelihood Empowerment Against Poverty; NHIS = National Health Insurance Scheme; SSNIT = Social Security and National Insurance Trust.

We also examine the sensitivity of marginal effects on poverty to the choice of the poverty line (overall and extreme) (table C.4 in appendix C). The estimates based on the extreme poverty line are uniformly less than are even the small effects discussed here in relation to the overall poverty line.

EFFECTIVENESS

One characteristic of marginal effects is that, all else being equal, programs with larger outlays have larger marginal effects.[11] A way to check the robustness of the incidence results based on marginal effects is to calculate a program's effectiveness—roughly, its "bang for the buck." As with marginal effects, information on who received a given social protection program benefit and how much was received is used for estimating effectiveness.

Impact effectiveness is defined as the ratio between the inequality or poverty reduction that a program actually achieves and the inequality or poverty reduction that it could achieve if all its outlay were distributed in the most progressive way possible. This perfect distribution of a program's spending would give enough of a benefit to the poorest person to bring their consumption up to the level of the second-poorest person, then give enough to both to bring their consumption up to the level of the third-poorest person, and so on, until the outlay is exhausted. Unlike the estimation of impact effectiveness, which holds the program's outlay constant, the estimation of spending effectiveness holds the inequality or poverty level constant and asks how much less we could spend and still attain that inequality or poverty level if we were to achieve the perfect distribution of program benefits as described above. Both effectiveness measures are based on a scale from 0 to 100 percent.[12]

We examine program impact and spending effectiveness with respect to inequality as measured by the Gini index and with respect to poverty, as reflected by the poverty gap and by poverty severity (table 4.2). The poverty gap and poverty severity measures are based on the overall poverty line.

TABLE 4.2 Program effectiveness
Percent

	INEQUALITY (GINI INDEX)		POVERTY GAP		POVERTY SEVERITY	
	IMPACT	SPENDING	IMPACT	SPENDING	IMPACT	SPENDING
	(1)	(2)	(3)	(4)	(5)	(6)
By program						
LEAP	69.2	69.3	65.1	65.1	35.1	33.4
LEAP, in LEAP areas	38.0	36.7	64.3	65.1	39.6	36.6
LEAP+	65.9	65.8	59.9	60.2	36.8	33.4
GSFP	57.4	57.1	47.8	47.8	27.7	24.2
GSFP, in GSFP areas	49.5	48.6	48.0	47.8	29.4	24.9
NHIS	28.7	27.5	22.1	21.9	16.0	10.5
SSNIT pensions	−24.5	0.0	1.0	1.0	0.4	0.2
NHIS, by membership category						
Indigent	47.9	48.1	45.5	46.1	27.0	26.4
FMC	29.7	30.0	21.0	20.2	9.1	8.4
Age <18 years	35.3	34.5	26.2	25.8	15.9	11.9
Age ≥70 years	27.3	27.3	21.9	21.6	10.4	9.1
SSNIT paid	−13.3	0.0	0.7	0.7	0.2	0.2
Self-paid	21.2	20.7	17.0	17.3	9.5	7.3
Employer paid	−10.2	0.0	4.5	4.9	1.9	1.7

Source: Original estimates based on data from the Ghana Living Standards Survey 2016–17.
Note: Table reports impact and spending effectiveness estimates with respect to inequality (measured by the Gini index), the poverty gap, and poverty severity, by program and by NHIS membership category. All poverty-related measures are estimated based on the overall poverty line. LEAP areas are primary sampling units of the GLSS 2016–17 with at least one LEAP program household. GSFP areas are primary sampling units of the GLSS 2016–17 with at least one GSFP household. LEAP+ refers to actual LEAP program households plus predicted LEAP program households, capped at the administrative statistic for the number of program households in January 2017. FMC = free maternal health care; GLSS = Ghana Living Standards Survey; GSFP = Ghana School Feeding Programme; LEAP = Livelihood Empowerment Against Poverty; NHIS = National Health Insurance Scheme; SSNIT = Social Security and National Insurance Trust.

The LEAP program is quite effective at reducing both inequality and the poverty gap, whether we use impact or spending effectiveness. It is 69 percent as effective as a perfect transfer would be at reducing the Gini index and 65 percent as effective as a perfect transfer at reducing the poverty gap. However, it is less effective at reducing poverty severity, performing only 35 percent and 33 percent as well as a perfect transfer would for impact and spending effectiveness, respectively. The results are similar for LEAP+.

GSFP is moderately effective at reducing inequality and the poverty gap but, again, is less effective at reducing poverty severity. Both the LEAP program and GSFP seem to be less effective at reaching the poorest-of-the-poor population than they are at reaching the poor population.

Furthermore, for both the LEAP program and GSFP, if we limited our analysis to areas covered by the program, the effectiveness at reducing poverty is similar to the results for the country as a whole, but the effectiveness at reducing inequality is lower. The explanation for this is that program beneficiaries are less poor relative to those who live in the targeted areas (which are poorer) than they are to the national population, so the benefit they receive does less to equalize the distribution in targeted areas than it does to equalize the national distribution.

SSNIT pensions increase inequality and do nothing to reduce poverty.

NHIS is uniformly less effective at reducing poverty or inequality than are the LEAP program and GSFP. NHIS effectiveness at reducing inequality is only about 30 percent of the effect of a perfectly targeted transfer, and its effectiveness at reducing poverty is even less. This is not necessarily a criticism, as the purpose of NHIS is to facilitate use of health care services, not to be a transfer scheme, although it does favor some groups we might have expected to be in the relatively poor group with premium waivers.

NHIS membership provided (for free) to the indigent population is a little less than half as effective as is a perfect transfer at reducing inequality and the poverty gap—48 percent for impact and spending effectiveness with respect to the Gini index and 46 percent for both impact and spending effectiveness, in relation to the poverty gap—but is less effective at reducing poverty severity. The other membership categories aimed at certain demographic groups we might consider to be needy—children, pregnant women, and elderly people—are less effective at reducing inequality and poverty, while the categories associated with the formal sector—SSNIT pensioners and employer-paid beneficiaries—are almost completely ineffective at reducing poverty (and actually increase inequality).

We also examined the sensitivity of effectiveness in poverty reduction to the choice of poverty line (overall and extreme) (table C.5 in appendix C). The LEAP program, GSFP, and NHIS are only about half as effective at reducing either the extreme poverty gap or extreme poverty severity for both impact and spending effectiveness. SSNIT pensions remain completely ineffective.

SIMULATED REFORMS TO THE LEAP PROGRAM

The LEAP program has small effects on poverty and inequality mainly because of its limited coverage and low benefit levels. Table 4.3 reports results for 12 simulated reforms in LEAP program targeting, coverage, and benefit levels in line with the directions that the MOGCSP is exploring. All simulated reforms take as a base the set of LEAP+ households.

TABLE 4.3 Effects of simulated reforms to the LEAP program, LEAP+ program households

INDICATOR	LEAP+	(1)	(2)	(3)	(4)	(5)	(6)	(7)	(8)	(9)	(10)	(11)	(12)
Concentration coefficient[a]	-0.485	-0.725	-0.592	-0.723	-0.587	-0.725	-0.554	-0.725	-0.592	-0.723	-0.587	-0.725	-0.554
Inequality (Gini index) (ppt change)		0.07	0.02	0.07	0.01	0.06	-0.05	0.06	0.00	0.06	0.00	0.05	-0.08
Overall poverty rate (ppt change)		0.10	0.00	0.11	0.00	0.10	-0.10	0.10	-0.01	0.11	-0.01	0.10	-0.12
Overall poverty gap (ppt change)		0.10	0.02	0.10	0.02	0.09	-0.07	0.09	-0.01	0.08	-0.01	0.07	-0.11
Extreme poverty rate (ppt change)		0.09	0.00	0.09	-0.03	0.09	-0.13	0.07	-0.03	0.07	-0.06	0.06	-0.19
Extreme poverty gap (ppt change)		0.09	0.02	0.08	0.02	0.07	-0.03	0.08	0.00	0.07	0.00	0.06	-0.06
Program outlay (change in million cedis)[b]	102	-73	-23	-70	-19	-66	38	-68	-8	-64	-4	-59	64
Program outlay (change in percent)		-72.6	-23.0	-68.9	-19.0	-65.3	37.5	-67.4	-8.4	-63.0	-3.6	-58.7	63.6
Share of all HHs losing benefits (percent)		1.9	1.1	1.9	1.3	1.9	1.1	1.9	1.1	1.9	1.3	1.9	1.1
Share of LEAP HHs losing benefits (percent)		69.0	39.1	71.3	50.0	69.0	39.1	69.0	39.1	71.3	50.0	69.0	39.1

Source: Original estimates based on data from the Ghana Living Standards Survey 2016–17.

Note: Table reports the results of simulations of various coverage and benefit-level reforms in the LEAP program, based on the LEAP+ population. LEAP+ refers to actual LEAP program households plus predicted LEAP program households, capped at the administrative statistic for the number of program households in January 2017. Column (1): Improved-targeting-only simulation, in current LEAP program areas (primary sampling units of the GLSS 2016–17 with LEAP program households), providing benefits to the PMT-extreme-poor population only. Column (2): Same as column (1) but with program benefits to PMT-poor population only. Column (3): Targeting improvement and partial scale out, in main LEAP program regions (Northern, Upper East, and Upper West), providing benefits to the PMT-extreme-poor population only. Column (4): Same as column (3) but with program benefits to the PMT-poor population only. Column (5): Targeting improvement and full scale out, in Ghana as a whole, providing program benefits to the PMT-extreme-poor population only. Column (6): Same as column (5) but with program benefits to the PMT-poor population only. Columns (7) to (12): Correspond to columns (1) to (6) but with program benefits scaled up by 19 percent to account for inflation from 2015 to 2016–17 (the GLSS 2016–17 period). GLSS = Ghana Living Standards Survey; HHs = households; LEAP = Livelihood Empowerment Against Poverty; PMT = proxy means test; ppt = percentage point.

a. Concentration coefficient calculated on household consumption per adult equivalent.

b. Program outlay (change in million cedis) is the difference between the current LEAP program outlay, column (1), and the outlay needed for the simulation. Negative values indicate a budgetary savings.

In the first simulation, we assume that the LEAP program maintains the geographic targeting in effect in 2016/17 but discards the current within-community targeting criteria and replaces them *solely* with the proxy means test (PMT) based on the GLSS 2016–17 currently being used by the MOGCSP, selecting all those whom the PMT finds in the extreme-poor group. The second simulation takes the same approach but selects all those whom the PMT finds in the poor group. The third and fourth simulations use the same two PMT approaches but scale up the LEAP program to all areas in the main program regions of Northern, Upper East, and Upper West (region classification per Ghana's 2010 population and housing census [GSS 2012]). The fifth and sixth simulations again use the same two PMT approaches but scale up the program across all areas in the country. The seventh through twelfth simulations are the same as the first through sixth but with program benefits scaled up by 19 percent to account for inflation between 2015, when the benefit levels were established, and 2016/17, when the GLSS 2016–17 was conducted.

The concentration coefficients are remarkably consistent. Providing program benefits to the PMT-extreme-poor group only yields an extremely progressive coefficient of about –0.72 to –0.73, regardless of the areas covered. Providing program benefits to the PMT-poor group only yields a coefficient of about –0.55 to –0.59, regardless of the areas covered. By comparison, the concentration coefficient for the LEAP program is –0.49. Thus, using the PMT, the LEAP program can be scaled up to all areas of the country without diluting the progressivity of the program.[13]

All of the simulations that provide program benefits to the PMT-extreme-poor population only (the odd-numbered columns) yield substantial reductions in spending, even if the program is rolled out nationally (column 5) and benefit amounts are adjusted for inflation (column 11). The simulations that provide program benefits to the PMT-poor population only (the even-numbered columns) yield much less budgetary savings, and rolling the LEAP program out nationally would actually require a 38 percent increase in outlay (column 6), or a 64 percent increase if the benefit amounts are adjusted for inflation (column 12).

Table 4.3 also includes the changes in inequality and poverty statistics for each reform possibility. The most notable point about these results is that all the changes are small, mostly around one-tenth of a percentage point or smaller. Even if the program were expanded to all areas across the country, the size of the LEAP program in terms of outlay would not be large enough to have a significant impact on poverty or inequality. It is also notable that providing benefits to the PMT-poor population only in existing LEAP program areas actually increases poverty and inequality by a small amount. Even though the targeting of this program is excellent, the outlay reduction it implies more than offsets the better targeting. Providing program benefits to the PMT-extreme-poor population only while expanding either to all areas of the main LEAP program regions or to all areas of the country also increases the poverty rate slightly but improves the other distributional statistics, also slightly. It is also notable that increasing the value of LEAP program benefits to account for inflation between 2015 and 2016/17 decreases poverty and inequality only slightly. (Compare, for example, column 4 to column 10 or column 6 to column 12.) Much larger program benefit increases would be needed to have a larger impact on poverty and inequality.

Finally, we note that retargeting the LEAP program with the PMT only would result in a substantial share of existing LEAP program households losing their benefits. If the LEAP program were to shift to providing benefits to the PMT–extreme-poor population only (any of the odd-numbered columns in the table), 69–71 percent of current program beneficiaries would lose their benefits. Even if the program were to switch to providing benefits to the PMT–poor population only (any of the even-numbered columns), 39–50 percent of current program beneficiaries would lose their benefits.

LEAP program benefits are low (see the discussion of absolute and relative benefit levels in the "Incidence" section in this chapter). This partly explains the LEAP program's limited effect on poverty despite its excellent targeting. Figure 4.19 shows the effect on poverty levels of increasing the generosity of LEAP program benefits. Two results are striking. First, even with very large increases in LEAP program benefits—up to 500 percent of the existing benefit

FIGURE 4.19

Poverty effects of simulated percent increases in LEAP program benefits, LEAP+ households

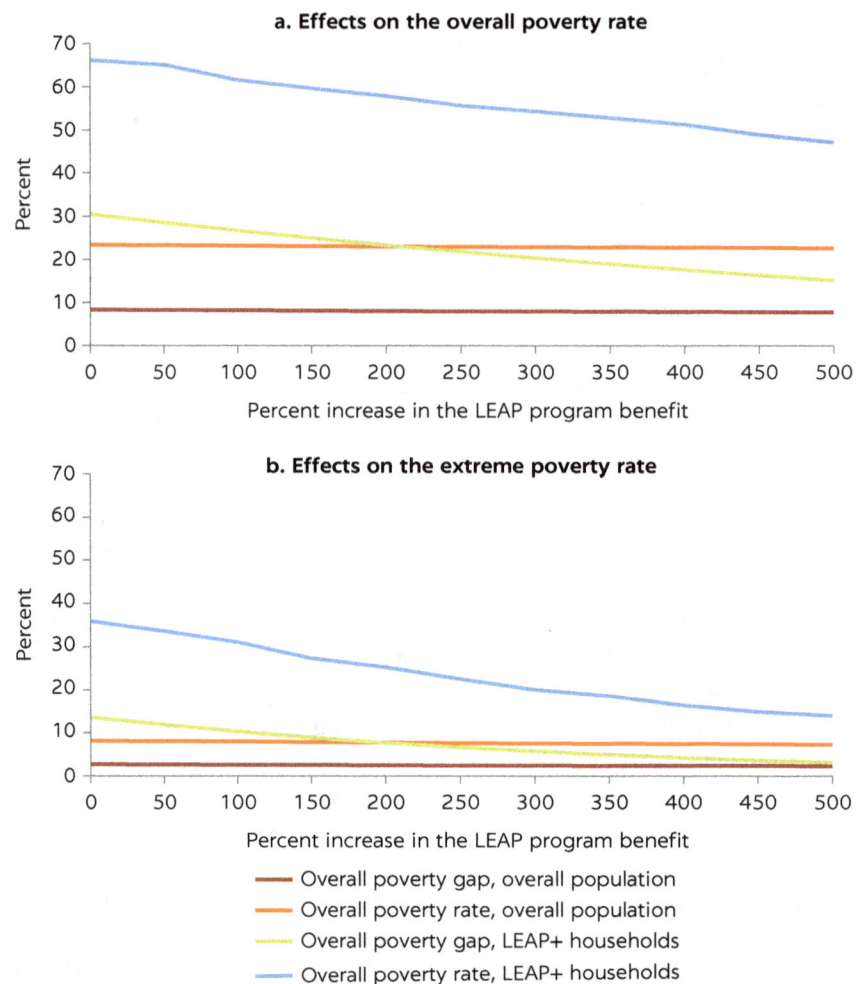

Source: Original estimates based on data from the Ghana Living Standards Survey 2016–17.
Note: Figure shows simulated changes in the extreme and overall poverty rates for LEAP+ households and for the overall population as LEAP benefits are increased. LEAP+ refers to actual LEAP program households plus predicted LEAP program households, capped at the administrative statistic for the number of program households in January 2017. LEAP = Livelihood Empowerment Against Poverty.

level—overall and extreme poverty levels among LEAP program households remain high. Second, the effect on overall and extreme poverty levels in the national population of even substantial increases in LEAP program benefits is small because the existing number of beneficiaries is limited. These results, combined with the earlier results on the LEAP program's marginal effects, suggest that, to have a large effect on poverty, the LEAP program would need large increases in coverage and benefit generosity and, therefore, budgetary outlays.

Our empirical simulations of LEAP program coverage reforms are based on PMT-based targeting; the government already uses this targeting method. Other targeting methods have been used independently or in combination with PMT-based targeting, including in Ghana, such as for the LEAP program, the LIPW program, and GSFP. Grosh et al. (2022) have discussed various targeting methods for countries that cannot use actual means testing. Despite skepticism from some researchers (for example, Brown, Ravallion, and van der Walle 2018), available rigorous research tends to find that PMT-based targeting performs about as well as other targeting methods and often marginally better. Specifically, the research comprises evidence from field experiments comparing PMT-based targeting to community-based targeting (Alatas et al. 2012; Premand and Schnitzer 2021).

Several studies also have shown that a variety of machine learning algorithms do not consistently outperform traditionally developed PMT models by much, if at all. (For a summary of these studies, see Hernani-Limarino 2022.) An important exception to this conclusion is Hernani-Limarino (2022), who found that a random forest algorithm augmented with oversampling techniques did much better at identifying the poor population in several Latin American countries. At our request, Hernani-Limarino ran the GLSS 2016–17 data through his algorithm and found that it does not perform consistently better than the PMT model we apply here for our analysis.

SHOCKS AND SOCIAL ASSISTANCE PROGRAM PARTICIPATION

The GLSS 2016–17 does not include questions about economic shocks respondents have experienced, precluding an analysis at the household level of the correlation among such shocks, poverty status, and social assistance program participation status.[14] Nxumalo and Raju (2022) combined drought and flood risk data from high-resolution maps produced by the Norwegian Embassy, Ghana's National Disaster Management Organisation, and United Nations Development Programme (Norwegian Embassy, NADMO, and UNDP 2015) with administrative data on household beneficiaries for the LEAP program and the LIPW program.[15] These data were matched at the district level to examine the correlation between drought and flood risk, on the one hand, and program participation, on the other.

Under current climate conditions, many parts of Ghana are susceptible to damaging floods and droughts (USAID 2017). The Global Facility for Disaster Reduction and Recovery indicated that Ghana is rated "high" (the highest level on a 4-point scale) for different climate shocks, including water scarcity and flooding.[16] A rating of high for flooding implies an expectation of potentially damaging flooding every 10 years, and a corresponding rating for water scarcity implies an expectation of drought every 5 years.

FIGURE 4.20

District drought and flood risks, by region, 2010

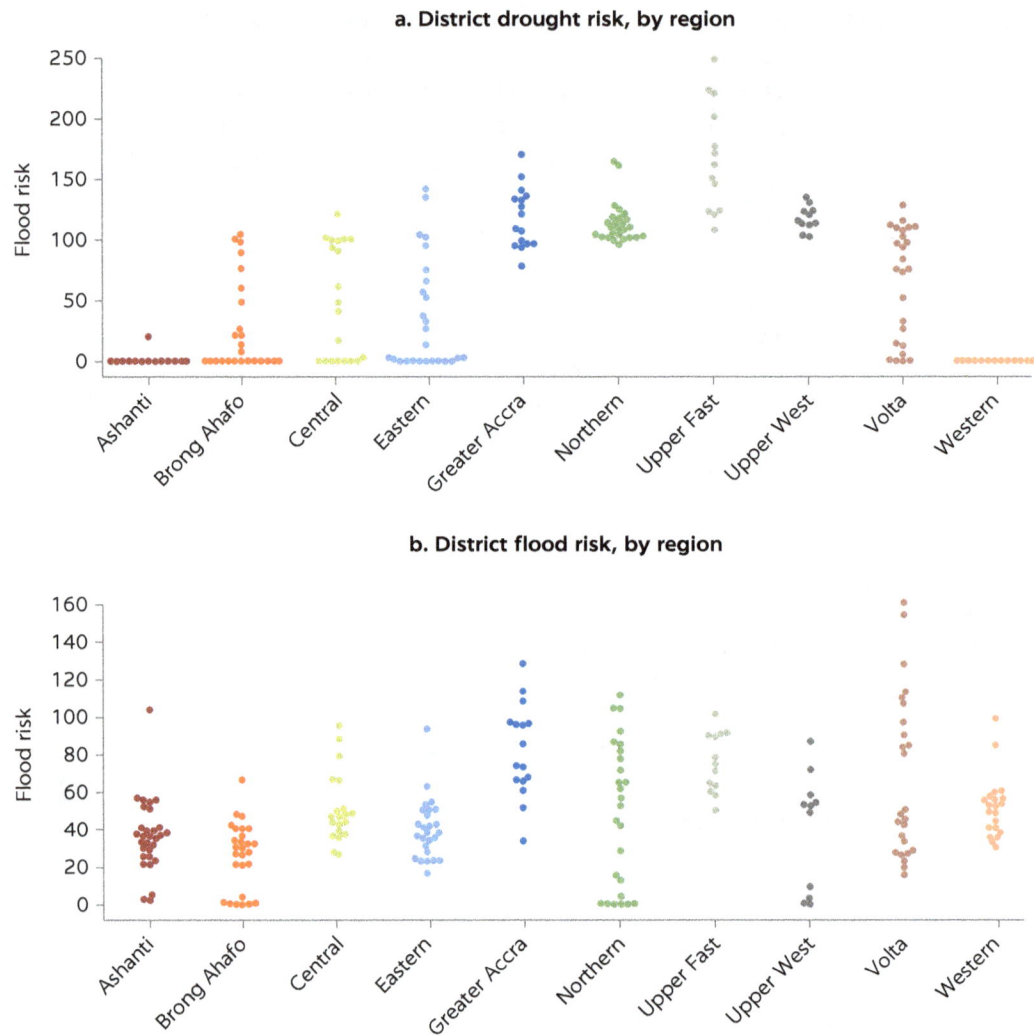

a. District drought risk, by region

b. District flood risk, by region

Source: Reproduced from Nxumalo and Raju 2022.
Note: Figure shows the distribution of district-level drought and flood risks separately by region. The scales for flood and drought risks represent district-level totals of pixel-level risk scores, which range between 0 and 249 for drought risk (panel a) and 0 and 160 for flood risk (panel b). For details on risk scores and summations for drought and flood, see Norwegian Embassy, NADMO, and UNDP (2015). Region indicators and district observations are per Ghana's 2010 population and housing census (GSS 2012).

The United Nations Office of Disaster Risk Reduction and the CIMA Research Foundation (2019) also have presented information on the current and expected climate conditions for the country in terms of floods and droughts, as well as on the estimated and predicted direct impacts from these climate events. Under current climate conditions, on average, every year, floods affect about 0.16 percent of the population and generate a loss of 0.23 percent of national income. The economic losses mainly occur in the services sector, followed by the agriculture and housing sectors. Furthermore, on average, every year, droughts affect about 13 percent of the population and produce a loss of 15 percent of national income. These economic losses predominantly occur in crop farming and livestock rearing. Under predicted future climate conditions (specifically, a predicted significant increase in temperature), droughts and their direct impacts on population and income are expected to increase substantially.

Figure 4.20 plots district-level drought and flood risks in 2010 by region, based on the underlying district totals of pixel-level risk values, which range from 0 to 249 for drought risk and from 0 to 160 for flood risk. Nxumalo and Raju (2022) noted several patterns. First, drought risk around the country is highly skewed, with most districts having negligible risks, while some have very high risk. This pattern is often repeated within a region, except in those with very low average risk of drought (Western and Ashanti regions) and those with very high average risk (Northern, Upper East, and Upper West regions). For flood risk, there is no apparent skewness, but variance within regions is large, and the regions are more similar to one another than is the case for drought risk. It is also apparent that drought risk is concentrated in the northern districts (Northern, Upper East, and Upper West regions) and in the southeast (Greater Accra and Volta regions), while flood risk is spread more evenly across the country.

FIGURE 4.21

District-level pairwise correlations between flood and drought risks and LEAP program participation measures

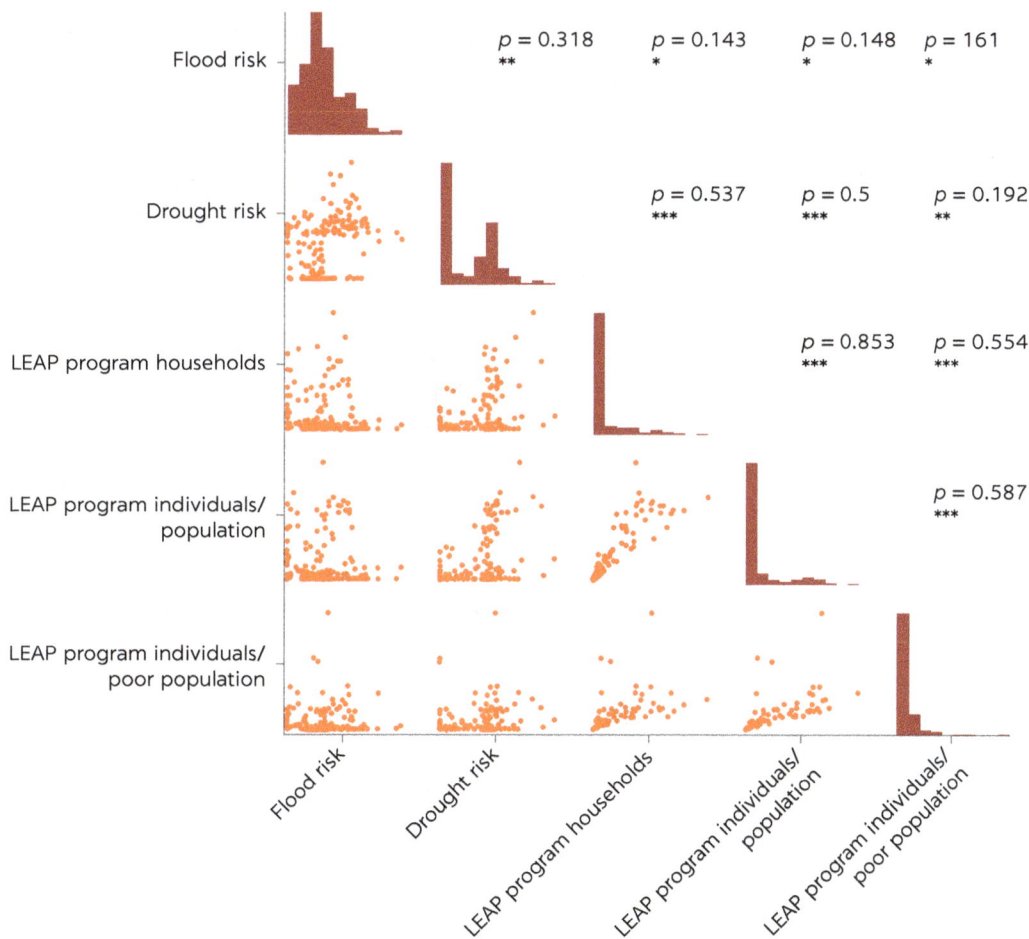

Source: Reproduced from Nxumalo and Raju 2022.
Note: Figure presents bivariate scatterplots, univariate distributions through histograms, and pairwise correlation coefficients. LEAP = Livelihood Empowerment Against Poverty; p = pairwise correlation coefficient. Significance level: * = 10 percent, ** = 5 percent, *** = 1 percent.

LEAP program household numbers in Nxumalo and Raju's (2022) analysis are as of 2020; LIPW program household numbers are cumulative from 2011 (when the program was started) through 2020, as the LIPW program provides temporary support to different cohorts of beneficiaries across years. The household rolls of the LEAP and LIPW programs are not disjointed, as eligibility rules for the LIPW program privilege LEAP program households.

Figure 4.21 shows district-level scatterplots between flood and drought risks and LEAP program participation indicators, accompanied by pairwise correlation coefficients. Figure 4.22 shows the same information in relation to the LIPW program. Drought risk is positively associated with LEAP and LIPW program participation. The associations between flood risk and the alternative measures of LEAP and LIPW program participation are positive but either weakly significant or not significant statistically.

FIGURE 4.22

District-level pairwise correlations between flood and drought risks and LIPW program participation measures

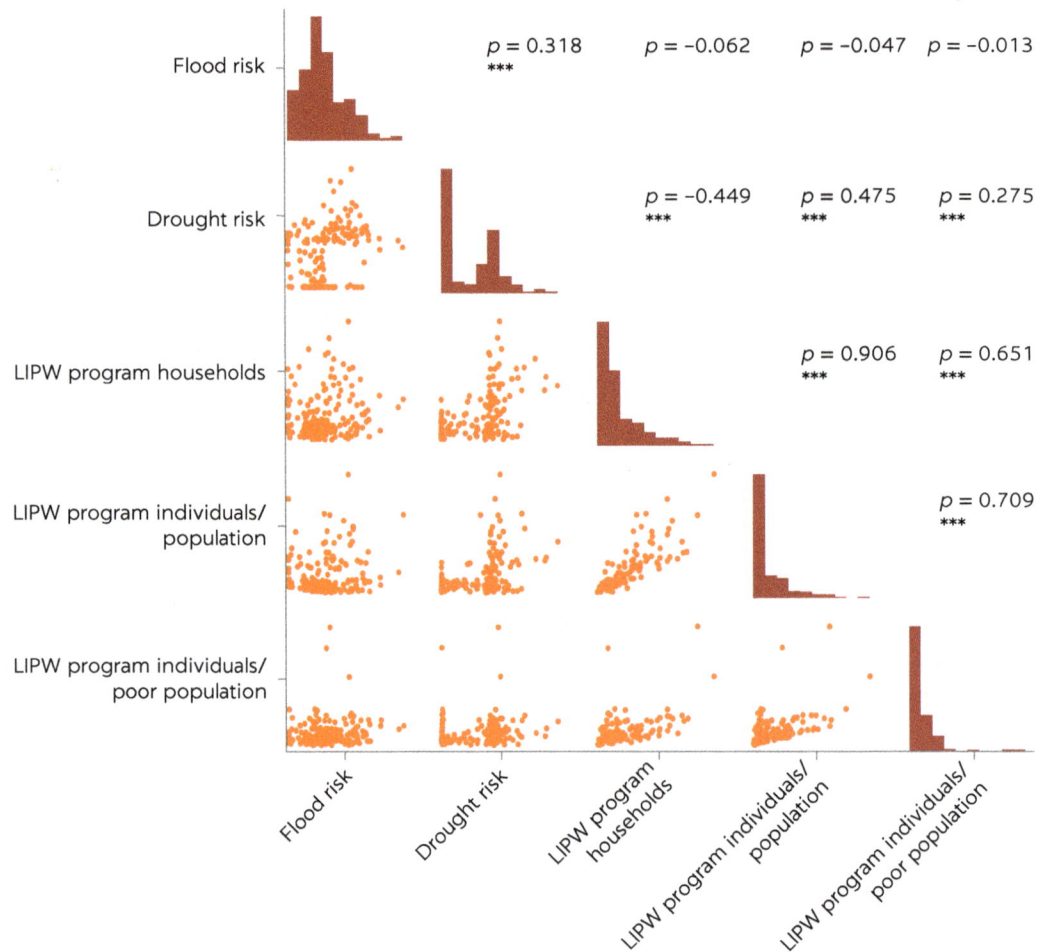

Source: Reproduced from Nxumalo and Raju 2022.
Note: Figure presents bivariate scatterplots, univariate distributions through histograms, and pairwise correlation coefficients. LIPW = Labor-Intensive Public Works; ρ = pairwise correlation coefficient. Significance level: * = 10 percent, ** = 5 percent, *** = 1 percent.

The results suggest that participation in the selected social assistance programs is higher in areas with drought risk. The corresponding results for flood risk are weaker, presumably due to flood risk being more scattered across the country and linked to river systems and coastal areas, while coverage by the social assistance programs is predominantly in the northern parts of the country.

Nxumalo and Raju (2022) interpreted the link between household participation in the LEAP and LIPW programs and drought risk as stemming from preshock program coverage of drought-prone areas, achieved indirectly through the intentional coverage of poor areas. However, in the case of the LIPW program, they indicated that the association might be an element of ex post response at work. The location, type, and scale (including workforce size) of the public works subproject may be influenced by local drought risk considerations. The district authority and the community jointly determine the nature of the subproject in the community.

As discussed in the "Labor-Intensive Public Works Program" section in chapter 3, possible subproject types include the construction or rehabilitation of small dams and dugouts, reforestation and afforestation, catchment and watershed protection, and biodiversity conservation. These subproject types can help address drought risk. In most years, these subproject types are the typical public works selected by district authorities and the communities.

The preshock coverage of drought-prone areas by the social assistance programs can make any post-shock responses through these programs, or through the delivery infrastructure these programs have rolled out, more efficient than when preshock coverage is absent. Even more efficient is preshock coverage that allows for a *preshock response* through the programs (or through the underpinning delivery infrastructure) by, for example, adjusting transfers before a shock occurs, predicted by early warning systems.

NOTES

1. These international averages are likely a large underestimate given that total spending is estimated based solely on reported relevant data from household surveys (that is, without any corrections for coverage or benefit-level discrepancies vis-à-vis administrative data or for missed programs). Household surveys tend to capture relevant information on programs that offer regular cash transfers over extended periods; relevant information is frequently absent in these surveys on programs that offer monetary benefits but allow for short-duration participation and on programs that offer in-kind benefits, such as food transfers.
2. For program coverage rates of households separately by household consumption quintiles, see table C.3 in appendix C. The table also reports program coverage rates of households separately for rural and urban areas.
3. In LEAP program households, each member is considered covered.
4. As a comparison, in a sample of program households for an evaluation of the LEAP program, Handa et al. (2017) found that across program households, program benefits received in 2016 as a percentage of the household's total consumption in 2010 averaged 18.3 percent.
5. We obtained the household poverty line for each household by multiplying the stipulated individual poverty line by the number of adult equivalents in the household. See appendix A for more information on the poverty lines.
6. For a definition of the measure, see appendix B.
7. The average concentration coefficient value for direct transfers of any type among 55 countries is –0.27, and the lowest coefficient value is –0.63. See CEQ Data Center on Fiscal Redistribution, https://commitmentoequity.org/datacenter (accessed May 15, 2022).

8. This could be because indigent people who lack a fixed address are not captured in the GLSS 2016–17 sampling frame.

9. For reference, the concentration coefficients for being younger than 18, 70 or older, or pregnant are –0.11, –0.01, and 0.02, respectively.

10. For a more detailed definition of the measure, see appendix B.

11. This is not quite true, as explained in Lustig (2018), but the intuition serves our purposes here.

12. For a more detailed discussion of these measures, see appendix B.

13. Concentration coefficients are not affected by proportional scaling, so the results for simulations 7–12 are identical to the results for simulations 1–6.

14. Boko, Raju, and Younger (2021) and Raju and Younger (2021) include such analysis.

15. Similar data for other social safety net programs in Ghana were not available.

16. See the Ghana page of Think Hazard, https://thinkhazard.org/en/report/94-ghana (accessed January 20, 2022).

REFERENCES

Alatas, Vivi, Abhijit Banerjee, Rema Hanna, Benjamin A. Olken, and Julia Tobias. 2012. "Targeting the Poor: Evidence from a Field Experiment in Indonesia." *American Economic Review* 102 (4): 1206–40.

Boko, Joachim, Dhushyanth Raju, and Stephen Younger. 2021. "Welfare, Shocks, and Public Spending on Social Protection Programs in Lesotho." Social Protection and Jobs Working Paper 2102, World Bank, Washington, DC.

Brown, Caitlin, Martin Ravallion, and Dominique van de Walle. 2018. "A Poor Means Test? Econometric Targeting in Africa." *Journal of Development Economics* 134: 109–24.

Grosh, Margaret, Phillippe Leite, Matthew Wai-Poi, and Emil Tesliuc. 2022. *Revisiting Targeting in Social Assistance: A New Look at Old Dilemmas.* Washington, DC: World Bank.

GSS (Ghana Statistical Service). 2012. *2010 Population and Housing Census: Summary Report of Final Results.* Accra: GSS.

Handa, Sudhanshu, Gustavo Angeles, Gean Spektor, Robert Darko Osei, and Richard de Groot. 2017. *Livelihood Empowerment against Poverty Programme: Endline Impact Evaluation Report.* Chapel Hill: Carolina Population Center, University of North Carolina at Chapel Hill.

Hernani-Limarino, Werner. 2022. "Augmented Proxy Mean Tests: Can Machine Learning Improve Targeting Effectiveness?" Unpublished manuscript.

Lustig, Nora, ed. 2018. *Commitment to Equity Handbook: Estimating the Impact of Fiscal Policy on Inequality and Poverty.* New Orleans: CEQ Institute at Tulane University; Washington, DC: Brookings Institution Press.

Norwegian Embassy, NADMO, and UNDP (National Disaster Management Organisation and United Nations Development Programme). 2015. *National-Level Flood and Drought Risk Assessment and Mapping: Technical Report.* Accra: Norwegian Embassy, NADMO, and UNDP.

Nxumalo, Mpumelelo, and Dhushyanth Raju. 2022. *Shocks and Social Safety Net Program Participation in Ghana: Descriptive Evidence from Linking Climate Risk Maps to Program Beneficiary Rolls.* Washington, DC: World Bank.

Premand, Patrick, and Pascale Schnitzer. 2021. "Efficiency, Legitimacy and Impacts of Targeting Methods: Evidence from an Experiment in Niger." *World Bank Economic Review* 35 (4): 892–920.

Raju, Dhushyanth, and Stephen D. Younger. 2021. "Social Assistance Programs and Household Welfare in Eswatini." Social Protection and Jobs Working Paper 2106, World Bank, Washington, DC.

UNDRR (United Nations Office of Disaster Risk Reduction) and CIMA Research Foundation. 2019. *Disaster Risk Profile: Ghana.* Nairobi: UNDRR and CIMA Research Foundation.

USAID (United States Agency for International Development). 2017. *Climate Change Risk Profile—Ghana. Fact Sheet.* https://www.climatelinks.org/sites/default/files/asset/document/2017_USAID_Climate%20Change%20Risk%20Profile%20-%20Ghana.pdf.

5 Conclusion

OVERVIEW

This study examines the performance of social protection program spending in Ghana based on an analysis of household survey and government administrative data and through a review of relevant literature. Rather than summarize the main findings again (as we do in chapter 1), we conclude by using them to inform some general observations about social protection policy in Ghana. Foremost, it is important to note that the government of Ghana gets many things right in its social protection programs. Public expenditure reviews tend to focus on what is wrong with public policy and recommend fixes, but there is much to be learned, in Ghana and elsewhere, from what is going well.

The government makes a genuine, often creative, and usually successful effort to target its social assistance program spending to the poor population. Benefits from the Livelihood Empowerment Against Poverty (LEAP) program and the Ghana School Feeding Programme (GSFP) are highly concentrated among the poor population, and they are effective at reducing poverty and inequality in the sense that they obtain a substantial impact for each cedi spent. We are unable to make the same claims about the Labor-Intensive Public Works (LIPW) program due to the lack of data, but the program design and existing program reviews offer no reason to believe that it is different.

While it may seem obvious that social assistance program spending should effectively target the poor population, programs in many countries are co-opted for political reasons and end up with less effective targeting. Such pressures also exist in Ghana, of course, but the government has usually been able to resist them.

Another reason for Ghana's success with social protection programs is that most have been carefully studied by researchers and practitioners and, importantly, the government uses this information to improve program design. This study provides several examples of the impact of evaluative and operational research available to policy makers as they set and refine the parameters of social protection programs, especially the LEAP program and the National Health Insurance Scheme (NHIS). This technocratic approach also improves the targeting of the social assistance programs.

An important problem for the social assistance programs in Ghana is that funding is low, which limits coverage and makes the benefits rather low. This means that, despite strong targeting, the actual reductions in poverty and inequality that these programs induce are small. An obvious recommendation, then, is to increase the outlays for these programs. Unfortunately, that runs head on into a difficult macroeconomic and budgetary environment that, because of high debt burdens, seems unlikely to improve considerably in the medium term. Thus, the government is left with a frustrating trade-off: It has proven tools to reduce poverty and inequality effectively but must balance those with the exigencies of fiscal deficit reduction. The recent government announcements of large increases in the benefit amounts of the LEAP program and GSFP do not in any way imply that this trade-off is less severe.

We note that as inflation has accelerated in Ghana, the real value of the (already low) transfers made by the LEAP program and GSFP become smaller still.[1] The occasional ad hoc adjustments to program benefit amounts have not kept up with rising prices. For a government facing severe fiscal constraints, it may seem useful to reduce the real value of its program costs, but this undercuts further the poverty-reducing impact of both programs.

Coverage of elderly individuals by Social Security and National Insurance Trust (SSNIT) pensions is also low, as is its distributional impact, although for a very different reason. SSNIT pensions are actually generous, but because program beneficiaries must have contributed for at least 15 years and, until recently, this had to be in the formal sector, the eligible population is quite limited. Furthermore, SSNIT is not constrained by the public sector's fiscal situation, as it is independently funded and managed. There are, however, concerns about its sustainability.

We make a few more observations about targeting. First, the LEAP program and GSFP, and probably the LIPW program,[2] have made good use of geographic targeting. Both the LEAP program and GSFP have better targeting nationally than they do within the geographic areas they intentionally target. That is, both programs chose the areas in which to operate well given their intention to reach the poor population. As these programs expand in national coverage, as both have done over the past decade, they will lose their effective geographic targeting, which may worsen their targeting overall. On the other hand, the government has been using a proxy means test (PMT) to target the LEAP program, and our simulations show that its sole use can be as or more effective than the prior multilevel, multimethod targeting strategy used by the program.[3] Thus, there is every reason to believe that the LEAP program will continue to have highly pro-poor targeting.

GSFP, however, cannot target individual children; it is a school-level intervention. Expansion to nationwide coverage, then, will certainly dilute its targeting effectiveness. This issue suggests the need for a policy adjustment: The government could concentrate its social assistance program spending meant to alter the distribution of income directly in the LEAP program and perhaps the LIPW program, where the PMT can be used to target the poor population effectively. GSFP, on the other hand, would cease to be a transfer program. Instead, it could be assigned to schools where it is most likely to improve children's nutritional status and academic performance, based on the evaluation results in the academic literature. Of course, these schools would have many poor children, but the redistributional effects would be a side benefit, not the main purpose, which would be nutrition, school enrollment, school attendance, and academic achievement.

NHIS presents the most daunting problems we found in this study. Unlike the other social protection programs, NHIS is meant to be universal (that is, to provide health insurance for all). Yet over the past 15 years, membership has covered only 30 percent to 40 percent of the population. Even with such limited membership, NHIS has had difficulty covering its expenses. By far the most common criticism of any social protection program in Ghana is that NHIS pays health care providers late or not at all for the services they provide to NHIS members, a point we come back to later. If NHIS is to be truly universal, it will need substantially more resources, probably more than twice its current budget. Once again, this collides with the macroeconomic and fiscal situation. It seems unlikely that the government can allocate the additional resources needed to make NHIS universal.

What other options are there for NHIS? Raising fees and premia might seem to be the obvious answer. They are very low, covering less than 5 percent of NHIS expenditures. Yet, it is also true that operational evaluations and survey data suggest that fees and premia, however small, are the main impediment to people registering or reregistering for NHIS. We have been unable to collect enough information to assess whether large reductions in administrative costs are possible, but it seems unlikely. Lacking this, NHIS must accept that it will not cover everyone, reduce the scope of the coverage it offers, or obtain an implausibly large allocation from the central government budget, possibly through an increase in the national health insurance levy.

SSNIT is also far from universal. In the past few years, SSNIT has made an effort to draw in more informal sector workers, but the response has been minimal. Furthermore, there is a lesson from the NHIS experience: The government probably cannot and will not fund a universal pension, so any expansion of SSNIT pension membership will require actuarially fair premia payments from new members, something that will probably discourage them from joining.

We began this conclusion stressing the many things that are right about Ghana's social protection programs. We conclude with one pervasive and chronic problem: The government often accumulates substantial arrears to its service providers. Over the previous decade, the government failed to pay more than GH¢3 billion it owed to SSNIT for its employees' premia. NHIS is so slow to reimburse health care providers that many now refuse to accept NHIS patients, or they charge them illegal copays. GSFP caterers have sometimes experienced long delays in payments as well. The convenience of these arrears for a cash-strapped government is understandable: They constitute an interest-free loan and also hide the true size of the fiscal deficit, for a while. However, arrears have real costs in terms of program effectiveness. The arrears to SSNIT reduce its investment earnings, jeopardizing its already doubtful ability to pay pensions in the future. The arrears to health care providers cause them to deny NHIS members the free health care that NHIS is supposed to guarantee. Unpaid caterers must cut corners in the meals they provide.

Resorting to arrears will not be an easy habit to break. Furthermore, doing so will not generate an immediate willingness of health care providers and caterers to provide the services that NHIS and GSFP are meant to give. Once burned, twice shy. Still, it is an effort that the government needs to make, consistently, if it wants its social protection program spending to reach its full potential.

NOTES

1. LIPW program wage payments are tied to national daily minimum wages, which is indexed to inflation.
2. Recall, we do not have the same survey information for the LIPW program.
3. The multimethod targeting strategy included targeting individuals with specific sociodemographic characteristics as well as those living in poor areas.

Data and Variable Construction

INTRODUCTION

Analysis of the social protection program performance in the study is based on data from the seventh Ghana Living Standards Survey (GLSS), commonly called GLSS 7, but here referred to as GLSS 2016–17. Initiated in 1987/88 and conducted periodically since then by the Ghana Statistical Service (GSS), the survey gathers data on the living conditions and well-being of the country's population.

The GLSS 2016–17 was conducted between October 22, 2016, and October 17, 2017. The survey successfully interviewed 14,009 households (of an originally planned sample of 15,000 households) from 1,000 primary sampling units across the country (GSS 2019). The number of bona fide members in the interviewed households was 58,844.

The GLSS 2016–17 follows a two-stage stratified sampling design. In the first stage, stratified by administrative region and urban versus rural, enumeration areas are selected based on probability proportional to population size to form primary sampling units. A complete listing of households in the selected primary sampling units is then undertaken to form secondary sampling units. A fixed, uniform number of households (secondary sampling units) are selected systematically from each primary sampling unit (GSS 2019).

The survey is representative at the national and administrative region-by-area (urban, rural) levels. At the time of the survey, there were 10 administrative regions.

While the GLSS 2016–17 gathered data through different types of questionnaires, the data used in this study come from the household questionnaire only.

WELFARE, POVERTY, AND INEQUALITY

Welfare, poverty, and inequality are measured following the approach by the GSS (2018).

"Welfare" is defined as household consumption per adult equivalent.

Ghana has two poverty lines: (a) an upper poverty line, to measure overall poverty status, and (b) a lower poverty line, to measure extreme or food poverty status. The overall poverty line is GH¢1,760.9 per adult equivalent per year, and the extreme poverty line is GH¢984.2 per adult equivalent per year, both in 2016/17 prices (GSS 2018).

Households with welfare below the extreme poverty line are classified as "extreme poor," and those with welfare below the overall poverty line are classified as "poor." Households with welfare between the extreme and overall poverty lines are classified as "moderate poor." Households with welfare between the overall poverty line and 1.5 times the overall poverty line are classified as "near poor," while those with welfare above 1.5 times the overall poverty line are classified as "other nonpoor."

"Inequality," measured by the Gini index in our analysis, is also based on household consumption per adult equivalent.

SOCIAL PROTECTION PROGRAMS

Household members were asked about receipt of Social Security and National Insurance Trust (SSNIT) pensions and Livelihood Empowerment Against Poverty (LEAP) program benefits in the previous 12 months in section 11.C of the household questionnaire. For each program (as relevant), each member was asked when they had enrolled in the program, when they received their last payment, how much they received in their last payment, and how many times they received payments in the preceding 12 months.

SSNIT pension scheme

A household member who received SSNIT pension benefits in the preceding 12 months is classified as a beneficiary. No age floor is imposed because, according to the rules, SSNIT pension benefits can be received by the SSNIT scheme member on early retirement or in the case of permanent physical or mental disability, as well as by the scheme member's dependents in the case of the member's death before age 75.

To calculate the pension benefit, we annualized the most recently reported payment, multiplying it by 12, rather than using the number of times it was received in the preceding 12 months. In doing this, we assumed that, for those who had recently begun to receive a pension benefit (and so report fewer than 12 payments in the previous 12 months), their poverty status at the time of the survey reflects the full value of the pension benefit.

In certain cases, SSNIT pension beneficiaries can receive lump-sum benefits. We found one observation with a much larger reported pension value than the rest of the sample, which was received only once. For this observation, we assumed the reported payment was received only once.

LEAP program

A household that reported receiving LEAP program benefits in the previous 12 months is classified as a LEAP program household.

Statutory payments for each payment round in 2016 and 2017 range from GH¢64 for LEAP program households with one eligible member to GH¢106 for LEAP program households with four or more eligible members. If the most recent payment reported by the program household was smaller than GH¢64, we raised it to GH¢64. If the most recent payment reported by the program household was larger than GH¢106, we reduced it to GH¢106.

A household could have reported a larger payment than GH¢106 if it missed a past payment. (The Ministry of Gender, Children, and Social Protection [MOGCSP] reports that missed payments by program households was an uncommon occurrence in 2016 and 2017.) The reported values greater than GH¢106 do not follow a clear pattern (multiples of statutory payment values) that would allow us to ascertain the household's payment level. The ceiling of GH¢106 helps reduce the extent of bias in reported benefit values.

After the corrections for "too low" and "too high" reported payments, payment values are annualized by multiplying by 6, given that there were 6 payment rounds annually in both 2016 and 2017 as reported by the MOGCSP. (We did not use the information reported by the household on the number of times payments were received in the previous 12 months.)

NHIS

In section 3.B of the household questionnaire, several options exist to classify a household member as a National Health Insurance Scheme beneficiary, including whether the member is registered with NHIS (question 1), covered by NHIS (question 3), and has a valid NHIS card (question 6). We chose the most conservative option—namely, that the person has a valid NHIS card (response option 1 to question 6). In addition, we also classified children who are younger than age 3 months and have mothers who are NHIS beneficiaries as NHIS beneficiary themselves, in line with NHIS eligibility rules.

We valued the benefits of NHIS membership to be equal to total NHIS expenditures on claims for members in 2017 divided by the total number of active NHIS members (that is, active membership at the end of 2017). This calculation yields an estimated benefit of GH¢124 per year per member.[1]

Some NHIS members, however, must pay a premium for membership, which is GH¢15 per year in rural areas and GH¢22 in urban areas, and still more must pay a processing fee of either GH¢8 or GH¢5 to join or renew (Nsiah-Boateng and Aikins 2018). These values are reported separately in question 9a (for the premium payment) and question 9b (for the processing fee) in section 3.B of the household questionnaire.

However, there seems to be a considerable amount of confusion on the part of respondents as values that look like the processing fee (GH¢5 or GH¢8) are recorded under the question on the premium payment and vice versa, along with some that look like combinations of the two types of payments (e.g., GH¢30 under the question on the premium payment). To deal with this, we combined the values in questions 9a and 9b into a single payment value. If this total payment value was less than GH¢5 but greater than zero, we increased it to GH¢5, the minimum possible processing fee. We maintained zero values because some people are exempt from both fees. We also capped the total payment at GH¢30 for an urban respondent and GH¢23 for a rural respondent, the maximum possible payments.

For each NHIS beneficiary, we then subtracted their total payment from the assumed benefit of GH¢124 per year to obtain the beneficiary's net benefit from NHIS participation.

While there is a question that can be used to identify respondents who are exempt from paying the processing fee or the premium (question 8, section 3.B), we did not use this information. In our analysis, respondents who are "exempt" are those whose calculated total payment value is zero.

GSFP

The household questionnaire asks about the receipt of school meals (specifically "free food at school") (question 24, section 2.A) for each household member ages 3–12 years attending either preschool or primary school. On the basis of this question, members who report that they received school meals from the government (response option 1 to question 24) are classified as GSFP beneficiaries.

For each beneficiary, we assigned an annual benefit value of GH₵160 (GH₵0.8 per meal for 200 school days per year). The value of GH₵0.8 per meal per student was in effect during the academic years that overlap with the reference period for the GLSS 2016–17, as reported by the MOGCSP.

Table A.1 compares estimates of the number of beneficiaries and total spending on benefits obtained from the GLSS 2016–17 to corresponding statistics obtained from government administrative data. Across all programs, survey estimates for the number of beneficiaries fall short of administrative statistics, particularly for the LEAP program followed by SSNIT pensions (figure A.1). The survey estimate is 33 percent of the administrative statistic for 2017 for the LEAP program and 57 percent for SSNIT pensions. The lower estimated numbers of beneficiaries in the GLSS 2016–17 are largely behind the lower estimated total spending on benefits in the survey compared to administrative statistics. Among the programs, the survey estimates for NHIS come closest to its administrative statistics. However, we found significant differences in the degree of correspondence between the survey estimate for the number of beneficiaries and the administrative statistic across NHIS membership categories (table A.2). The survey estimate comes close to the administrative statistics for the under age 18 and other membership categories; it is far greater than the administrative statistic for the 70 years and above category and far lower than the administrative statistics for the SSNIT-paid category (which is consistent with the survey undercount of the SSNIT pension beneficiaries reported in table A.1), as well as those in the free maternal care and, especially, the indigent.[2]

TABLE A.1 Program beneficiary numbers and total spending on benefits, survey estimates versus administrative information

		BENEFICIARIES (THOUSANDS)			BENEFITS (MILLION GH₵)		
			ADMINISTRATIVE DATA			ADMINISTRATIVE DATA	
		GLSS 2016–17	2016	2017	GLSS 2016–17	2016	2017
PROGRAM	LEVEL	(1)	(2)	(3)	(4)	(5)	(6)
LEAP	Household	66	198	198	31	75	93
GSFP	Individual	1,125	1,645	1,672	180	366	259
NHIS	Individual	9,345	11,027	10,655	1,036	1,054	1,325
SSNIT pensions	Individual	107	174	190	779	1,749	2,189

Source: Survey values are original estimates based on the Ghana Living Standards Survey 2016–17. Administrative information on the LEAP program and GSFP was obtained from the Ministry of Gender, Children, and Social Protection; NHIS from the National Health Insurance Authority; and SSNIT pensions from SSNIT.

Note: Table reports estimates from the *Ghana Living Standards Survey* 2016–17 of the number of beneficiaries and total spending on benefits, by program. It also reports corresponding statistics from program administrative information for 2016 and 2017. Administrative information on LEAP program household numbers is for the last payment round in each year. For NHIS, the administrative statistics for beneficiary numbers correspond to active membership numbers at the end of the year. Likewise, for the LEAP program, the administrative statistics for beneficiary numbers correspond to the numbers of program households that were included in the last payment round of the year. GLSS = Ghana Living Standards Survey; GSFP = Ghana School Feeding Programme; LEAP = Livelihood Empowerment Against Poverty; NHIS = National Health Insurance Scheme; SSNIT = Social Security and National Insurance Trust.

FIGURE A.1

Beneficiaries and benefit spending, ratio of GLSS 2016–17 estimates to administrative statistics in 2017, by program

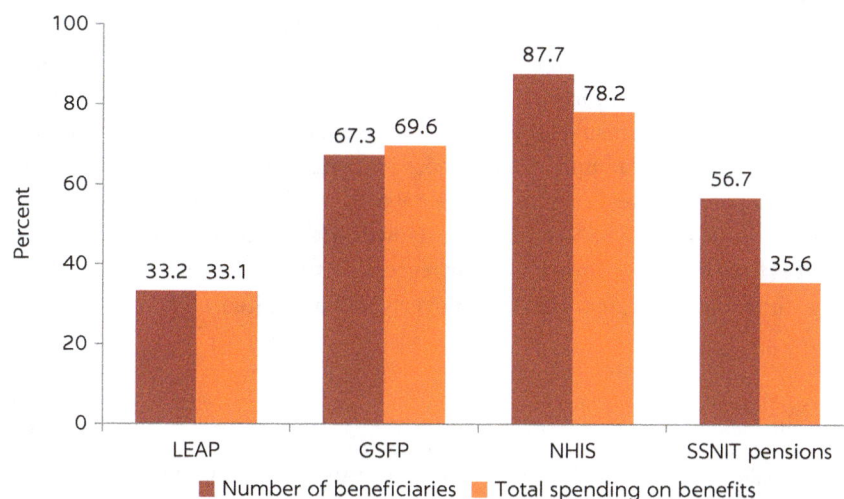

Source: Survey values are original estimates based on the Ghana Living Standards Survey 2016–17. Administrative information on the LEAP program and GSFP was obtained from the Ministry of Gender, Children, and Social Protection; NHIS from National Health Insurance Authority; and SSNIT pensions from SSNIT.
Note: Figure shows the ratio (in percent terms) in survey estimates for 2016/17 to administrative statistics for 2017 in the number of beneficiaries and total spending in benefits, by program. GLSS = Ghana Living Standards Survey; GSFP = Ghana School Feeding Programme; LEAP = Livelihood Empowerment Against Poverty; NHIS = National Health Insurance Scheme; SSNIT = Social Security and National Insurance Trust.

TABLE A.2 NHIS beneficiary numbers, by membership category, survey estimates versus administrative information

	BENEFICIARIES (THOUSANDS)		
		ADMINISTRATIVE DATA	
	GLSS 2016–17	2016	2017
CATEGORY	(1)	(2)	(3)
Age <18 years	4,490	4,564	4,852
Age ≥70 years	691	481	502
SSNIT paid	254	538	600
Other	3,509	3,131	3,400
Free maternal care	311	778	831
Indigent	33	1,534	677

Source: Survey values are authors' estimates based on Ghana Living Standards Survey 2016–17. Administrative information obtained from National Health Insurance Authority.
Note: Table reports estimates from the GLSS 2016–17 of the number of NHIS beneficiaries by membership category. It also presents corresponding statistics (active membership at the end of each applicable year, by membership category) from program administrative information for 2016 and 2017. GLSS = Ghana Living Standard Survey; NHIS = National Health Insurance Scheme; SSNIT = Social Security and National Insurance Trust.

Diagnosing the drivers of the shortfalls is difficult. For programs that are spatially targeted, a potential reason for the shortfalls is the design of the GLSS itself. The LEAP program is targeted to poor districts and communities. The GLSS 2016–17 is designed to be nationally representative (and representative of regions and rural and urban areas within them), but the survey is not explicitly designed to be representative of LEAP program communities. The same concern applies to GSFP, because the program is also targeted to poor districts and communities. Another potential reason applicable to all programs is that the design or implementation of section 11.C of the household questionnaire has shortcomings that unintentionally contribute to underreporting of program participation status.

There are no straightforward analytical solutions to correct for the shortfalls. When reviewing the results, it is important to keep in mind that the coverage, marginal contribution, and effectiveness statistics are underestimates.[3] The underestimates are severest for the LEAP program but are also of significant concern for GSFP and SSNIT pensions. However, for SSNIT pensions, because benefits from this program are strongly regressive, the impact of the shortfalls on the estimation of marginal effects on poverty will be limited.

NOTES

1. We applied this benefit to all those insured, not just to those who actually used NHIS to pay for health care services. Barofsky and Younger (2022) compared using the "insurance value" of public spending on health versus the "use value." We used the former here, assuming that, even if an insured person had not utilized NHIS in the previous 2 weeks (the GLSS 2016–17 recall period for the use of health care services), eventually, the benefits will average out to the cost per insured person.
2. If indigent individuals lacked a fixed address, they were excluded from the GLSS 2016–17 sampling frame.
3. The direction of bias for incidence is not clear.

REFERENCES

Barofsky, Jeremy, and Stephen D. Younger. 2022. "The Effect of Government Health Expenditure on the Income Distribution: A Comparison of Valuation Methods in Ghana." In *Commitment to Equity Handbook: Estimating the Impact of Fiscal Policy on Inequality and Poverty*. 2nd ed., edited by Nora Lustig, 3–51. Vol. 2. Washington, DC: Brookings Institution Press; New Orleans: CEQ Institute, Tulane University.

GSS (Ghana Statistical Service). 2018. *Poverty Trends in Ghana, 2005–2017*. Accra: GSS.

GSS (Ghana Statistical Service). 2019. *Ghana Living Standards Survey (GLSS) 7: Main Report*. Accra: GSS.

Nsiah-Boateng, Eric, and Moses Aikins. 2018. "Trends and Characteristics of Enrolment in the National Health Insurance Scheme in Ghana: A Quantitative Analysis of Longitudinal Data." *Global Health Research and Policy* 3: 32.

Description of Measures

INTRODUCTION

This appendix is reproduced from Boko, Raju, and Younger (2021). While there are many measures of inequality, poverty, and social protection program benefit incidence, this review uses only a few. For inequality, we use the Gini coefficient. For poverty, we use the Foster–Greer–Thorbecke (FGT) poverty measures (Foster, Greer, and Thorbecke 1984). For social protection program benefit incidence, we use concentration coefficients and the marginal effect of a benefit on poverty and inequality. For effectiveness, we use measures developed in Enami (2022) that calculate how much inequality or poverty reduction a government gets from a program relative to the size of its budget.

PROGRAM COVERAGE

Coverage measures the total number of beneficiaries of a social protection program divided by the target population for that program. This denominator may be the entire population or some subset. For example, for Social Security and National Insurance Trust (SSNIT) pensions, we take the number of people receiving such pensions divided by the population age 60 years or older.

INEQUALITY MEASURE: GINI COEFFICIENT

The Gini coefficient is the most common measure of inequality. The easiest way to understand this measure is to first construct a Lorenz curve: Order the data by our welfare measure—consumption per adult equivalent (from here on, consumption)—from poorest to richest, and then plot the cumulative share of the sample on the horizontal axis against the cumulative share of consumption on the vertical axis. Table B.1 provides some illustrative data for 10 people.

Because there are 10 people, the first person represents 10 percent of the sample, the first two people represent 20 percent, and so on, producing column 2. Column 3 reports each person's consumption, and we can see that the data are ordered from poorest to richest. The sum of all consumption is 1,000, so we obtain the consumption shares in column 4 by dividing each person's consumption by 1,000. Column 5 reports the cumulative consumption shares.

TABLE B.1 Illustrative data for a Lorenz curve and the Gini coefficient

OBSERVATION	CUMULATIVE POPULATION SHARE	CONSUMPTION	CONSUMPTION SHARE	CUMULATIVE CONSUMPTION SHARE
(1)	(2)	(3)	(4)	(5)
1	0.100	1	0.001	0.001
2	0.200	3	0.003	0.004
3	0.300	7	0.007	0.011
4	0.400	13	0.013	0.024
5	0.500	20	0.020	0.044
6	0.600	30	0.030	0.074
7	0.700	60	0.060	0.134
8	0.800	100	0.100	0.234
9	0.900	250	0.250	0.484
10	1.000	516	0.516	1.000
	Total	1,000		

Source: Boko, Raju, and Younger 2021.

FIGURE B.1

Illustrative Lorenz curve

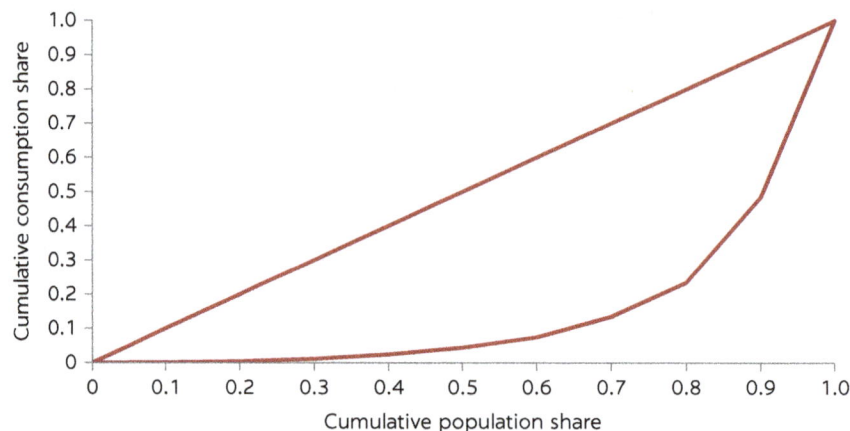

Source: Boko, Raju, and Younger 2021.

The Lorenz curve then graphs column 5 against column 2, as in figure B.1. Because both axes are shares, they range from 0 to 1, and because the data are ordered from poorest to richest, the Lorenz curve must be convex: The poorest person's consumption share cannot be greater than their population share and similarly for the poorest two people and so on.

Indeed, the more convex the Lorenz curve, the more unequal the distribution of consumption. In the extreme case, in which one person has all the consumption, the Lorenz curve would be a right angle, running along the horizontal axis until it reaches the last person in the sample, because everyone but that person would have 0 consumption. Conversely, if everyone has exactly the same consumption—representing complete equality—the cumulative consumption share would be equal to the cumulative population share, and the Lorenz curve would be a 45-degree line.

The Gini coefficient is the area between the 45-degree line and the Lorenz curve, multiplied by 2. With complete equality, where the Lorenz curve is on the 45-degree line, the Gini coefficient would be 0. With complete inequality, the Gini coefficient would be twice the triangle below the 45-degree line, or 1. Across countries in recent years, Gini coefficients are observed to range from around 0.23 to around 0.63.

POVERTY MEASURES: POVERTY RATE AND POVERTY GAP

The FGT measures—a group of related measures—are the most common measures of poverty. The first FGT measure, denoted by $FGT(0)$, is the *poverty rate* (or headcount ratio), which is the share of the population that is poor. The second FGT measure, denoted by $FGT(1)$, is the *poverty gap*, which is the average difference between the poverty line and a person's consumption, usually scaled by the poverty line itself. The poverty gap is expressed by the following equation:

$$poverty\ gap = \left(\frac{1}{N}\right)\sum_i \left(\frac{z-c_i}{z}\right)_+ ,$$

where z is the poverty line, c_i is the ith person's consumption, and N is the sample size. The plus sign indicates that we include the difference only if it is positive. The third FGT measure, denoted by $FGT(2)$, is the squared poverty gap, sometimes called *poverty severity*. It is calculated in the same way as the poverty gap but with the term in parentheses squared. In fact, the family of FGT measures can be written concisely as

$$FGT(\alpha) = \left(\frac{1}{N}\right)\sum_i \left(\frac{z-c_i}{z}\right)_+^{\alpha}.$$

If $\alpha = 0$, the term in parentheses is 1 if a person is poor and 0 otherwise, so that gives us the poverty rate. If $\alpha = 1$, we obtain the poverty gap, and if $\alpha = 2$, we obtain poverty severity.

Table B.2 illustrates the calculation of the poverty measures using the same data with which we derived the Lorenz curve and assuming that the poverty line is 21. Column 3 indicates whether a person is poor. Summing this column and dividing by the sample size gives the headcount ratio: 0.50. Therefore, half of the population is poor. Column 4 reports the absolute poverty gap for each person, the difference between the poverty line (21) and their consumption. This has an interesting interpretation because it shows how much money would be needed to bring every person's consumption to the poverty line. Column 5 scales each person's absolute poverty gap by the poverty line. Averaging that over the sample gives the poverty gap: 0.29. Finally, column 6 squares each person's scaled poverty gap. Averaging that over the sample gives the poverty severity: 0.22.

TABLE B.2 Illustrative calculation of FGT poverty measures

OBSERVATION	CONSUMPTION	POVERTY STATUS	ABSOLUTE POVERTY GAP	SCALED POVERTY GAP	SCALED POVERTY GAP SQUARED
(1)	(2)	(3)	(4)	(5)	(6)
1	1	1	20	0.952	0.907
2	3	1	18	0.857	0.735
3	7	1	14	0.667	0.444
4	13	1	8	0.381	0.145
5	20	1	1	0.048	0.002
6	30	0	0	0	0
7	60	0	0	0	0
8	100	0	0	0	0
9	250	0	0	0	0
10	516	0	0	0	0
	Sum	5		2.90	2.23
Average (FGT)		0.50		0.29	0.22
Poverty line		21			

Source: Boko, Raju, and Younger 2021.
Note: FGT = Foster–Greer–Thorbecke.

PROGRAM BENEFIT INCIDENCE

Concentration curve and coefficient

A concentration curve is similar to a Lorenz curve. We order the data from poorest to richest and then plot the cumulative share of a benefit against the cumulative share of the population. Table B.3 provides illustrative data for a benefit, and figure B.2 shows the corresponding curve graphing column 6 against column 2.

Unlike a Lorenz curve, a concentration curve can be either convex or concave. A concave curve would occur if poorer people receive a higher share of a benefit than richer people (which may well be the case for explicitly targeted benefits).

Like the Gini coefficient, the concentration coefficient for a social protection program benefit is the area between its concentration curve and the 45-degree line. This can range from –1 (the poorest person receives all the benefit) to 1 (the richest person receives all the benefit), with 0 representing a benefit spread evenly across the population. Benefits with a concave concentration curve (negative concentration coefficient) are usually referred to as pro-poor or absolutely pro-poor. Those with a concentration curve below the Lorenz curve (concentration coefficient greater than the Gini) are considered regressive. Also, benefits with a concentration curve between the Lorenz curve and the 45-degree line (concentration coefficient less than the Gini but positive) are relatively pro-poor.

Marginal effect

Another way to assess the incidence of a social protection program benefit is to see how it alone changes poverty or inequality. We refer to this as its *marginal effect*.

TABLE B.3 Illustrative data for a concentration curve

OBSERVATION	CUMULATIVE POPULATION SHARE	CONSUMPTION	BENEFIT RECEIVED	BENEFIT SHARE	CUMULATIVE BENEFIT SHARE
(1)	(2)	(3)	(4)	(5)	(6)
	0.00				0.00
1	0.10	1	30.0	0.300	0.30
2	0.20	3	20.0	0.200	0.50
3	0.30	7	15.0	0.150	0.65
4	0.40	13	10.0	0.100	0.75
5	0.50	20	5.0	0.050	0.80
6	0.60	30	5.0	0.050	0.85
7	0.70	60	5.0	0.050	0.90
8	0.80	100	5.0	0.050	0.95
9	0.90	250	3.0	0.030	0.98
10	1.00	516	2.0	0.020	1.00
	Total	1,000	100.0		

Source: Boko, Raju, and Younger 2021.

FIGURE B.2

Illustrative concentration curve

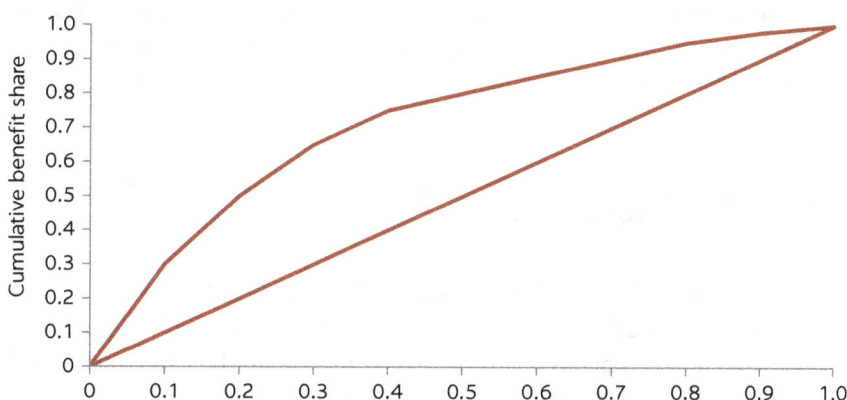

Source: Boko, Raju, and Younger 2021.

To determine it, we calculate a measure of poverty or inequality for household consumption per adult equivalent and then recalculate the same poverty or inequality measure after either adding or removing the social protection program benefit. The difference between the two measures is the marginal effect.

One important difference between the marginal effect and the concentration coefficient is that the marginal effect depends on the overall size of the social protection program benefit while the concentration coefficient does not. A larger program benefit, for example, can have a larger impact on inequality and especially poverty than a smaller one that is distributed to the same people and so has the same concentration curve.

PROGRAM EFFECTIVENESS

The last measure we consider is the effectiveness of a social protection program. Enami (2022) presents two measures: *impact effectiveness* and *spending effectiveness*. The impact effectiveness of a program benefit is the ratio of its marginal effect on a distributional statistic (we use the Gini coefficient and the poverty gap in this study) to the marginal effect of a perfectly targeted program benefit of the same size, that is, with the same total program budget. A perfectly targeted program benefit is one that transfers enough money to the poorest person in the country to bring their consumption up to that of the second-poorest person, then transfers enough to both of them to bring their consumption up to that of the third-poorest person, and so on, until the program budget runs out. Impact effectiveness is expressed by the following equation:

$$impact\ effectiveness = \frac{\pi_{with\ actual\ benefit} - \pi_{without\ actual\ benefit}}{\pi_{with\ perfect\ benefit} - \pi_{without\ actual\ benefit}},$$

where π is some distributional statistic. Because the actual benefit cannot improve the distributional statistic by more than the perfect benefit does, the measure is bounded above by 1. Also, if the actual benefit does not improve the distributional statistic at all, the measure is bounded by 0.[1]

Enami's (2022) second measure, spending effectiveness, is the ratio between the amount that would have to be spent on a perfect transfer to achieve the same reduction in the distributional statistic as is actually achieved by a benefit and the amount spent on the actual benefit. Spending effectiveness is expressed by the following equation:

$$spending\ effectiveness = \frac{budget\ needed\ to\ achieve\ \left(\pi_{with\ actual\ benefit} - \pi_{without\ actual\ benefit}\right) with\ a\ perfect\ transfer}{budget\ needed\ to\ achieve\ \left(\pi_{with\ actual\ benefit} - \pi_{without\ actual\ benefit}\right) with\ the\ actual\ benefit}.$$

This measure is also bounded by 0 and 1. If the actual benefit does not improve the distributional statistic of interest, then the numerator is 0: No spending is needed to achieve an equally good result. Also, if the actual benefit is distributed perfectly, the numerator and denominator are equal.

It is inappropriate to apply either of these effectiveness measures to the poverty rate. The most effective way to reduce the poverty rate is to give additional consumption to the poor person who is closest to the poverty line—that is, the *least poor* person—until their consumption reaches the poverty line, then transfer additional consumption to the *next poorest* poor person until that person's consumption reaches the poverty line, and so on. Because this "perfect" transfer favors the least poor of the poor population, it is not ethically defensible. On the other hand, the perfect transfer discussed earlier, which favors the poorest of the poor population, may well fail to bring anyone above the poverty line and so be judged as completely ineffective on the basis of the two effectiveness measures—because while it would benefit only the poor population, it would not reduce the poverty rate.

NOTE

1. We ignore cases in which the benefit actually worsens the distribution of consumption (per adult equivalent) and simply set their impact effectiveness to zero.

REFERENCES

Boko, Joachim, Dhushyanth Raju, and Stephen Younger. 2021. "Welfare, Shocks, and Public Spending on Social Protection Programs in Lesotho." Social Protection and Jobs Working Paper 2102, World Bank, Washington, DC.

Enami, Ali. 2022. "Measuring the Effectiveness of Taxes and Transfers in Fighting Inequality and Poverty." In *Commitment to Equity Handbook: Estimating the Impact of Fiscal Policy on Inequality and Poverty*, edited by Nora Lustig, 121–79. Washington, DC: Brookings Institution Press.

Foster, James, Joel Greer, and Erik Thorbecke. 1984. "A Class of Decomposable Poverty Measure." *Econometrica* 3 (52): 761–66.

APPENDIX C

Supplemental Figures and Tables

TABLE C.1 Coverage rates of individuals, by program and area

Percent

GROUP	LEAP PROGRAM			GSFP			NHIS			SSNIT PENSIONS		
	OVERALL	RURAL	URBAN	OVERALL	RURAL	URBAN	OVERALL	RURAL	URBAN	OVERALL	RURAL	URBAN
	(1)	(2)	(3)	(4)	(5)	(6)	(7)	(8)	(9)	(10)	(11)	(12)
By poverty status												
Extreme poor	6.7	7.2	0.0	9.9	10.1	6.3	31.7	30.7	45.8	0.0	0.0	0.0
Moderate poor	3.6	4.5	0.3	6.9	8.1	2.9	27.1	26.9	27.8	0.1	0.0	0.1
Near poor	1.6	2.5	0.2	5.1	5.6	4.4	33.4	30.3	37.9	0.1	0.1	0.2
Other nonpoor	0.2	0.5	0.1	2.2	3.6	1.5	35.4	32.4	36.9	0.6	0.2	0.8
By consumption quintile status												
First (poorest)	5.0	5.8	0.2	8.5	9.3	3.5	28.2	28.2	27.9	0.0	0.0	0.1
Second	1.8	2.7	0.2	5.0	5.6	4.0	33.0	30.1	37.7	0.1	0.1	0.1
Third	0.4	0.8	0.2	3.6	4.6	2.8	31.9	29.0	34.4	0.2	0.1	0.3
Fourth	0.1	0.2	0.1	2.0	3.1	1.4	36.0	34.0	37.0	0.5	0.3	0.6
Fifth (richest)	0.1	0.4	0.0	1.1	2.2	0.8	38.4	37.6	38.6	1.1	0.5	1.3
Overall	1.5	2.9	0.1	4.0	6.1	2.0	33.5	30.4	36.5	0.4	0.1	0.1

Source: Original estimates based on data from the Ghana Living Standards Survey 2016–17.
Note: Table reports coverage rates of individuals, by program and by area, for alternative poverty statuses and alternative consumption quintile statuses. The LEAP program benefit is treated as a household benefit; given this, all members in LEAP program households are considered beneficiaries. For definitions of the poverty statuses, see appendix A. GSFP = Ghana School Feeding Programme; LEAP = Livelihood Empowerment Against Poverty; NHIS = National Health Insurance Scheme; SSNIT = Social Security and National Insurance Trust.

TABLE C.2 **Coverage rates of individuals in target categories for GSFP and SSNIT, by target categories and area**

Percent

	GSFP						SSNIT PENSIONS		
	PUBLIC (PRE)PRIMARY STUDENT			PUBLIC (PRE)PRIMARY STUDENT IN GSFP AREA			AGES 60+		
	OVERALL	RURAL	URBAN	OVERALL	RURAL	URBAN	OVERALL	RURAL	URBAN
GROUP	(1)	(2)	(3)	(4)	(5)	(6)	(7)	(8)	(9)
By poverty status									
Extreme poor	36.8	37.4	24.9	64.2	64.1	65.3	0.5	0.6	0.0
Moderate poor	27.4	30.3	14.4	66.8	70.6	44.0	0.9	0.7	2.1
Near poor	23.3	22.8	24.2	57.7	57.0	59.2	1.7	1.3	2.4
Other nonpoor	20.6	22.0	19.2	56.5	59.3	53.6	7.7	2.8	10.8
By consumption quintile status									
First (poorest)	31.9	34.2	15.0	66.1	68.4	42.4	0.6	0.5	1.4
Second	23.0	23.0	23.0	58.0	57.3	59.9	1.5	1.1	2.2
Third	21.4	22.5	20.1	56.2	60.0	51.7	2.6	1.3	3.8
Fourth	19.6	20.9	18.4	60.0	58.2	62.2	6.9	3.6	9.4
Fifth (richest)	21.0	22.7	20.0	52.9	58.5	49.6	12.5	4.1	15.3
Overall	25.1	27.5	19.9	60.7	63.3	54.2	5.2	1.7	9.0

Source: Original estimates based on data from the Ghana Living Standards Survey 2016–17.
Note: Table reports GSFP and SSNIT pension coverage rates of individuals in target categories (where target categories are defined in the data by the authors) for alternative poverty statuses and alternative consumption quintile statuses. GSFP area refers to Ghana Living Standards Survey 2016–17 primary sampling units with at least one GSFP household. For definitions of the poverty statuses, see appendix A. GSFP = Ghana School Feeding Programme; SSNIT = Social Security and National Insurance Trust.

TABLE C.3 **Coverage rates of households, by program and area**

Percent

	LEAP PROGRAM			GSFP			NHIS			SSNIT PENSIONS		
	OVERALL	RURAL	URBAN	OVERALL	RURAL	URBAN	OVERALL	RURAL	URBAN	OVERALL	RURAL	URBAN
GROUP	(1)	(2)	(3)	(4)	(5)	(6)	(7)	(8)	(9)	(10)	(11)	(12)
By poverty status												
Extreme poor	6.0	6.5	0.0	28.1	29.0	17.4	58.9	58.7	60.8	0.3	0.3	0.0
Moderate poor	2.8	3.6	0.3	17.8	20.3	9.1	51.4	50.7	54.0	0.4	0.3	0.7
Near poor	1.3	2.0	0.2	12.5	13.1	11.5	53.8	49.9	59.5	0.6	0.5	0.8
Other nonpoor	0.2	0.4	0.1	4.3	6.9	3.0	46.4	44.2	47.5	1.7	0.7	2.2
By consumption quintile status												
First (poorest)	4.1	4.8	0.1	22.8	24.9	11.5	53.1	53.3	51.8	0.3	0.2	0.5
Second	1.5	2.3	0.3	12.4	13.3	10.9	54.2	50.6	59.9	0.5	0.4	0.7
Third	0.5	0.9	0.3	9.0	11.3	6.9	48.4	46.2	50.3	0.8	0.4	1.1
Fourth	0.2	0.3	0.1	4.2	6.4	3.0	47.5	44.4	49.1	1.5	1.0	1.8
Fifth (richest)	0.1	0.2	0.0	1.9	2.9	1.6	44.6	42.0	45.5	2.5	0.9	3.0
Overall	0.9	1.9	0.1	7.9	12.6	4.2	48.5	47.8	49.0	1.4	0.6	2.0

Source: Original estimates based on data from the Ghana Living Standards Survey 2016–17.
Note: Table reports household coverage rates, by program and by area, for alternative poverty statuses and for alternative consumption quintile statuses. For definitions of the poverty statuses, see appendix A. GSFP = Ghana School Feeding Programme; LEAP = Livelihood Empowerment Against Poverty; NHIS = National Health Insurance Scheme; SSNIT = Social Security and National Insurance Trust.

FIGURE C.1

Distribution of program beneficiaries, by consumption decile

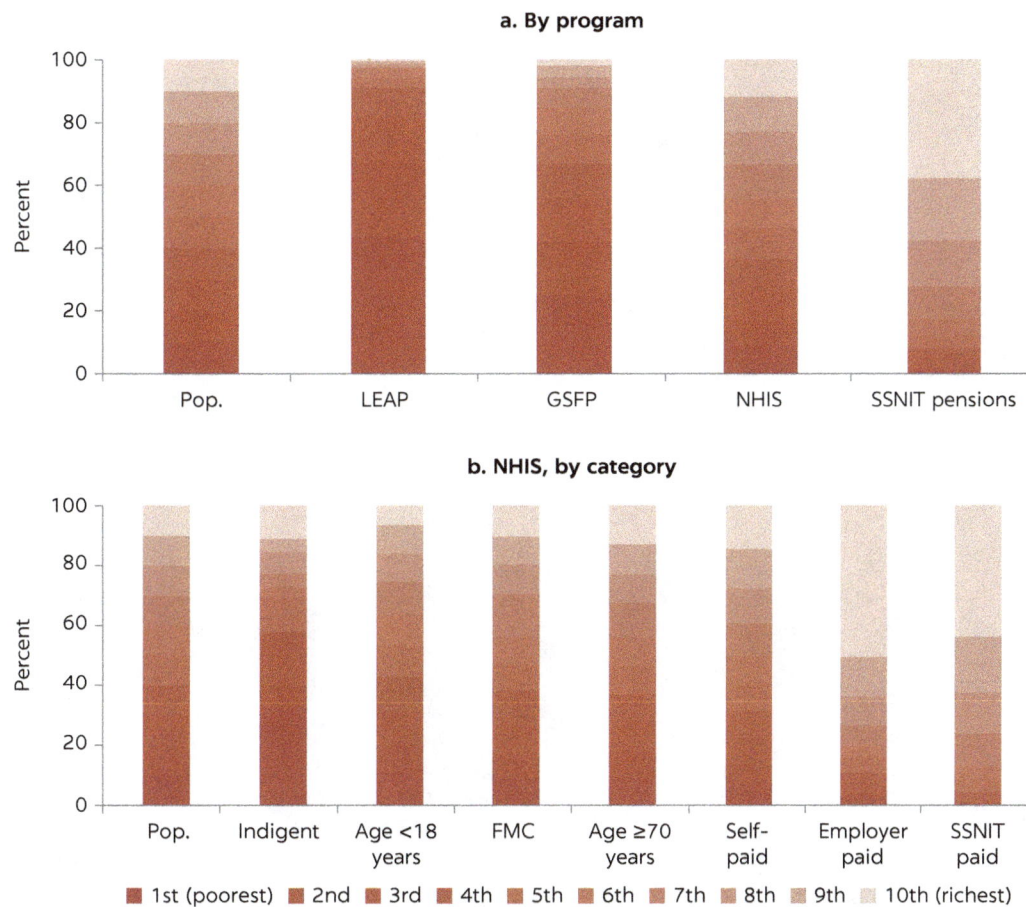

a. By program

b. NHIS, by category

Legend: 1st (poorest) · 2nd · 3rd · 4th · 5th · 6th · 7th · 8th · 9th · 10th (richest)

Source: Original estimates based on data from the Ghana Living Standards Survey 2016–17.
Note: Panel (a) shows the distribution of beneficiaries across consumption deciles, by program. Panel (b) shows the distribution of total NHIS beneficiaries across consumption deciles, by membership category. Consumption here refers to household consumption per adult equivalent. FMC = free maternal health care; GSFP = Ghana School Feeding Programme; LEAP = Livelihood Empowerment Against Poverty; NHIS = National Health Insurance Scheme; Pop. = population; SSNIT = Social Security and National Insurance Trust.

FIGURE C.2

Distribution of program benefits, by consumption decile

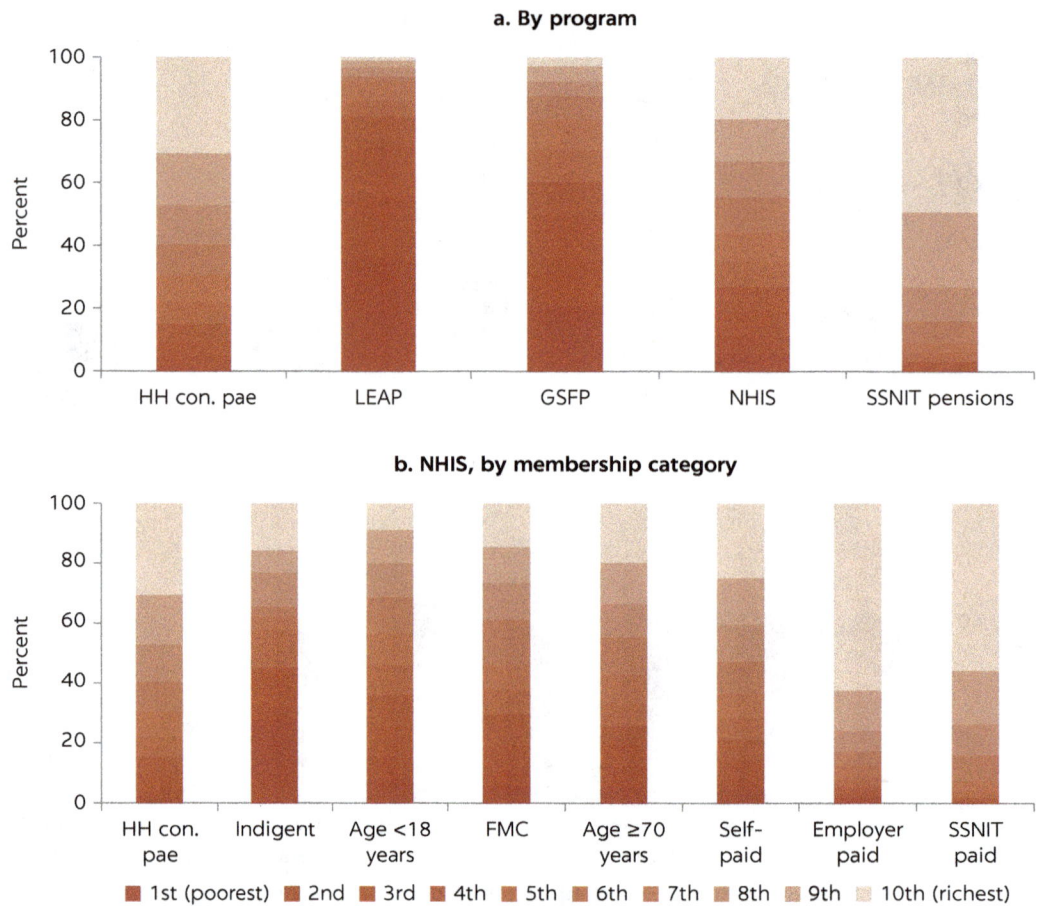

Source: Original estimates based on data from the Ghana Living Standards Survey 2016–17.

Note: Panel (a) shows the distribution of total benefits across consumption deciles, by program. Panel (b) shows the distribution of total NHIS benefits across consumption deciles, by membership category. Consumption here refers to household consumption per adult equivalent. FMC = free maternal health care; GSFP = Ghana School Feeding Programme; HH con. pae = household consumption per adult equivalent; LEAP = Livelihood Empowerment Against Poverty; NHIS = National Health Insurance Scheme; SSNIT = Social Security and National Insurance Trust.

TABLE C.4 **Sensitivity of marginal effect estimates to alternative national poverty lines**

Percentage points

	EXTREME POVERTY LINE		OVERALL POVERTY LINE	
	POVERTY RATE	**POVERTY GAP**	**POVERTY RATE**	**POVERTY GAP**
PROGRAM AND CATEGORY	**(1)**	**(2)**	**(3)**	**(4)**
Program				
LEAP	0.04	0.06	0.06	0.05
LEAP, in LEAP areas	0.59	0.72	0.82	0.83
LEAP+	0.14	0.21	0.13	0.17
GSFP	0.10	0.03	0.08	0.04
GSFP, in GSFP areas	0.19	0.09	0.27	0.11
NHIS	0.08	0.07	0.21	0.10
SSNIT pensions	0.00	0.02	0.03	0.18
By NHIS membership category				
Indigent	0.00	0.00	0.00	0.00
Free maternal care	0.00	0.00	0.01	0.00
Age <18 years	0.04	0.04	0.13	0.06
Age ≥70 years	0.01	0.01	0.02	0.02
SSNIT paid	0.00	0.00	0.00	0.00
Self-paid	0.03	0.02	0.06	0.03
Employer paid	0.00	0.00	0.00	0.00

Source: Original estimates based on data from the Ghana Living Standards Survey 2016–17.
Note: Table reports estimates of marginal effects in relation to the poverty rate and poverty gap, by program and by NHIS membership category. The poverty rate and the poverty gap are estimated based on two alternative poverty lines, the overall poverty line and the extreme poverty line. At the national level, the base levels for evaluating the marginal effects on overall poverty are 23.4 percent for the poverty rate and 8.4 percent for the poverty gap, whereas the base levels for assessing the marginal effects on extreme poverty are 8.2 percent for the poverty rate and 2.8 percent for the poverty gap. LEAP areas are GLSS 2016–17 primary sampling units with at least one LEAP program household. GSFP areas are GLSS 2016–17 primary sampling units with at least one GSFP household. LEAP+ refers to actual LEAP program households plus predicted LEAP program households, capped at the administrative statistic for the number of program households in January 2017. GLSS = Ghana Living Standards Survey; GSFP = Ghana School Feeding Programme; LEAP = Livelihood Empowerment Against Poverty; NHIS = National Health Insurance Scheme; SSNIT = Social Security and National Insurance Trust.

TABLE C.5 Sensitivity of effectiveness estimates to alternative national poverty lines

Percent

	EXTREME POVERTY LINE				OVERALL POVERTY LINE			
	POVERTY GAP		POVERTY SEVERITY		POVERTY GAP		POVERTY SEVERITY	
	IMPACT	SPENDING	IMPACT	SPENDING	IMPACT	SPENDING	IMPACT	SPENDING
PROGRAM AND CATEGORY	(1)	(2)	(3)	(4)	(5)	(6)	(7)	(8)
By program								
LEAP	33.6	33.8	18.0	15.2	65.1	65.1	35.1	33.4
LEAP, in LEAP areas	33.2	33.8	24.1	17.9	64.3	65.1	39.6	36.6
LEAP+	31.9	32.1	23.5	17.2	59.9	60.2	36.8	33.4
GSFP	22.2	22.3	15.2	9.8	47.8	47.8	27.7	24.2
GSFP, in GSFP areas	22.3	22.3	17.6	10.0	48.0	47.8	29.4	24.9
NHIS	13.6	8.5	19.0	4.3	22.1	21.9	16.0	10.5
SSNIT pensions	0.1	0.1	0.1	0.0	1.0	1.0	0.4	0.2
By NHIS membership category								
Indigent	30.5	30.9	16.9	15.9	45.5	46.1	27.0	26.4
Free maternal care	8.1	7.6	4.0	3.1	21.0	20.2	9.1	8.4
Age <18 years	10.1	10.0	12.3	4.8	26.2	25.8	15.9	11.9
Age ≥70 years	8.2	8.2	4.9	3.5	21.9	21.6	10.4	9.1
SSNIT paid	0.1	0.1	0.0	0.0	0.7	0.7	0.2	0.2
Self-paid	6.3	6.4	5.8	2.7	17.0	17.3	9.5	7.3
Employer paid	2.2	2.4	0.7	0.5	4.5	4.9	1.9	1.7

Source: Original estimates based on data from the Ghana Living Standards Survey 2016–17.

Note: Table reports impact and spending effectiveness estimates in relation to the poverty rate and poverty gap, by program and by NHIS membership category. The poverty rate and the poverty gap are estimated based on two alternative poverty lines, the overall poverty line and the extreme poverty line. LEAP areas are GLSS 2016–17 primary sampling units with at least one LEAP program household. GSFP areas are GLSS 2016–17 primary sampling units with at least one GSFP household. LEAP+ refers to actual LEAP program households plus predicted LEAP program households, capped at the administrative statistic for the number of program households in January 2017. GLSS = Ghana Living Standards Survey; GSFP = Ghana School Feeding Programme; LEAP = Livelihood Empowerment Against Poverty; NHIS = National Health Insurance Scheme; SSNIT = Social Security and National Insurance Trust.

Estimating Household Consumption in the Absence of SSNIT Pensions

Most of the social protection program benefits considered in this study are small, even relative to the consumption of the poor population, so ignoring behavioral responses to them provides a reasonable first-order approximation of the effect of the programs on welfare (for an explanation, see Lustig 2018). But Social Security and National Insurance Trust (SSNIT) pensions are large, both in absolute value and as a share of beneficiaries' household consumption. According to our survey data, SSNIT pension benefits average GH¢7,734 per year for beneficiary households, which is 60 percent of household consumption minus the benefit.

Because these benefits are so large, most beneficiary households end up seeming quite poor if we remove SSNIT pension benefits and assume that the household does nothing in response, even though the households are relatively well off after receiving the benefits. This large horizontal movement across the consumption distribution can confound estimates that use comparisons of consumption with and without the benefit of interest: the marginal effects and the effectiveness measures.

To avoid this "false poverty," we assume that beneficiaries of the program would, in fact, respond to a loss of the benefit by working more.[1] We estimate how much labor income beneficiaries would make in the absence of their pension benefit and add this labor income to their households' consumption in the "without benefit" state when calculating marginal effects and effectiveness measures.

The estimation uses a variant of coarsened exact matching (Blackwell et al. 2009). We calculate the median labor income of groups of people who are not SSNIT pension beneficiaries based on their age group (0–13, 14–17, 17–21, 21–25, 25–50, 50–60, and 60+), educational attainment (less than primary, primary graduate, lower secondary graduate, upper secondary graduate, postsecondary technical graduate, and university graduate), gender, and area of residence (urban, rural). We then add that median labor income to the households of SSNIT pension beneficiaries in the "without benefit" state when calculating marginal effects and effectiveness measures.

Because of the large amounts for these benefits, our adjustment has a substantial effect on the results. The concentration coefficient of the given benefit over ex ante household consumption (that is, household consumption removing the benefit) changes from –0.266 to 0.565 for SSNIT pensions.

The changes in marginal effects due to the adjustment are limited because of the small shares of individuals benefiting from the program. The marginal effect for the Gini index changes from 0.2 percentage points to 0 for SSNIT pensions. The marginal effect for the poverty rate changes from 0.10 to 0.03 percentage points for SSNIT pensions.

NOTE

1. We find nontrivial labor market activity in terms of labor force participation and hours of work among elderly individuals in the Ghana Living Standards Survey 2016–17, particularly for those who do not benefit from SSNIT pensions.

REFERENCES

Blackwell, Matthew, Stefano Iacus, Gary King, and Giuseppe Porro. 2009. "CEM: Coarsened Exact Matching in Stata." *Stata Journal* 9 (4): 524–46.

Lustig, Nora, ed. 2018. *Commitment to Equity Handbook: Estimating the Impact of Fiscal Policy on Inequality and Poverty*. New Orleans: CEQ Institute at Tulane University; Washington, DC: Brookings Institution Press.

Simulating LEAP+ Households

Based on the Ghana Living Standards Survey (GLSS) 2016–17, a household that reported receiving Livelihood Empowerment Against Poverty (LEAP) program benefits in the preceding 12 months is classified as a LEAP program household. The survey includes 330 households reporting LEAP program benefits, which, when expanded to estimate the total population of LEAP program households, comes to 65,729. This is only about one-third of the program households found in government administrative records during the survey period (roughly 198,000). To address this lower count of LEAP program households in the GLSS 2016–17, we augmented the total number of program households by selecting nonprogram households in the GLSS 2016–17 that are similar to reported program households and assigned them benefits as well. We do this on a regional basis so that the augmented set of program households is (almost) equal to the number of program households in administrative records. We refer to the joint set of actual LEAP program households and augmented LEAP program households as "LEAP+" households.

We selected the augmented set of program households by first estimating the probability that a household reports being a LEAP program beneficiary, regressing actual program beneficiary status at the household level on the characteristics used to target the LEAP program geographically—the poverty rate in each district—and the qualifying characteristics for household members (sociodemographic categorical targeting criteria): having a significant disability, being an orphan, being age 65 or older, or being a pregnant woman or a mother of an infant younger than 1 year old.[1] We also include indicator variables for the agroecological zone interacted with an urban or rural indicator.[2]

The sociodemographic categorical targeting criteria are applied at entry into the program but are not considered for continued participation in the program. Given this, the variables that reflect these categorical criteria are less meaningful if the household entered the program in the years preceding 2016/17, our data period. Arguably, this concern applies especially to the categorical targeting of mothers and infants.

The qualifying member characteristics, with the exception of being a pregnant woman or a mother of an infant, are statistically significant predictors of LEAP program beneficiary status. Households in all urban areas are significantly less likely to participate, while those in rural Savannah areas are significantly more likely to participate than households in other rural areas. Both of these predictions are consistent with the geographical targeting of LEAP program benefits circa 2017.

Once we estimated the probability of receiving LEAP program benefits, we then added predicted LEAP program households to the set of actual LEAP program households, starting with the highest-probability households and working down until the total estimated number of program households (reporting and predicted) was (almost) equal to the number of program households in administrative records for January 2017. We did this assignment region by region.

For the augmented set of program households, we assigned benefits by eligible members, according to the statutory rules and sociodemographic categorical targeting criteria.

Based on the calculations we discussed earlier, the average annual benefit in actual LEAP program households was GH¢469, whereas it was GH¢515 in LEAP+ households. Total LEAP program benefits relative to total household consumption averaged across households was 12.8 percent for actual LEAP program households and 15.7 percent for LEAP+ households.

NOTES

1. District poverty rates were obtained from GSS (2015).
2. It is impossible to use finer geographic indicators, that is, region, because some regions have few or no LEAP program households in the GLSS 2016–17.

REFERENCE

GSS (Ghana Statistical Service). 2015. *Ghana Poverty Mapping Report*. Accra: GSS.

www.ingramcontent.com/pod-product-compliance
Lightning Source LLC
Chambersburg PA
CBHW051425290326
41932CB00048B/3227